Ana-María Rizzuto, M.D., is a training and supervising analyst at the Psychoanalytic Institute of New England, East. She received the 1996 William C. Bier Award of the American Psychological Association and the 1997 Pfister Award of the American Psychiatric Association for her contributions to the study of religion. Among Dr. Rizzuto's previous publications is *The Birth of the Living God*, a study of the psychodynamics of religious belief.

Why Did Freud Reject God?

Why Did Freud Reject God?

a psychodynamic interpretation

Ana-María Rizzuto, M.D.

Yale University Press   New Haven and London

Designed by Sonia L. Scanlon
Set in Joanna type by The Composing Room of Michigan,
Inc., Grand Rapids, Michigan
Printed in the United States of America by
Book Crafters, Inc., Chelsea, Michigan
Library of Congress Cataloging-in-Publication Data
Rizzuto, Ana-María.
Why did Freud reject God? : a psychodynamic
interpretation / Ana-María Rizzuto
p.   cm.
Includes bibliographical references and index.
ISBN 0-300-07525-1 (cloth : alk. paper)
1. Freud, Sigmund, 1856–1939—Religion. I. Title.
BF109.F74R55 1998
200'.92—dc21   97-49877

A catalogue record for this book is available from the
British Library.
The paper in this book meets the guidelines for
permanence and durability of the Committee on Produc-
tion Guidelines for Book Longevity of the Council on Library Resources.

10 9 8 7 6 5 4 3 2 1

I offer this book to my friends and colleagues who, following Freud, dedicate their daily work to the never-ending discovery of the lasting psychic power of childhood impressions.

From that bondage [of religious illusion] I am, we are, free. Since
we are prepared to renounce a good part of our infantile wishes, we
can bear it if a few of our expectations turn out to be illusions.

Freud, "The Future of an Illusion" (1927)

My deep engrossment in the Bible story (almost as soon as
I learnt the art of reading) had, as I recognized much later, an
enduring effect upon the direction of my interest.

Freud, 1935 addition to An Autobiographical Study (1925)

contents

illustrations

preface

Why did Freud reject God? Fortuitous circumstances led to this question and the attempt to answer it in this book. From February 28 to April 5, 1992, the exhibition "The Sigmund Freud Antiquities: Fragments from a Buried Past," came to the Boston University Art Gallery, sponsored by the Freud Museum in London to commemorate the fiftieth anniversary of Freud's death. Scholars from the university and psychoanalysts from the Boston Psychoanalytic Society and Institute and the Psychoanalytic Institute of New England, East (PINE), were asked to lecture on related subjects.

Several years earlier (Rizzuto, 1979), I had published a book about the psychic conditions for the formation of God-representations and their implications for both belief and unbelief. More recently, a group of PINE colleagues and I had published a paper (Barron et al., 1991) that had required prolonged immersion in Freud's biography and theoretical writings. When Dr. Ira Lable, chairman of the PINE program committee, asked the faculty to suggest a lecturer on the antiquities collection, my colleagues proposed that I be asked to give a talk exploring Freud's motives as a collector. I was pleased to accept the assignment.

The exhibition featured sixty-five objects drawn from Freud's collection of more than two thousand ancient Egyptian, Roman, Near Eastern, and Asian artifacts. The selection, according to the fact sheet for the exhibition, "emphasize[d] the parallels between the procedures of archaeology and Freud's revolutionary theories of psychoanalysis, and demonstrate[d] that Freud's views on the history of civilization and the development of the human psyche were deeply rooted in his knowledge of archaeology and antiquity." In addition to the antiquities, prints pertaining to Freud's collection, archaeological books from his library, and photographs of Freud's consulting room and study in Vienna were displayed. The photographs, taken by Edmund Engelman in 1938, shortly before Freud's departure for London, vividly reveal the living environment Freud had created for himself and his collection. They offer convincing evidence that while Freud was engaged in the work of listening to patients, thinking, and writing, he was surrounded by antiquities, his "audience."

Also included in the exhibition was a copy of an annotated and illustrated edition of the Hebrew Bible, in Hebrew and German. In 1891 Freud's father, Jakob, who had owned the so-called Philippson Bible since 1848, gave his copy to Sigmund as a thirty-fifth birthday gift. The bible on display was not the one Jakob had given to his son but rather a three-volume edition of the same work published in 1858, which Freud himself had bought secondhand some time later. I had seen the antiquities exhibition at the spring meeting of the American Psychoanalytic Association the previous year, but there, as in Boston, the bible was protected by a glass case that made it possible to view only two pages. In preparation for my lecture, I requested permission to preview the exhibition and to examine the bible more closely. The permission was granted, but I soon realized that the abundance of illustrations in the bible—which contains more than five hundred engravings of animals, trees, objects, and landscapes mentioned in the biblical text—made it impossible to study it thoroughly in this context. I decided that I had to find a copy that could be examined over a period of time without concern for disturbing the exhibition. After some complex explorations, I located a copy of the 1858 edition at the Andover Library of the Harvard Divinity School.

With the exhibition catalogue in hand, I began to explore the three volumes of the bible. Soon I became aware that there were frequent similarities between the objects pictured in the catalogue and the illustrations in the bible. Rosenfeld (1956) had suggested that "it is not difficult to detect in his [Freud's] rich and almost complete Egyptian collection the old models of the Philippson's illustrations" (p. 104). Niederland (1988) also found correlations between the Philippson Bible illustrations and Freud's archaeological collection.

Before me were hundreds of biblical illustrations. The objects in the exhibition represented only slightly more than 3 percent of the Freud collection. This made it even more striking that so many of the objects on display evoked the biblical illustrations. I became convinced that Rosenfeld and Niederland were right: the biblical illustrations must have influenced Freud's choice of objects and perhaps even his passion for collecting.

It then became my task to provide a psychoanalytic explanation for the similarities. Following Freud's own method of inquiry, I explored the circumstances for his collecting, the explicit personal meaning of the objects, his probable unconscious motives, and the conscious satisfaction that the objects provided to their owner. This archaeological digging into Freud's collecting began to take shape in my mind as a reconstruction of the process that could have led to his passion for collecting.

In the summer of 1993 I visited the Freud Museum in London. Erica Davies, the director, graciously permitted me to pore over Freud's original bible, page by page, and gave me access to other relevant materials and information. To my astonishment, I discovered that some of the pictures of biblical figures had been colored by hand. The finding excited my imagination because as far as I could tell from the writing of Freud's oldest sister, Anna Freud Bernays, and his son Martin, neither Freud's siblings nor his children seem to have been involved with the Philippson Bible in the way that Sigmund was. I could imagine the young Sigmund learning to read, so deeply engrossed in the biblical stories that he was moved to give color to the illustrations. Upon my return to the United States, I decided to follow every lead I could find about the influence of the Bible and of God's stories on Freud's mind.

From there I was led from surprise to surprise. I found a letter from the adolescent Freud to his friend Eduard Silberstein fully imitating the style and content of the Book of Job. I discovered that even the arrangement of Freud's office and study resembled an illustration from his bible. These findings pointed to the Bible's deep impact on Freud's imagination. His father, Jakob Freud, had introduced him to the Philippson Bible as a young boy learning to read; later Jakob had given it to him, newly rebound, to celebrate his thirty-fifth birthday. Jakob wrote a poignant, scripturally profound dedication on the flyleaf, urging Sigmund to return to the Lord. My progressive discoveries now connected the bible not only to the antiquities but also to Freud's father.

Freud rejected his father's plea, but this did not stop him from theorizing about religion. Nor did it prevent him, at the end of his life, from returning to the biblical text to rewrite the story of Moses in his book *Moses and Monotheism*. Freud's theory that religion perpetuates the infantile illusion of being protected by a kind father closed the circle between father and son. Mature adults, Freud concluded, must free themselves from the childhood longing for such a father. He assumed that mature renunciation of infantile wishes and down-to-earth realism were reason enough for his adamant rejection of his father's God.

But a psychoanalyst has to go further. I learned that as a young boy, Freud, returning from services at the Catholic church to which his beloved nanny had taken him, would preach God to his parents. I found that at the age of seven Freud wrote to his half-brother Emmanuel: "I and my dear parents and sisters are thank God well" (my italics). These and other incidents strongly suggested that even before he was able to read Bible stories, Freud had formed in his mind a certain representation of a God who deserved to be preached and praised. My task was now to uncover the intrapsychic changes that had transformed Freud's childhood image of God as an object deserving of proclamation and gratitude to his mature denunciation of God as a wishful product of infantile longings. To carry out my investigation I decided to proceed as a psychoanalytic detective would: to start out with the findings that called attention to the need to examine an unusual event, and then, step by step, to follow the clues until enough facts were in hand to permit me to formulate a meaningful explanation. This book traces the course of my investigations and discloses the results. In keeping with my methods of detection, the chapters are arranged neither chronologically nor thematically; rather, each chapter pursues the questions raised by the preceding one.

I am aware that by writing this book I have joined in a complex dialogue with several communities of intellectuals. I am grateful to those scholars whose sustained interest in Freud's atheism has invited this exploration of the dynamic sources of his unbelief. I also appreciate the work of colleagues in the psychology of religion who have continued to lament Freud's rejection of religion in spite of his illuminating contributions to the field. And I am indebted to the many psychoanalytic institutes in the United States and abroad that have invited me to present my ideas on the psychodynamic processes involved in religious belief. Discussions with these colleagues and their challenging questions have contributed greatly to the evolution of my thinking and have inspired my quest to understand Freud's rejection of religion.

This book would not have been written without the invitation from Dr. Lable to present a lecture during the exhibition of the Freud antiquities at Boston University. From that moment on, I received constant help from people in the United States and abroad. I owe gratitude to Laura Whitney, librarian at the Andover-Harvard Library at the Harvard Divinity School, who generously allowed me to use that facility and to study the Philippson Bible at my leisure. Sanford Gifford, M.D., searched on my behalf for entries about the Philippson Bible and the Philippson family at Harvard's Widener Library and offered me unflagging encouragement. Ann Menaschi, librarian of the Boston Psychoanalytic Society and Institute, gave me unfailing help in researching sources and finding what I needed in the briefest possible time. Erica Davies, director of the Freud Museum in London, facilitated my research at every step. During my visit to the museum she put at my disposal all that I requested and more. Later, when I faxed requests for further help in tracing sources, she was always efficient and courteous. I also owe gratitude to T. K. Davies, librarian at the Freud Museum, who assisted me in looking at Freud's bible and tracing reference sources. Allan D. Satin, reference librarian at the Hebrew Union College in Cincinnati, reviewed the different editions of the Bible in his collection and confirmed that the figure of the Egyptian jumper existed in the edition of the Philippson Bible to which Freud was exposed as a child. The Leo Baeck Institute in New York also permitted me to study its copies of the Philippson Bible.

Among my colleagues, I am especially indebted to Dr. Ernst Falzeder of Salzburg, who alerted me to several of Freud's references to God in his correspondence. Professor Gerhard Fichtner, of the Institut für Geschichte der Medizin in Tübingen, Germany, generously provided me with a comprehensive listing of Freud's references to God in his letters. Dr. Eva Laible of

Vienna sent me the original publications in German of J. Sajner's papers about Freud's childhood circumstances, thus giving me direct access to sources I knew only through secondary references.

My deepest gratitude is to my colleagues in the United States. Dr. Gary Goldsmith patiently read the drafts of the manuscript, offering invaluable suggestions and corrections and pointing out inconsistencies. Drs. Axel Hoffer and Michael Robbins gave me much support in moments of doubt. Dr. Arnold Richards encouraged me with his enthusiasm when I discussed the outline of the book with him. I am also indebted to the many friends who lent a sympathetic ear to my reflections and ponderings.

Katherine M. Messina offered invaluable help by editing the manuscript, tightening up sentences, polishing phrases, and smoothing out the flow of ideas. Last but not least, I also owe gratitude to Gladys Topkis of Yale University Press, for her unfailing ability to put every detail in place and for her skill in helping to shape my convoluted sentences into readable English prose.

introduction

Why did Freud reject God? This question formed slowly in my mind when I was going from surprise to surprise in discovering the connections between the Philippson Bible illustrations and many of the pieces in Freud's collection of antiquities. How could it be that a man who worked surrounded by objects seemingly out of his childhood bible had rejected the central subject of the biblical text, the God of Abraham, Isaac, and Jacob? Freud insisted that God was nothing but the wishful emotional clinging to an exalted childhood father transformed into a supernatural being. This conviction led him to a mission, presented in *The Future of an Illusion* (1927), aimed at helping immature believers: "Men cannot remain children forever; they must go out into 'hostile life.' We may call this '*education to reality*.' Need I confess to you that the sole purpose of my book is to point out the necessity for this forward step?" (p. 49).

The antiquities collection pointed to deep emotional connections between the childhood Bible and the father who had introduced his young son to the sacred book. The mystery of Freud's religious evolution from his "deep engrossment in the Bible story" to his missionary atheism demanded an explanation. The researcher had a difficult task ahead: to trace the process of Freud's internal psychic transformation from childhood belief to mature passionate unbelief.

Starting from the evidence at hand, I had to determine first when and how Freud began his collection and what meaning it had for him. In Chapter 1, "Freud's Compulsion to Collect Antiquities," we see that Freud started his collection immediately after the death of his father and kept it close to him until his own death. That these precious objects provided joy and companionship for him demands a psychoanalytic answer to three questions: What personal life circumstances, early and later, led Freud to find deep emotional satisfaction in his antiquities? What was the relation between his collecting and the death of his father? What was the nature of the relationship between father and son?

After Chapter 2, "Family History," I explore in Chapter 3, "Jakob and the 'Catastrophe,'" a key event in the family history that marked young Sigmund for life. Another episode, much later in life, directly linked Jakob, Sigmund, and the Philippson Bible. On the occasion of Sigmund's thirty-fifth birthday, Jakob had his copy of the Philippson Bible bound in leather and gave it to his son with a moving and scripturally profound plea for his return to the Lord. The scant biographical information we have about Jakob makes this dedication a precious document, revealing the father's feelings and wishes for his now fully adult son. To unveil the paternal feelings more clearly, I offer, in Chapter 4, "Jakob, Man and Father," a composite picture of Freud's father as portrayed by his grandchildren and his son.

In Chapter 5, "The Dedication and Freud's Response," I trace the lines to scriptural sources and their meanings. Why did Freud pay no attention to his father's plea? Was it out of ignorance of the deep meaning of Jakob's religious injunction, or did it reflect conflict between father and son? In Chapter 6 I investigate "Freud's Childhood Impressions from the Philippson Bible" and his dreams based on images he saw in its pages. Gifted with an excellent visual memory, Freud seemed to have been able to register, at least in his unconscious mind, a large number of the Philippson Bible's illustrations.

Once all this information was available, I could put together in Chapter 7, "The Philippson Bible and Freud's Antiquities Collection," an interpretation of Freud's relationship with his father, his father's Bible, and the antiquities that he was compelled to collect and surround himself with.

But this interpretation did not yet explain how Freud became an atheist. I had to seek further answers in a different field. A systematic exploration of "Freud's Religious Evolution," in Chapter 8, was the most fruitful approach. Freud began his religious career as a toddler preaching God to his family after returning from the church services he attended with his nurse. He became an official atheist in the middle years of his medical studies, after undergoing a deep philosophical battle between potential theism and determined atheism. The religious crisis was precipitated by his attendance at Professor Franz Brentano's lectures demonstrating "scientifically" the existence of God.

I consider another source of insight into Freud's internal processes of religious transformation—his writings on religion—in Chapter 9, "Freud's Theories About Religion." His theorizing, the lines of reasoning, and the arguments set forth, often in disguised theoretical form, help us to understand his intellectual and emotional stance in reference to the psychodynamic processes involved in belief in God. Freud's theories link all religious beliefs (or the rejection of such beliefs) to the child's relationship with his father. The figure of the mother in the psychodynamic process of formation of religious feelings and beliefs is conspicuously absent. The omission called for an investigation of Freud's relationship with his own mother. Chapter 10, "Amalie Nathansohn Freud," presents Freud's mother as she was described by those who knew her. In Chapter 11, "Amalie Freud, Nature, God, and Death," I describe Freud's objective and internal relationship with his mother—in particular, his persistent linking of his mother to death.

The material presented in the preceding chapters offered enough elements for me to formulate, in Chapter 12, "Why Did Freud Reject God?" a psychodynamic interpretation of the internal processes that led Freud not only to reject God but to urge others to follow him in repudiating the infantile belief in a protecting and benevolent divine being.

chapter one
Freud's Compulsion to
Collect Antiquities

In June 1896 Jakob Freud was seriously ill. Sigmund Freud (1887–1904) wrote to Fliess on June 30: "My old father (age eighty-one) is in Baden[1] in a most shaky state. . . . I do not dare make any plans now that would take me a day's journey away from Vienna. To be sure, he is a tremendous fellow, and should he still be granted a span of well-being, as I hope he will, I should

use it for our meeting." Two weeks later, on July 15, Freud confided to Fliess: "The old man's condition, by the way, does not depress me. I do not begrudge him the well-deserved rest that he himself desires. He was an interesting human being, very happy with himself; he is suffering very little now, and is fading with decency and dignity. I do not wish him a prolonged sick bed."

On October 26 Freud informed Fliess of his father's death: "Yesterday we buried the old man, who died during the night of October 23. He bore himself bravely to the end, just like the altogether unusual man he had been."

Freud was not prepared for the intensity of his reaction to his father's death. He seemed surprised by his response, as he disclosed in the November 2 letter to Fliess:

I find it so difficult to write to you just now that I have put off for a long time thanking you for the moving words in

1. A spa near Vienna.

your letter. By one of those dark pathways behind the official consciousness the old man's death has affected me deeply. I valued him highly, understood him very well, and with his peculiar mixture of deep wisdom and fantastic light-heartedness he had a significant effect on my life. By the time he died, his life had long been over, but in [my] inner self the whole past has been reawakened by this event. I now feel quite uprooted.

The letter mentions "a nice dream I had the night after the funeral" in which Freud read a sign saying: "You are requested to close the eyes."

His immediate recognition of the workings of the "dark pathways," the "reawakening" of the past, and the "uprooted" feeling did not fully convey the impact of his father's death on Freud's psychic stability. After his self-analysis, and as late as 1908, he described it in the preface to the second edition of his *Interpretation of Dreams* as "the most important event, the most poignant loss, of a man's life" (1900, xxv).

On December 4 he confided to Fliess: "My bad time has run its course in typical fashion; I am fully occupied, with every half-hour taken, and am not in the least interested in life after death." This disclaimer is followed in the letter by four "proud words" to introduce some future publications. The mottoes clearly reveal Freud's concerns with gods, accountability to God, the infernal regions, and doomsday. They seem to be obscure and defended unconscious derivatives of what Freud did not want to think about. They deserve full citation to illustrate the distress they reveal in Freud's conflicted thinking.

The first, intended for some future writing on the psychology of hysteria, is from Aristotle's *De partibus animalium*, 1:5, 20. These are the words spoken by Heraclitus to visiting strangers who were afraid to join him in the kitchen where he was warming himself: "Introite et hic dii sunt" ("Enter—for here too are gods").

The second quotation is supposed to introduce another future chapter on something Freud called "summation":

Sie trieben's toll, ich fürcht' es breche
Nicht jeden Wochenschluss macht Gott die Zeche.
(You are acting wildly, I fear it may break,
Not every weekend will God settle the account.)[2]

This incomprehensible passage comes from Goethe's "Spruche in reimen," as Walter Schönau has shown (1968, pp. 80–83). It seems to have been a popular saying at the time, but no German-speaking person I have asked about it recognizes it. It is hard to imagine what Freud had in mind; he never wrote anything on "summation" except in his correspondence with Fliess, posthumously published as the *Project for a Scientific Psychology* (1950).

The third motto, from Virgil's *Aeneid* (7:312), was in fact used by Freud in *The Interpretation of Dreams* four years later, although his letter indicates that he intended it for a work on symptom formation. Juno, feeling humiliated and vanquished by the actions of Aeneas, exclaims that she will not refrain from seeking help from any power anywhere: "Flectere si nequeo superos, Acheronta movebo" (If I cannot bend the higher powers, I will move the infernal regions).

Finally, the fourth motto, intended for some writing on resistance, is from Goethe's *Zahme Xenien*:

2. Otto Hoffer and Leon Wurmser helped with the translation of these obscure words. They concur that the expression means that God is not such a bad host or innkeeper that he would harass the guest.

Mach es kurz!
Am jüngsten Tag ist's doch nur ein———.
(Cut it short!
On doomsday it won't be worth a———).

Freud omitted the last word, *fart*, in the letter. The words are spoken in Goethe's text by God the Father, replying to Satan's charges against Napoleon. Freud used this quotation in 1914 as the epigraph for chapter 3 of his essay "On the History of the Psychoanalytic Movement."

Clearly, six weeks after his father's death, Freud was trying very hard *not* to think about the afterlife, heaven and hell, and God. His efforts were to no avail: God, gods, doomsday, the infernal regions, returned to his mind in the epigraphs he had proposed. The loss of his father had in fact taken some very dark pathway within him, and extreme measures were required to reorganize the reawakened past.

In his customary active way of mastering intense distress, Freud responded to the internal challenge with three creative moves. The first, reported to Fliess on December 6, was the acquisition of the first known objects of his antiquities collection, which he placed in the "new quarters" in his home to which he had moved his office in late November: "I have now adorned my room with plaster casts of Florentine statues. It was a source of extraordinary invigoration [*Erquickung*, meaning, also, comfort] for me; I am thinking of getting rich, in order to be able to repeat these trips [to Naples and Pompeii].³ A congress on Italian soil!" (1887–1904, p. 214). The buying of the statues and their consoling function suggests some relation to his father's death (Cassirer Bernfeld, 1951; Gamwell, 1989).

The other two moves—his self-analysis and the writing of

3. Jones (1953) states that Freud visited Florence for a week in the summer of 1896 (p. 333).

The Interpretation of Dreams—prompted Freud to attend to his inner world, where "the whole past" had been reawakened by his father's death. Twelve years later he acknowledged the connection among these events in the preface to the second edition of the "dream book" (1900): "For this book has a further subjective significance for me personally—a significance which I only grasped after I had completed it. It was, I found, a portion of my own self-analysis, my reaction to my father's death—that is to say, to the most important event, the most poignant loss, of a man's life" (p. xxvi).[4] Such an enormous, original, creative power of self-discovery is evidence of the inner turmoil elicited by his father's disappearance from his life. Why should this be? What psychic function did the presence of his father serve that his death led Freud to revise his entire early history, scrutinize his dreams, and collect antiquities while denying his interest in life after death?

The first objects Freud acquired, either on his short trip to Florence or from a local Viennese art dealer, induced in him, as noted, a feeling of "extraordinary invigoration." We may assume that the psychic function of the objects, which he bought six weeks after Jakob's death, went beyond the esthetic pleasure they provided. Lynn Gamwell (1989) concludes: "To consider that he began his collection in some sense as a reaction to his father's death seems unavoidable" (p. 23). Indeed, a central thesis of this book is that Freud's collecting of antiquities was a

---

4. In this book I shall not discuss Freud's self-analysis or his self-disclosures in *The Interpretation of Dreams*. Anzieu (1986) has written a comprehensive book about Freud's self-analysis. Grinstein (1980) and many others have studied in great detail the biographical background to Freud's dreams and the multiple connections they have to his rich and complex relationship with his father. I shall use the results of their research as needed in the exploration of Freud's relationship to the antiquities, his father, and God.

compulsory activity motivated by irresistible and unrecognized deep emotions, emotions that could be assuaged only by the physical presence of the objects and their reassuring psychic meaning.

The collection of archaeological objects, as Freud acknowledged in a letter to Stefan Zweig on February 7, 1931, was for him as compelling a need as smoking: "Despite my much vaunted frugality I have sacrificed a great deal for my collection of Greek, Roman and Egyptian antiquities, have actually read more archaeology than psychology, and that before the war and once after its end I felt compelled to spend every year at least several days or weeks in Rome, and so on" (1960, p. 403). Smoking was also compelling for Freud and seems to have helped to provide a necessary context for his work. Max Schur (1972), his personal physician, called it an addiction at the service of his creativity, and Freud himself wrote: "I ascribe to the cigar the greatest share of my self-control and tenacity in work."

It is important to notice that these are solitary activities that do not require, in and of themselves, the participation of another person. Their obligatory, compulsory nature reveals psychic needs that seek substitutive satisfaction in them. The actions must be repeated because they are not adequate compensation for unfulfilled needs. Smoking is easily recognized as an oral need; collecting antiquities, as described by Freud and the friends who observed him, offered him a needed joy and excitement not supplied by any other activity. The compulsory yearly visit to Rome as well as other trips was always an exhilarating occasion to search for antique objects.

Freud's first exposure to archaeology occurred during his early university years, at the time when the discipline made its entrance into the scientific world. Heinrich Schliemann's findings in Troy occurred in 1873, the excavation of King Minos's labyrinth in Crete in 1900, and the opening of Tutankhamen's tomb in Egypt in 1922. These discoveries were headline news in the daily press (Gamwell, 1989, p. 22). Freud had seen Greek and Roman antiquities when he visited Paris in 1885, not only in the Louvre but also at the home of his teacher Jean Martin Charcot. There is no evidence that he bought at the time any object or archaeological book.

His first reference to archaeology as a metaphor for analytic technique appears in 1893 in the case history of Fräulein Elisabeth von R.: "This procedure was one of clearing away the pathogenic psychic material layer by layer, and we like to compare it with the technique of excavating a buried city" (1893–95, p. 139). Freud did not buy his first archaeological book until 1899. He wrote to Fliess on May 28: "I gave myself a present, Schliemann's *Ilios*, and greatly enjoyed the account of his childhood. The man was happy when he found Priam's treasure, because happiness comes only with the fulfillment of a childhood wish." Seven months later, in his December 21 letter to Fliess, Freud applied the archaeological description to his self-analysis: "Buried deep beneath all fantasies, we found a scene from his primal period[5] (before twenty-two months) which meets all the requirements and in which all the remaining puzzles converge. It is everything at the same time—sexual, innocent, natural, and the rest. I scarcely dare believe it yet. It is as if Schliemann had once more excavated Troy, which had hitherto been deemed a fable. . . . For this piece of work I even made him the present of a picture of Oedipus and the Sphinx." Once more an archaeological object had the quality of an emotional reward given by a playful, loving, and approving superego.

The first archaeological reward Freud gave himself was the selection of Florentine statues that so invigorated him six weeks

5. Freud refers to himself in both the third person and the first person plural.

after his father's death. One of these replicas is of Michelangelo's *Dying Slave*. His son Martin photographed Freud sitting next to the statue and published the picture in his book *Glory Reflected* (1957). The photograph (fig. 1.1) was believed to be from about 1912, but Gamwell (1989) concludes, on the basis of contextual evidence, that it was taken around 1905 in the ground-floor study that Freud used from 1891 to 1907 (p. 25). She believes that the statue in the photograph is one of the Florentine pieces because when Freud moved his study to the second floor of the house in 1907, he did not take *The Dying Slave* there. It is unknown what happened to it.

The Dying Slave was one of three major pieces that Michelangelo made for the tomb of Pope Julius II. (*The Rebellious Slave* and *Moses* were the others.) The psychoanalyst Robert Liebert (1983) believed that the statue was inspired by the discovery of the *Laocoön*, a late Hellenistic marble group that dramatically portrays the kinship in death between father and sons. *The Dying Slave* "is closely patterned after the dying younger son to the left of the father" in the *Laocoön* (p. 170). It is not known whether Freud knew about the relation between the *Laocoön* group and Michelangelo's statue.

What could have prompted Freud to buy *The Dying Slave* at this particular moment of his life? What meanings did it have for him? What "invigorating" comfort could it bring to his bereavement?

Writing about the seventeenth-century painter Christoph Haizmann, Freud (1923) observed: "His father's death had made him lose his spirits and his capacity to work; if he could only obtain a father substitute he might hope to regain what he had lost" (p. 82). Haizmann made a pact with the Devil in his efforts "to feel secure": "He followed the path which led from his father, by way of the Devil as a father-substitute, to the pious Fathers of the Church" (p. 104). Freud did not lose his spir-

1.1 Freud, about 1912, sitting next to the Florentine statue. Freud Museum

its when his father died, but he did respond with the same need Haizmann expressed to regain what he had lost. Gamwell (1989) interprets Freud's purchase of The Dying Slave as "placing an idealized statue of his father in his study" (p. 26).

It is not difficult to understand that the subject matter of the statue might have satisfied Freud's need to let his father die peacefully. The slave is shown serenely dying, as Freud's father had died, with "decency and dignity." But it is unclear how the statue could restore his vigor. This can be better understood if we view the statue as also representing Jakob's actual presence in the office, in the way that a photograph or an object pertaining to a deceased person frequently restores a sense of presence. Freud's Erquickung may have come from the reappearance of his father's "fantastic light-heartedness."

The statue itself may offer another clue. The sense of slavery, of belonging to an "alien" race, was a feeling Freud had known in childhood and adolescence. His most poignant memory dates to age ten or twelve, when, in an intimate conversation, his father told him a personal story. Freud (1900) describes his father's account and his response:

> "A Christian came up to me and with a single blow knocked off my cap into the mud and shouted: 'Jew! get off the pavement!'" "And what did you do?" I asked. "I went into the roadway and picked up my cap," was his quiet reply. This struck me as unheroic conduct on the part of the big, strong man who was holding the little boy by the hand. I contrasted this situation with another which fitted my feelings better: the scene in which Hannibal's father, Hamilcar Barca, made his boy swear before the household altar to take vengeance on the Romans. Ever since that time Hannibal had had a place in my phantasies. (p. 197)

Freud had seen in the Philippson Bible, his father's book, the illustration of a naked jumper standing on his head on the back of a crocodile (fig. 1.2). If we compare The Dying Slave with the illustration we can see a physical resemblance between the two, particularly in the heads. Both are human males accompanied by an unusual animal—an ape in the sculpture, a crocodile in the illustration. We might speculate that Freud unconsciously remembered the illustration when choosing what statue to buy. This speculation becomes a conviction on reading the biblical text the figure illustrates. In the Book of Job, 40:29–32, the Lord confronts Job with his inability to deal with Leviathan, the primeval monster and mythical symbol of evil:

> 5 Will you play with him as with a bird, or will you put him on leash for your maidens?

6 Will traders bargain over him? Will they divide him up among the merchants?

7 Can you fill his skin with harpoons, or his head with fishing spears?

8 Lay hands on him; think of the battle; you will not do it again!

Ein ägyptischer Springer; antiker Marmor im brittischen Museum.

1.2 An Egyptian jumper. Antique marble at the British Museum. Philippson Bible, vol. 3, p. 614

I find it highly likely that Freud read this passage, alone or with his father, or possibly at the Gymnasium, where the Book of Job was assigned reading for the eighth grade (Rainey, 1975, pp. 44–45). The lines referring to traders and merchants must have impressed him, for Jakob had pursued these occupations. He must have thought, like Hannibal, that the revenge of Leviathan should befall anyone who dared to touch a Jew. The reference to being enslaved is explicit: "Will traders bargain over him?"

There is evidence that in his late adolescence Freud knew several passages of the Book of Job by heart. For example, on August 16, 1873, he wrote to his friend Eduard Silberstein: "Yesterday, when I had to suffer an Egyptian darkness for an hour because I could not lay my hands on flint or matches and because, as the Book of Job puts it, I cannot send lightnings to make light for me, I thought up the following conversation" (1871–81, p. 37). The reference is to Job 38:35: "Can you send forth lightnings, that they may go and say to you, 'Here we are'?" The speaker, God, confronts Job with his impotence compared with God's power over nature. It is part of the long answer God gives to Job's questioning, an answer that continues in the next chapters, where the passage illustrated by the Egyptian jumper is found. Freud here identifies with Job's impotence; he cannot command nature, as the Lord can.

On January 30, 1875, he reported to Silberstein that the journal he and three friends had founded "has passed peacefully into the keeping of the Lord." In the next paragraph he comments: "It was I who delivered the death blow; it had been ailing for a long time and I took pity on its suffering. I gave it life and I have taken its life away, so blessed be my name, for ever and ever, Amen" (p. 86). The reference is to Job 1:21: "Naked I came from my mother's womb, and naked shall I return; the Lord gave, and the Lord has taken away; blessed be the name of the Lord." In his transformation of the quotation, Freud takes the place of the Lord, celebrating his Godlike power to give and to take the life of the journal and imagining his name as eternally blessed. The impotent light maker has become the omnipotent giver and taker of life. The two quotations illustrate well Freud's intense and playful identification with the two main characters of the Book of Job.

The Philippson Bible illustration of Job's versicles seems to defy the meaning of the biblical warning against tampering with Leviathan; it presents a jumper "playing with him," "showing his art on the back of the crocodile," Philippson says. The illustration for the Lord's confrontation of Job, the questioning, suffering Jew, is an *Egyptian* marble statue found at the British Museum. Freud's "Egyptian darkness" and his assumption of the Lord's position may have found a precedent in this illustration. The contradiction between the biblical text and the Egyptian jumper illustration suited Freud's need to find an object that in form and content could encompass his diverse and complex feelings about his dead father. By its presence in his study, the Florentine *Dying Slave* could evoke simultaneously the longed-for presence of his father, Freud's reaction to Jakob's meek submissiveness, and his own willful defiance of all monsters. The Egyptian jumper certainly portrays a "fantastic light-heartedness" by taking the crocodile as his plaything. No wonder Freud felt so invigorated by a statue that may have brought him not only a reminder of his father but also symbolic satisfaction of wishes related to the father-son relationship—perhaps the wish that his father had defied the anti-Semite.

The collection inaugurated by *The Dying Slave* was to increase steadily until the end of Freud's life, eventually numbering more than two thousand objects. Freud bought most of them himself, principally from dealers in Vienna and in the places he visited on his many trips throughout Europe. His pleasure in collecting became public knowledge, prompting friends to search out suitable objects to add to the collection. Marie Bonaparte gave him several of the finest pieces of his collection. His passion was so well known that upon his arrival in London, Freud received as gifts several valuable antiques from people who were uncertain whether he would retrieve his collection from Vienna (Jones, 1957, pp. 229–30).

These gifts were always personal presents to Freud, to be placed in his office or study, not in the living quarters he shared with his wife and children. In fact, there was a striking contrast between house and study, as Spector (1975) observed: "Martha Freud . . . decorated their house in conformity to the current fashion of covering floors and sofas with sumptuous-looking Persian rugs (easily available in Vienna) and walls with richly colored and textured hangings. The couple's conservative taste largely bypassed Jugendstil, the Viennese counterpart of Art Nouveau; the austere Sachlichkeit of such important Viennese architects as Otto Wagner and Adolf Loos never affected them" (p. 22). The office and the study were also decorated with Oriental rugs, but they differed from the family apartment in that every available surface was densely covered with archaeological pieces, and there were several cabinets exclusively dedicated to containing and displaying the objects, both on top and within (fig. 1.3). The visitor could not avoid noticing them.

At first Freud bought a few Renaissance reproductions. But his heart was soon set on archaeological objects. He became a personal customer of the four or five antiquarian dealers in Vienna (Gamwell, 1989, p. 29, note 9). Freud's fondness for antiquarian stores was so great that he tended to misread shop signs, as he said in a paragraph added in 1907 to the second edition of The Psychopathology of Everyday Life: "There is one misreading which I find irritating and laughable and to which I am prone whenever I walk through the streets of a strange town on my holidays. On these occasions I read every shop sign that resembles the word in any way as 'Antiquities'. This betrays the questing spirit of the collector" (1901, p. 110).

Freud was prudent with his money and a good bargainer. Not being wealthy, he devised a method of rationalizing his purchases: "Anything he earned from single consultations he regarded as a bonus and felt justified in reserving it for his favorite hobby—the collecting of antiquities. To Ferenczi Freud used to refer to such sums as proceeding from the *National geschenk* (Public Donation)" (Jones, 1955, pp. 389–90). The objects were of course not as expensive at that time as they are now. According to Robert Lustig, a Viennese dealer who sold Freud hundreds of objects, Freud bought *Isis Suckling the Infant Horus*, one of the most beautiful pieces in his collection, for the price of its worth as metal (Gamwell, 1989, p. 23). Freud was intent upon obtaining pieces of quality and, Lustig said, insisted that the dealers authenticate each one.

Freud collected primarily sculptures of humans and animals, which prompted Spector to comment: "One cannot help associating this group of figurines with the sculptured ancestor-figurines of primitive religions" (1975, p. 23). Freud also possessed about fifty prints portraying archaeological sites and approximately one hundred ancient vases, lamps, steles, and contemporary photographs, not to mention fragments of paintings on plaster, papyrus, and linen, and three engravings by Rembrandt. The Freud Museum in London has not yet issued a comprehensive catalog of the collection, but we know that it encompasses Egyptian, Greek, Roman, Near Eastern, and Asian objects, plus a half-dozen Jewish objects. Later in life Freud collected Oriental art. Egyptian art prevails over all others, constituting 50 percent of all the objects. I will further explore this very significant fact in Chapter 7.

What the collection lacks is as important as what it includes.

1.3 Looking through a doorway from Freud's Vienna consulting room into his study, 1938. Photo copyright © Edmund Engelman

1.4 Freud's desk in Vienna, with his antiquities arranged like an audience, 1938. Photo copyright © Edmund Engelman

Absent are objects representative of modern art, as well as paintings and sculpture from any period of later European art. There is no primitive art, no children's or psychotic's art. There are no objects illustrating bisexuality, hermaphrodites, phallic cults, explicit eroticism, or any other aspect of the ubiquitous sexuality of humankind, even though sexuality was of central interest to Freud's investigations.

Scholars have asked whether there was an organizing principle behind Freud's passion for collecting antiquities. Richard Wells (1989), cocurator of the Freud Museum exhibition, says that the collection is not "tied together" and thus reflects the interests of a collector who "was buying with little time or money but with a passion." Lorelei H. Corcoran (1991) observes that Freud had no serious academic commitment to archaeology, did not subscribe to or read the academic journals in the field, and did not update his archaeological library (pp. 20–21). Many pieces provide undeniable esthetic pleasure but others do not; beauty seems not to be the source of the intense pleasure the antiquities gave their owner. S. Astropoulos (1989) concludes that "Freud's collecting agenda was not governed by a desire to acquire fine works of art, but was motivated by an ardent desire to accumulate objects which, for Freud, embodied certain concepts important to his theories" (cited in Corcoran, 1991). Freud rarely referred to his collection or to particular objects in his writings. He used some of the objects to make a point to his patients, who obviously could not avoid seeing them in the office. To the Wolf Man (1918), for example, Freud said: "The psychoanalyst, like the archaeologist in his excavations, must uncover layer after layer of the patient's psyche, before coming to the deepest, most valuable treasures" (Gardiner, 1971, p. 139).

Wells (1989) suggests that Freud's intellectual breadth suffices to explain his passion for antiquities: "Freud the humanist and Freud the scientist are linked in his favorite image of himself as the great explorer-conqueror of the mysteries of the human psyche." But this does not explain the intensity of the emotions involved in collecting and in the collection itself. The passion and addictive need to collect certain objects appear more emotional than intellectual.

Most authors agree that the objects were "his silent, loyal, immensely rewarding companions" (Gay, 1989, p. 15), his "audience," "whose gaze creates a conscious presence" (Gamwell, 1989, p. 27). And, indeed, Freud related to them as if they were alive. On July 17, 1899, he wrote to Fliess: "The ancient gods still exist, because I obtained . . . recently . . . a stone Janus who looks at me with his two faces in a very superior manner." Jones (1955) describes Freud's "habit of bringing his latest purchase of an antiquity, usually a small statuette, to the dinner table and placing it in front of him as a companion during the meal. Afterwards it would be returned to his desk and then brought back again for a day or two" (p. 393).

The statuettes, as Freud told Fliess in his August 1, 1899, letter, "participated" in his creative work: "My old and grubby gods, of whom you think so little, take part in the work as paper weights for my manuscripts." For Freud these "gods" had the full and playful life of true transitional objects, capable of making him feel accompanied, be it by their "superior manner" or by their "work as paper weights." Freud, it can truly be said, was never alone as long as he was with his antique objects.

According to Paula Fichtl, the maid who cleaned his office and study from 1929 until his death, "The professor especially loved a Chinese porcelain statue. He used to say that this statuette smiled at him every morning and that he could do nothing but to return the smile" (Berthelsen, 1986, my translation). Freud actually played with the statue, not unlike a child playing with a doll or a tin soldier. He also "stroked his marble Baboon of Thoth, god of learning, like a pet" (Salisbury, 1989). Acquiring a piece for his collection always lifted his mood. He wrote to Fliess on August 6, 1899: "On the next rainy day I shall tramp on foot to my beloved Salzburg, where I actually unearthed a few Egyptian antiquities last time. These things put me in a good mood and speak of distant times and countries." The objects also had a soothing function for him. Gamwell found and transcribed a February 16, 1927, letter to Max Eitingon in which Freud describes being fitted for a new prosthesis after oral surgery: "I got myself an expensive present today, a lovely little dipylon vase—a real gem—to fight my ill humor. (Spending money is indicated not only for states of fear.)" Gamwell (1989, p. 30, note 15) suggests that the object is the Mycenaean stirrup jar shown as figure 7.13.

The objects, particularly those on his desk, had to be kept in the places to which he had assigned them (fig. 1.4). Paula Fichtl knew the great importance of the task and took pride in knowing precisely where each piece belonged. She was probably the only person allowed to touch them. After their arrival in London she "arranged the wall bookshelves and the glass cabinets filled with Professor Freud's collection (Assyrian, Egyptian, Chinese, and Roman figures) in the same manner as they were in Austria, so that the Professor could feel at home when he arrived at Maresfield Gardens" (Berthelsen, 1986, my translation). This comment reveals her awareness that to Freud "home" meant his office, with his beloved antiquities and his books.

Among the members of the audience on his desk he had a "favorite." The American poet Hilda Doolittle (H.D.) was seeing him as a patient because of her writing block. One day Freud took the statuette of Athena from the end of the semicircle and said to her: "This is my favorite. She is perfect, only she has lost her spear." H.D. did not understand the comment.

She later wrote, "He might have been talking Greek" (Doolittle, 1956, pp. 68–69). She did not understand that Freud was alluding to his theory of female sexuality. In Greek mythology Athena was the *motherless* who sprang from the head of the male god Zeus. Pinsent (1969) describes the goddess: "Athena is not a name but a title. It means 'the Athenian one' and refers to another manifestation of the pre-Greek mother-goddess worshipped . . . in the Parthenon on the Acropolis at Athens. She was, however, quite literally absorbed by Zeus, who by pure thought brought her to birth from his forehead, fully armed in his own magic goat-skin, the aegis, though Hephaestus cleft his head open with an axe to effect the delivery" (pp. 31–32).

Freud (1922) noticed that Athena, a virgin goddess, wears the horrifying head of the Medusa and "thus she becomes a woman who is unapproachable and repels all sexual desires—since she displays the terrifying genitals of the mother" (pp. 273–74). He was committed to the view that male norms and the phallus prevail and that women are castrated males greatly dissatisfied with their maimed condition. Was this enough to make Athena his favorite? Other explanations are required because Athena was also a "protector" for him. He asked Marie Bonaparte to smuggle the statue out of Austria before the other antiquities were sent to London. He wrote to her on June 8, 1938, immediately upon his arrival in England, after spending a day in Paris in Bonaparte's house, where he was reunited with Athena. He described the trip from Paris this way: "Surrounded by love for twelve hours, we arrived proud and rich under the protection of Athena" (Schur, 1972, p. 564). The description suggests once more the soothing function of the objects of the collection, but without unveiling Freud's motive for favoring Athena.

After the Nazis invaded Austria, in March 1938, Freud reluctantly accepted the need to leave his country. There was much to be disposed of. He could take with him only a limited number of books. After he selected those to be sent to England, there remained eight hundred volumes that had to be sold.[6] Freud seems to have parted from the bulk of his library without any expressed suffering.

It was another matter for him to think of being separated from the antiquities. On May 14, 1938, he confided in a letter to his sister-in-law Minna Bernays: "In the fateful first days of next week the commission on which the fate of the collection depends is supposed to come here. The shipper is lurking in the background" (Gay, 1989, p. 15). After a period of anxious waiting the permission was given. He wrote to Minna on May 23: "My collection has been released. Not a single confiscation, a minimal levy of RM 400. . . . The shipper can start with the packing without delay." Hans Demel, director of the Kunst historisches Museum in Vienna, had given a low appraisal to the whole collection—RM 30,000, a considerable amount but not enough to tempt the authorities to confiscate them.

By the time Freud arrived in London he was terminally ill. Max Schur wrote that during August 1939 "everything went downhill." Freud, growing weaker by the day, had to give up seeing patients. When the study was no longer his workplace it became "his sick bay" (Schur, 1972, p. 526), the place where he chose to die. He was "home" there, with his couch, his books, his statuettes, looking at him, smiling at him, and "protecting" him with their unobtrusively friendly and mysterious companionship—from the time of the death of his father to his own death.

6. He handed them over to the Viennese bookseller Heinrich Hinterberger, who advertised them discretely as the collection of a "scientific explorer" and asked 1,850 German marks—sixty cents per volume—for them. Fortunately, Dr. Jacob Schatzky, librarian of the New York State Psychiatric Institute, guessed that Freud might be the "explorer" and arranged to buy the collection and ship it to New York before the end of 1939 (Clark, 1980, p. 511).

In a will written on July 28, 1938, Freud left "to my daughter Anna my collection of antiquities as it is defined by the catalogue" (1991, p. 638).[7] Anna Freud, in turn, decided at the end of her life to create the Freud Museum in commemoration of her father's life and work, and to give a permanent home to his beloved antiquities.

7. The will, which was made public for the first time in 1991, does not clarify who made this catalog or how comprehensive it was.

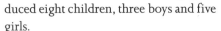

Sigmund Freud was the fourth son and the fifth child of the twelve offspring of Jakob Freud. The first four children were from Jakob's first marriage, at age sixteen, to Sally Kanner. The two eldest, Emmanuel and Philipp, survived, but their siblings, a boy and a girl, died in infancy (Krüll, 1986, p. 234, table 3). Jakob's second marriage, to a woman we know only as Rebekka, apparently brought him no children. His third marriage produced eight children, three boys and five girls.

Sigmund Freud was the first child born to Amalie Nathansohn Freud, a woman not yet twenty years old in 1855, at the time of her marriage to the thirty-nine-year-old Jakob. Like the biblical patriarch Jacob and his son Joseph, Jakob seemed to have loved Sigmund "more than all his brothers" (Genesis 37:4). The most intriguing confirmation of this favoritism comes from Jakob's handwritten annotations in the family bible. Sigmund's birth and circumcision are the only entries about children registered on the commemorative page (Gedenkblatt) of the bible. Furthermore, as we have seen, Jakob gave this bible to Sigmund as a very special gift for his thirty-fifth birthday, though he had eight other living children who presumably had equal claims to such an heirloom.

In 1856, when Sigmund was born, Jakob Freud had already lived forty of his eighty-one years. He was precisely in the middle of his life's journey when his marriage to Amalie Nathansohn offered him a new beginning. His new start, however, began with the closing of an era: his own father, Shlomo (Salomon) Freud, died on February 21, 1856, at Tismenitz, in the Austrian region of Galicia, ten weeks before the birth of Jakob's first son from the new marriage. We have no information about Shlomo's death—whether it was expected or the result of sudden illness, how old he was at the time, or which, if any, of his four children attended his funeral. It is almost certain that Jakob, the firstborn son, was unable to attend; if so, he could not fulfill the filial obligation of closing his father's eyes and saying Kaddish at the funeral service. Jakob did document Shlomo's death, however, in a Hebrew inscription, the first he made on the commemorative page of the bible (fig. 2.1).

Next to Jakob Freud's inscription an unnamed translator (E. Freud et al., 1985, p. 324) has rendered it into German. In English it reads: "My father Rabbi Shlomo of blessed memory, son of Rabbi Ephraim Freud, entered into his heavenly home on the 6th day of the week, Friday, at 4 o'clock in the afternoon, on the 6th day of the month of Adar 616, and on the 18th of the same month was buried in the town of Tismenitz, where I was born. According to Christian reckoning he died on February 21 and was buried on February 23, 1856" (E. Freud et al., 1985, p. 46). The inscription connects the death of Shlomo the father to the birth of Jakob the son by the reference to Tismenitz, where one was buried, the other born. The next inscription connects, through their shared name, the birth of Shlomo Sigmund to the death of his grandfather.[1] The two entries are

1. The name Sigmund appears in German on the inscription page translating Jakob's entry, but Jakob's Hebrew said clearly Sigismund. Freud's name was registered in school documents as Sigismund. Ernst Freud (1985) reports that "as Dr. Eva Laible of Vienna has told us, 'Sigmund Freud' does not appear until 1870" (p. 325, note 12).

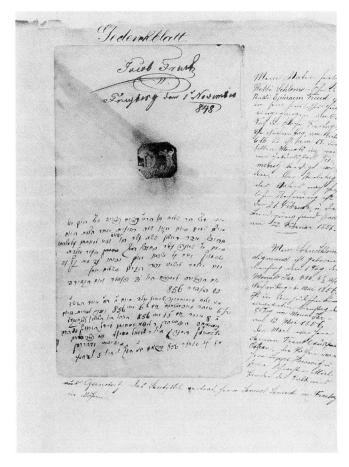

2.1 Commemorative page in the family Bible. Freud Museum

placed on the page in such a manner that the second appears as a continuation of the first. The handwritten translation of the second entry reads: "My son Shlomo Sigmund was born on Tuesday, the first day of the month of Iar 616 at 6:30 in the afternoon = May 6, 1856. He entered the Jewish community on

Tuesday, the 8th day of the month of Iar = May 15, 1856. The Moel [who circumcises the child] was Herr Samsom Frankl from Ostrau, the godparents were Herr Lippa Horowitz and his sister Mirl, children of the Rabbi from Czernowitz. The Sandykat [the duty of holding the child during the circumcision] was taken by Herr Samuel Samueli in Freiberg in Moravia" (E. Freud et al., 1985, p. 46).

Emmanuel Rice had the original Hebrew text retranslated by Rabbi Jules Harlow, who found that the last sentence of the Hebrew entry about Shlomo's death had been omitted from Ernst Freud's (1985) official translation. Jakob had written: "He who walked a straight course shall have peace on his resting place until the time of the end, until the day when He shall say to those who sleep in dust: 'Awake in peace.' Amen" (Rice, 1990, p. 34). Rabbi Harlow also suggests that in the part of the text describing Freud's birth, the phrase translated as "entered the Jewish community" is more accurately rendered by "entered into the covenant." The omission in the first entry and the translation of "covenant" by "community" in the second remove the explicitly religious connotations of the two events. When these are restored, it becomes clear that Jakob viewed Shlomo Sigmund, his son, as having entered into the covenant between the Jewish people and God, and Shlomo, his father, as destined to be awakened by God after peaceful rest. According to Harlow, then, Jakob Freud conceived of both his father's death and his son's life as related to God's call and covenant.

The three generations are linked by their joint appearance on the Gedenkblatt, connecting birth and death from generation to generation. Shlomo the elder had completed his life journey in peace because he had walked "a straight course." What course had Jakob walked in the first forty years of his life? What course did he expect Shlomo Sigmund, newly entered into the covenant, to follow? We have no evidence of Jakob's explicit wishes. The psychoanalyst, however, cannot ignore the fact that Shlomo Sigmund was born to a father mourning his own father—that is, facing "the most important event, the most poignant loss, of a man's life" (1900, xxvi [1908 preface])— whose name the newborn inherited. And both names were written in the family bible, the book that shows how to walk "the straight course." Thus Shlomo Sigmund entered this world enveloped in the psychic presence of his dead grandfather. While he was growing through the earliest attachments and sensory organization of his psychic reality, his father was immersed in the task of grieving his own father.

In the small Eastern European Jewish communities (*shtetls*) of Jakob Freud's early years, the civil restrictions imposed on Jews by law excluded them from the professions and most common trades and crafts. They were forced to live in poverty and were constantly watched over by the hostile neighbors who surrounded them everywhere. What made them Jews and kept them Jewish was their religion. Its strict dietary laws, its 613 commandments (*mitsvos*), the Sabbath observance, and the shared religious language of Hebrew precluded any assimilation with their Christian neighbors.

The Torah was the very center of Jewish life. "Torah study was a lifelong task for every pious Jew, his only true purpose in life" (Zborowski and Herzog, 1952, quoted by Krüll, 1986, p. 81). The Jew "was encouraged to marry early so that once his physical need had been satisfied, he could again devote himself wholeheartedly to the word of God." Couples frequently married as young as sixteen or seventeen. The Jewish religion was lived in a community context and involved every moment of the day. This enhanced the need for cohesion and resulted in very strict control of individual behavior through social pressure. The addition of extreme poverty to these religious circumstances meant that interdependence, mutual support, and

solidarity were not only religious imperatives but were necessary for survival. In such extreme situations as prevailed in Galicia, many Jews died of starvation in spite of community efforts.
Galicia "was set aside as a market for the products—chiefly the
so-called 'inferior' goods for the 'use of Galicia'—that the in-
dustrial areas in the monarchy produced. . . . The consumption
in Galicia of such staples as grain, meat and potatoes was one
half of that in Western Europe. According to income-tax figures the per capita income of the population of Galicia was one-
tenth that of the rest of Austria" (Mahler, 1990, pp. 126–27).

The commitment of Orthodox Jews to the study and interpretation of the Torah and the Talmud was accompanied by
great fear of secular learning: "Students were forbidden to read
any secular literature that could be perceived as posing the re-
motest threat to their beliefs" (Rice, 1990, p. 87). As a result
Orthodox children could not attend secular schools. "In 1787,
Joseph II charged Naphtali Herz Homberg . . . to open German-
language Jewish schools in Galicia" as envisaged in the Toler-
anz-Patent, which granted Jews equal rights and privileges
(Krüll, 1986, p. 76). The Bible would continue to be taught in
these schools, but only in German; in addition, the children
would be introduced to subjects other than those typically offered in the kheyder (Hebrew school) or yeshiva (rabbinical academy). The creation of these public educational institutions for
Jews reflected the spreading of the influence of the European
Enlightenment movement in Austria.

Rabbinical Jews—those with especially strong adherence to
the Torah and the Talmud—feared that secular knowledge, neglect of the Hebrew language, and the change of mores caused
by opening the closed Jewish community to the culture at large
would erode their ancestral heritage. Their response was an almost total boycott of these schools and bitter hatred of anyone

who tried to turn Jewish children away from Judaism by means of such institutions. Such was the Orthodox community in which Freud's father was born and lived until his late thirties. Jakob Freud, or Kallaman² Jakob, was born on December 18, 1815. All that is known about his mother is her name—Pessel (Peppi) Hofmann—and that she was the daughter of Zisie (Siskind) Hofmann, herself born in either 1775 or 1768 and a resident of Tismenitz. The Freud family has been traced to Buczacz, a town thirty-five miles east of Tismenitz, where they lived for four generations. The patronymic Freud was probably adopted in 1787, when all the Jews of Galicia were required to assume family names. It is presumably a derivative of Freide, the name of Shlomo Freud's great-grandmother. Shlomo Freud was the first in the family to move to Tismenitz, perhaps as a yeshiva student (S. Blond, in Krüll, 1896, p. 89).

Jakob's maternal grandfather, Siskind Hofmann, was a merchant, as was his son-in-law Shlomo Freud. Hofmann started traveling between Galicia and Moravia as early as 1804. After 1838 Shlomo accompanied him. Krüll (1986) speculates that "they had that characteristic Jewish relationship between father-in-law and son-in-law which was often so much easier than that between father and son" (p. 89). Nothing is known about the relationship between Shlomo Freud and his father, Ephraim, who continued to live in Buczacz. Jakob mentioned his paternal grandfather for the first time—the only documented time—when he entered the death of his father in the Gedenkblatt of the Philippson Bible.

Jakob was his father's firstborn son. He had two younger

2. Many of the names and patronymics are spelled differently in the original documents consulted by various authors and in the languages these authors employed to write their reports. The spellings presented here come from the comprehensive research compiled by Krüll, 1986.

brothers, Abae, whose date of birth is not known, and Joseph, ten years Jakob's junior, as well as a sister. Jakob must have entered a kheyder at the age of four. That he read and wrote Hebrew with full understanding and was clearly steeped in the reading of the Talmud suggests that he may also have attended the respected Tismenitz yeshiva. His granddaughter Judith Heller (1973) described him as "reading a great deal—German and Hebrew (not Yiddish)" and dividing his "time between reading the Talmud (in the original) at home, sitting in a coffee house, and walking in the parks" (p. 335). In addition, Jakob's ability to write German suggests that as a young man he may have attended the local Jewish Enlightenment school established by Homberg under orders of Josef II. In his twenties he signed the papers required for his travel and work permits in German; his grandfather Siskind Hofmann, by contrast, signed in Hebrew (Krüll, 1986, p. 90).

Nothing is known of Jakob's life in Tismenitz. This is surprising because Emmanuel and Philipp, his surviving children by his first wife, remained in contact with the family and could have provided information even if their father did not. The town apparently had a synagogue dating from the end of the seventeenth century (Blond, 1974), where Jakob must have participated in the Sabbath and High Holiday services. Freud's only reference to his father's religious background does not appear until 1930. Responding to A. A. Roback, an American Yiddishist, who had sent him one of his own books with a dedication written in Hebrew, Freud wrote: "It may interest you to hear that my father did indeed come from a Chassidic background. He was forty-one when I was born and had been estranged from his native environment for almost twenty years. My education was so un-Jewish that today I cannot even read your dedication, which is evidently written in Hebrew. In later life I have often regretted this lack in my education" (1960, p. 395).

This brief reference permits several inferences: first, that Jakob Freud had a "native environment" different from the one Freud had known and that he became "estranged" from it in his twenties; second, that he had been exposed to Hasidism but had left it behind; and, finally, that Freud could not read Hebrew at the time and presumably never could—a surprising remark from a man who taught himself Spanish at the age of fifteen and who had had a solid grounding in the Hebrew language in his childhood. If Jakob was exposed to Hasidism, as the letter implies, it must have occurred in his adolescence, not during his childhood, for "only from 1840 onward did the Hasidic movement begin to make some headway in Galicia" (Friedmann, 1929, p. 41, as quoted in Krüll, 1986, p. 75). Jakob's childhood education therefore could not have been Hasidic.

Freud must have known much more about his father and about his half-brothers' childhood background than he was willing to disclose to the world. Nevertheless, as a generation, his grandparents appear neither in his dreams nor in his conscious statements. The only reference to his maternal grandfather's death in his entire work, including his known correspondence, was as the occasion for the dream of "People with Birds' Beaks." Life for Freud seems to have begun with his parents. It is hard to assess the conscious and unconscious motives for this omission. In any case, it deprives the Freud scholar of any help in understanding Freud's psychic elaboration of the influence of his ancestors and specifically of his paternal grandfather, whose name he inherited (de Mijolla, 1981).

Jakob Freud's name appears for the first time in a document issued on April 30, 1844, giving him and his grandfather Siskind Hofmann a short-term permit to stay and do business in the city of Freiberg. Apparently he was replacing his own father, who had been Hofmann's earlier associate. Perhaps Jakob's "estrangement" from Tismenitz began as the result of these trips to Moravia, where "the Austrian authorities were . . . determined to ensure Jewish assimilation" (Krüll, 1986, p. 91). The application for this permit lists their occupation as "selling various products such as wool, hemp, tallow, honey, furs, and the buying of untreated cloth and seeing to its complete finishing." Each man owned a trading tax certificate. They seemed to have no relatives in town because they stayed at the "town hostelry" (Krüll, 1986, p. 92). Jakob's name in this document appears as Kallaman Jakob.

To a second application by the two merchants on June 24, 1844, the local magistrate appended an affidavit by the Cloth Makers' Guild. The document deserves full citation because it reveals the spirit of the time and illuminates Jakob's life as a traveling merchant:

> Siskind Hoffman and his grandson Kallmann Freud are known to us as honorable and trustworthy merchants, who purchase the products of local cloth masters, have them finished locally and forward them to Galicia, and import Galician products in return. The presence of these merchants in Freiberg is of great benefit both to the local inhabitants and also to the surrounding villages because the products of the cloth makers can invariably be sold through them. By virtue of the presence of these merchants in our midst, local commerce benefits considerably so that we feel in duty bound to endorse the application for a certificate of toleration by Siskind Hoffman and Kallmann Freud.[3] (Sajner, 1968, p. 169, translated by Krüll, 1986, p. 93)

Jakob was twenty-eight years old at this time, and his grandfather must have been at least in his mid-sixties.

3. These documents mentioned by Krüll were discovered by J. Sajner and R. Gicklhorn in the District Archive of Neu Titschein.

On October 19, 1847, Jakob applied on his own for a certificate giving him permission to stay in Freiberg for six months. Apparently the request was denied. He applied again on February 22, 1848, under the auspices of the Cloth Makers' Guild, and mentioned in this new application that he was in partnership with his grandfather. He described himself as "merely the appointee of Abraham Halpen in Stanislaus, who sends me these articles, and further of Nathan Tenner and M. N. Herdan of Tismenitz." Jakob assured the authorities, who were instructed by police regulations to expel Jews without passports, that his income tax certificate was "in the hands of my [wife] Fanny Freud in Tysmenitz" (Sajner, 1968, p. 170, translated by Krüll, 1986, pp. 94–95). At this time Jakob was issued a toleration certificate limited to three months. It is obvious that he had difficulty obtaining a certificate as an independent merchant.

The year 1848 was a critical one for the Austro-Hungarian Empire. The spirit of the Enlightenment was making itself felt in political, social, and intellectual life. A series of movements and revolutions resulted in significant changes, like the end of the feudal system of land tenure and the establishment of universal suffrage, freedom of the press, and the official use of regional languages. Austrian Jews were granted full political and civil rights. The restrictions on traveling and choice of residence that Jakob's permit application documents were removed. Jews were faced with the choice of either integrating into an emancipated and educated bourgeoisie or retreating into a secluded, homogeneously observant Jewish community.

Jakob Freud seemed to have preferred the first option. As a student of the Torah, he moved from the orthodoxy of the shtetl, with its Hebrew Torah, to the bilingual Hebrew and German edition of the Bible produced by Ludwig and Phoebus

Philippson. As a citizen he used his newly acquired freedom of residence to leave the shtetl of Tismenitz and move to Freiberg. It is not known when he made the move, but on October 31, 1852, the "Register of Jews shows him as a holder of a certificate of domicile issued by the Klogsdorf municipality, which bordered on Freiberg. It is likely, however, that Jakob Freud never actually lived in Klogsdorf, merely acquiring domiciliary rights there because such rights were easier to obtain in a village than in a town" (Krüll, 1986, p. 95).

At that time Freiberg (renamed Příbor after the end of the First World War) had approximately five thousand inhabitants, four thousand of them Catholic and one hundred Protestant. Twenty-nine Jewish families were registered there (Krüll, 1986, p. 95). The town is located at the foot of the Carpathian Mountains, along the Lubina River, 150 miles from Vienna (Clark, 1980, pp. 5–6). The Church of Mariae Geburt (The Birth of Mary) in the small central square dominates the town with its imposing presence and famous tower chimes. Jakob had moved into a Gentile town.

The 1852 Register of Jews Resident in Freiberg lists Jakob's household as consisting of himself, thirty-eight years old, his thirty-two-year-old wife, Rebekka, his sons Emmanuel and Philipp, aged twenty-one and sixteen, respectively, and Emmanuel's wife, Maria, aged eighteen. Jakob's occupation is given as "produce dealer." This document has the ages wrong: Jakob was in fact thirty-six years old at the time, and Emmanuel and Philipp were nineteen and eighteen, respectively. When Jakob married Amalie Nathansohn, in 1855, the official marriage certificate states that he had been a "widower since 1852." Rebekka is not listed in the 1854 Register of Freiberg inhabitants (Sajner, 1968, p. 171).

Whether Rebekka ever existed or was the result of a clerical error is much less important than the fact that Emmanuel, Philipp, and Sigmund himself never mentioned a public word about their father's wives. Sally (Fanny?) and the mysterious Rebekka were swallowed in deep secrecy. Freud's curiosity about his father's marriages is revealed only once, in a dream in which he described his father's recollection of having been drunk once in 1851: "'So you used to drink as well?' I asked; 'did you get married soon after that?'" (1900, p. 436).

The same mystery envelops the transition period in Jakob's life between 1844 and 1848, when he was commuting between Tismenitz and Freiberg. Did his grandfather–traveling companion die? Did his wife Rebekka die? Did Jakob go through a personal crisis of separation and loneliness or a religious and moral crisis during this period of upheaval? There is no historical document to reveal Jakob's inner state as he moved from the life of the shtetl to Gentile Freiberg. The known facts are these: the 1852 certificate of domicile shows Jakob on his own for the first time, not as "merely the appointee" of another merchant. Perhaps settling in Freiberg and starting his own business required him to break old commercial and family ties. This would have been an opportunity not available to him before. One year after his thirty-fifth birthday, the year when he reached full maturity as a Jewish male, Jakob declared that he was an independent man. It was the right time for new beginnings on all levels: in religion, work, and family.

There are few pieces of information about Jakob Freud's business. The district archives show that between 1852 and 1855 he imported sheep's wool, tallow, and honey; in fact, he was listed as one of the top six importers in Freiberg. This does not signify a large business but simply shows that Jakob functioned among the best of his peers in their small import operations. In December 1853 he transferred his business to his son

Emmanuel, who took full charge and paid the taxes in January of 1854 (Krüll, 1986, pp. 97–98). The register indicates that Jakob continued to import sheep's wool, tallow, and honey.

His new family life began on July 29, 1855, when he married Amalie Nathansohn, the youngest child and only daughter of Jacob and Sara Wilenz Nathansohn. Amalie was born in Brody, in northeast Galicia, and was taken to Odessa as a small child and then to Vienna.[4] Apparently her father was a "business agent" (Clark, 1980, p. 8), and it may be that it was through business connections that Jakob met her.

His photographs indicate that Jakob Freud was an attractive man. His 1847 passport description presents him, in the laconic words of any official portrayal: "Figure slim, face oval, hair blond, eyes brown, nose turned up" (Gicklhorn, 1976, table 1). Jacob Nathansohn was exactly ten years older than his son-in-law, whose first grandchild, Johann (John), was born to Emmanuel and Maria just two weeks after Jakob's marriage to Amalie.

All Freud's biographers wonder how the marriage contract was arranged between the bride, an attractive and spirited young woman of not quite twenty, and the thirty-nine-year-old bridegroom. In the 1850s most marriages between Orthodox Jews were of two contemporary and very young adults. It is legitimate to consider whether her parents may have thought that Amalie had tuberculosis. Her brother Julius died of the disease on March 15, 1858.[5] Jones mentions that after her marriage Amalie made frequent visits to Roznau, a spa in Moravia, ne-

4. This information is found in the marriage certificate as presented in W. Aron, *Notes on Sigmund Freud's Ancestry and Jewish Contacts*, YIVO Annual of Jewish Studies, New York, 1956–57, as quoted by Krüll (1986), table 7.

5. The information comes from a Freud-Nathansohn family tree at the Sigmund Freud archives of the Library of Congress in Washington, D.C. It was found by Peter and Julia Swales and given to Krüll (1986, p. 270).

cessitated by her tuberculosis (1953, p. 15). Sajner (1989) was able to find records of a total of twenty-four visits that Amalie made to Roznau, alone or with other children. The first documentation of such a visit is an entry in the Roznau Register of Spa Visitors for June 5, 1857, indicating that Amalie was there with her child Sigmund and a maid, Resi Wittek (Sajner, 1981). Nothing is known about who paid her expenses during those visits. Amalie's eldest daughter, Anna Freud Bernays, wrote: "Every Easter, Mother started to cough, and would then go to recuperate for three months in Roznau, a health resort in Moravia, invariably taking her weakest child with her, leaving me, the rest of the children, and Father in town for the summer" (ca. 1930, p. 8). Freud himself, in letters to Silberstein, to Martha, and to Fliess, mentioned several occasions on which his mother was suffering from a lung condition. For example, on February 27, 1875, he wrote to Silberstein: "My mother is suffering from a protracted illness admitting of no quick improvement: infiltration of the lungs; she is bedridden and weak, and will be going to Roznau at the beginning of May" (1871–81).

Tuberculosis was a terrible plague in the nineteenth century. Those who had it would certainly die, which foreclosed such future plans as marriage. Is it possible that Amalie's parents thought that she had no future and thus were willing to accept Jakob's marriage offer? Could she have had some other chronic lung condition that only simulated tuberculosis? The bacillus of tuberculosis was not isolated until 1882, and until then there were no scientific means of making a differential diagnosis between tuberculosis and other lung conditions.

Whatever the Nathansohns' motives for accepting such an unlikely husband for their daughter, the marriage took place under the full auspices of both Jewish and civil law. Rabbi Isaac Noah Mannheimer, who officiated, was known to be "conservative in his religious views" and was the "only person in the 1850s who could give legal sanction to a Jewish marriage because of the authorization given to him by the civil authorities to do so" (Rice, 1990, p. 57). The marriage certificate is in German, which indicates that it was a legal document, and there was a Jewish marriage contract as well.

The couple moved to Freiberg, where they lived in a rented room on the first floor of a house at Schlossergasse 117 (E. Freud et al., 1985, p. 45). J. Zajic, the owner, lived with his family in the other first-floor room, while the ground floor housed his locksmith shop. Philipp Freud, who was unmarried, lived across the street, also in a rented room, while Emmanuel and Maria Freud and their infant son, John, lived at no. 42 Markplatz (Krüll, 1986, p. 108).

Exactly nine months after the wedding Amalie delivered her firstborn, Shlomo Sigismund, who was to become "his mother's undisputed darling," her "golden Sigi." The meaning of the event for Jakob is recorded only in the entries about Sigmund's birth and circumcision in the Gedenkblatt of the Philippson Bible, below the notation of his father's death.

Could there have been a connection between this new son, new beginnings, and Jakob's leaving behind the strict Jewish orthodoxy of Tismenitz to search for the broader horizons suggested in the Philippsons' Bible and commentaries? It is known that Emmanuel and Philipp remained Orthodox Jews and in the late 1860s even participated in founding a new synagogue in South Manchester (Rice, 1990, p. 58). Was Jakob, by inscribing his son's name in the bible, affirming not only his own religious evolution but also his wish that Shlomo Sigismund would join the new Jewish world, becoming the new Jew dreamed of by those who believed in the full integration of Jews into the everyday life of their contemporaries?

chapter three
Jakob and the "Catastrophe"

In 1847 Ludwig Philippson, the rabbi of Magdeburg and the principal translator and editor of the Philippson Bible, delivered a series of twelve lectures entitled *The Development of the Religious Idea in Judaism, Christianity and Mahomedanism*. Anna Maria Goldsmith, the English translator, wrote in her preface that one of the purposes of the lectures was to "remove religion from the ideal station assigned to it, into the position to which it belongs—into life." According to Gold-

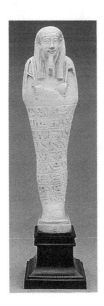

smith, Philippson believed that society and religion "must be reunited . . . until society collectively shall have become religious" (Philippson, 1855, p. ix). Judaism must lead in this movement because it alone had remained faithful to God's mandate. The time to achieve this change had arrived, and Judaism itself was going through a period of transition. "We see that Rabbinism has become wholly inoperative, if indeed it is not virtually defunct; while, on the other hand, we perceive that throughout its domain, Judaism is everywhere quickening into active life . . . [and] the causes actually in operation must inevitably produce a new phase of Judaism" (p. 15).

In Philippson's conception, "the Creator is in indirect relation with the world" but "in direct relation" with the human soul created after his likeness; this "is self evident from the constitution of the human mind" and its "free development." Man is capable of cooperating with a God who "offers continual providential guidance of the destiny of mankind" as it is so clearly "declared in every page of the Mosaic writings" (p. 43). Moreover, God is the maker of all that exists: "The Religious Idea teaches us that God is supermundane, and that nature is the work of God" (p. 232). The moderate form of Judaism endorsed by Philippson is "the special vehicle of the Religious Idea" and its connection with life (p. 244). To carry that Idea into life is the essential goal of Judaism (p. 259); on the other hand, "ceremonial law has no real and absolute value." The mission of Judaism is to produce "the unity of the whole race of man."

Philippson believed that the Religious Idea would triumph in the end and that the time had come for those Jews who were capable of casting off the ceremonial law to bring about that triumph (p. 265). The tidings of history were propitious for the first time in centuries:

> It was during the first half of the last century that the first rays of light fell on the benighted isolation of the Jews. The dissemination of these stray beams was aided by the position of some among them as members of the medical profession. Then the intellectual culture of the Jews increased both within and without, with almost magical rapidity. . . . What was at that time the attribute of few Jewish intellects became, in the course of the century, the universal property of the Jewish mass, thereby raising the whole of the next generation to the intellectual European standard, and consequently far above and beyond the domain of Talmudism. This intellectual cultivation could not fail to re-awaken the Idea, and to cause the right of private judgment and the claims of individual freedom, in opposition to Talmudism, to be fully recognized. (pp. 238–39)

This conception of Judaism and the new freedom of judgment accorded to Jews prompted Philippson to produce a faithful and elegant German translation of the Hebrew Bible with extensive commentaries illustrating God's creation and the works of humanity under God's guidance. The commentaries were meant to give the reader all the information needed to fully grasp the human and divine teachings in the biblical text. And, as we have noted, the bible included more than five hundred carefully chosen woodcuts, in violation of God's stern prohibition against using images:

> Take heed to yourselves, lest you forget the covenant of the Lord your God, which he made with you, and make a graven image in the form of anything which the Lord your God has forbidden you. For the Lord your God is a devouring fire, a jealous God. . . . If you act corruptly by making a graven image in the form of anything . . . I call Heaven and earth to witness against you this day, that you will soon . . . be utterly destroyed. And the Lord will scatter you among the peoples, and you will be left few in number among the nations where the Lord will drive you. (Deuteronomy 4:23–27)

The Philippson Bible even included pictures of Egyptian gods.

Jakob Freud had been strictly schooled in God's prohibitions against the making of any images. There is no documented information to help us understand the drastic change from his early Orthodox learning to the tides of the new Jewish times. Obviously he did not find it incongruous to write a reverent account of his Orthodox father's death and burial in a bible that defied God's law. This attests to his capacity to change, to join the "new intellectual culture of the Jews." Mayer Halevi (1958–59) claims to have found some letters written by Jakob to Zevi Menahem Pineles, a Tismenitz scholar who, influenced by the teachings of the great Moses Mendelssohn, had moved from being a Hasidic Jew to an adherent of the Haskala (Jewish Enlightenment). Perhaps Jakob had become a member of the Reading and Cultural Circle founded in Tismenitz in 1848, "whose object it was to spread secular knowledge and the ideas of the Enlightenment" (Blond, 1974, p. 155). In fact, it appears from the date written on the flyleaf that Jakob must have bought his Philippson Bible in the year the Reading Circle was founded.

By buying the Bible, Jakob had joined those Jews who wanted full integration with the wider culture while remaining faithful to God, to Judaism, and to the Torah—understood broadly as the Jewish covenant with God—as well as to the belief that God was at work in nature and history. Jakob was obviously an intelligent man, self-taught, who seemed to have shared some dreams of grandeur with his wife, Amalie. According to Martin Freud, his father had told him that it was no coincidence that Jakob's birthday was the same as Bismarck's and that Amalie's coincided with Emperor Franz Josef's. Both had selected the dates intentionally when they had to translate their birthdays from the Jewish calendar to the Gregorian calendar (Jones, 1953, p. 192). The wish to have something in common with great men may have prompted both Jakob, beginning anew, and Amalie, the young mother of a first son, to place on the newborn their dreams and ambitions for a better life, the hope for greatness, open now to all Jews of good intellect. The new Shlomo Sigismund would be a Jew fit for the new world, a great leader espousing the Religious Idea, a modern master of nature and its sciences, making discoveries while revering God's creation.

In the Gedenkblatt of the Philippson Bible, Jacob wrote another entry about his new son: "On the fourth of [?] [1]856 my son mentioned above, long may he live, got three teeth" (Rice, 1990, p. 34). This must have been in late November or early December, when Freud was six or seven months old. The report on Shlomo Sigismund's teeth is a moving evidence of Jakob's attentiveness to the infant.

Something must have changed after that because Jakob wrote no more in the bible. We know that in June 1857 Amalie, pregnant with Julius, went to Roznau with Sigmund and her maid. Had Amalie's tuberculosis become active, disrupting the new couple's everyday life? Up to that point their lives seem to have followed a simple family pattern. Amalie and her daughter-in-law and contemporary, Maria, had between them three small children, Sigmund, John, and Pauline. An older local woman, Monika Zajic (Sajner, 1968, pp. 173–74), or perhaps Resi Wittek (Sajner, 1981, p. 143), took care of Sigmund and possibly of John and Pauline as well. The woman, who was Catholic and Czech, frequently took Sigmund to the Mariae Geburt Church, where the services must have been in Latin and the preaching in Czech.

Family life and business seem to have proceeded normally during the family's residence in Freiberg; an 1859 affidavit from Klogsdorf states that "Herr Jacob Freud and his wife are of good repute in every way and . . . nothing untoward in their conduct has ever become known" (Sajner, 1968, p. 176, translated by Krüll, 1986). But at home, the family was confronted with some very significant deaths: that of Shlomo Freud, Jakob's father, on February 21, 1856, was followed by the death of Julius Nathansohn, Amalie's favorite brother, on March 15, 1858. His name had already been given to the couple's second son, probably because Amalie knew that her brother was dying. On April 15, 1858, an intestinal infection took little Julius at six months of age, leaving an indelible mark on the mind of his twenty-three-month-old brother Sigmund. We have no information about the effect of this death on the parents, still mourning earlier deaths. What is important is that during the first two years of Sigmund Freud's life his parents suffered very significant losses: a father, a favorite brother, and a son.

Freud's childhood recollections include playing with John

and Pauline, visiting the Catholic church with his caretaker, and enjoying the town and its surroundings. Freud (1960) described those years in a letter to the Mayor of Příbor (Freiberg): "It is not easy for the now seventy-five-year-old man to recall those early days of whose rich content only a few fragments reach into his memory, but of one thing I am certain: deep within me, although overlaid, there continues to live the happy child from Freiberg, the first born son of a youthful mother, the boy who received from this air, from this soil, the first indelible impressions" (pp. 408–9). The psychoanalyst cannot fail to observe that Freud presents himself only as his mother's son, omitting his father and the bewildering confusion of generations between his paternal half-brothers, his mother, and his coetaneous nephew and niece.

In the second half of 1859, when he was three years old, "the happy child from Freiberg" met "the original catastrophe" that from then on affected "his whole existence" (1899, p. 314). This catastrophe was the family's move from the open air of Freiberg to Leopoldstadt, the impoverished Jewish ghetto of Vienna. For Sigmund the move meant permanent separation from all his relatives except his immediate family and the permanent loss of a relatively comfortable economic situation. What prompted Jakob Freud to move his family from pleasant Freiberg to the slums of Vienna? And what caused his two oldest sons to emigrate to Manchester, England, at the same time? Most biographers relate the moves to bad economic times. Krüll has shown, however, that the economic situation of Freiberg had not declined and that there were no repressive measures against the Jews that could justify the need for departure (1986, pp. 144–45). Ignaz Fluss, another wool merchant from Tismenitz and a family friend, was in a similar economic situation yet "managed to establish himself in Freiberg as the owner of a successful textile mill, with a branch in Vienna" (p. 143). The young Freud revealed his admiration for Fluss's well-run business in a September 14, 1872, letter to Silberstein. Krüll also speculates about a possible liaison between Philipp, Jakob's bachelor son, and Amalie that could have led Philipp to emigrate. It may also be that Emmanuel and Philipp moved to avoid being drafted into the Austrian Army. Exile of the brothers would not have required Jakob to leave as well, assuming that he could provide for the family without their help. If he was unable to carry the business on his own, then the move to Vienna might have been motivated by the wish to be close to Amalie's parents, who lived nearby, according to the address given in Amalie's marriage certificate.

Although Jakob had been moderately successful as a merchant when he was associated with his grandfather or his sons, it appears that he was unable to manage the difficult and complex importing and selling operations on his own. Perhaps the best evidence of this point comes from Freud's January 10, 1884, letter to his fiancée: "Yesterday I met Father in the street, still full of projects, still hoping. I took it upon myself to write to Emmanuel and Philipp urging them to help Father out of his present predicament. He doesn't want to do it himself since he considers himself badly treated. So I sat down last night and wrote Emmanuel a very 'sharp letter'" (1960, p. 86). This suggests that Jakob Freud felt entitled to help from Emmanuel and Philipp and was indignant about not receiving it, and, further, that Sigmund agreed it was their obligation to help. It also discloses Freud's dismay at his father's incompetence and his conviction that Jakob's "projects" were futile. Earlier, on August 14, 1882, he wrote to Martha about his father: "When he isn't exactly grouchy, which alas is very often the case, he is the greatest optimist of all us young people" (p. 22).

The picture that emerges is of an impractical, unrealistic man whose "projects," hopes, and great optimism were based mainly on well-intended imaginings. From the time Jakob moved to Vienna until his death, no researcher has been able to find any evidence of a trade or business that occupied him, either in Freiberg or in Vienna. Furthermore, no one seems to have dared to ask about it directly, not even Jones, who had Freud close at hand. All biographers facing this strange conspiracy of silence have wondered how Jakob Freud managed to feed and clothe his family. The probable answer is that, in spite of his effort to be part of the Enlightenment, to partake of the new opportunity offered to Jews, he seems to have required charitable help from others in order to survive at least the first years in Vienna. His son Sigmund, like the rest of the family, lived in utter poverty and was also forced to accept charity, as is painfully documented in his letters to Martha, until he managed to establish a practice.

The move to Vienna was the beginning of a dark and painful period. Freud describes it in his disguised autobiographical paper "Screen Memories" (1899): "The branch of industry in which my father was concerned met with a catastrophe. He lost all his means and we were forced to leave the place and move to a large town. Long and difficult years followed, of which, as it seems to me, nothing is worth remembering" (p. 312). Freud might have recalled that the family first lived in horrifyingly overcrowded conditions, as subtenants of Selig Freud, a relative, at 3 Obere Weissgärberstrasse. This continued until perhaps 1861, when they moved to 114 Weissgärberstrasse (Krüll, 1986, p. 148). The extreme crowding was exacerbated by Amalie's frequent pregnancies. In addition to Sigmund and Anna, born in Freiberg, she delivered Rosa in March 1860, Mitzi a year later, Dolfi in July 1862, Paula in May 1864, and Alexander in April 1866. Thus the "youthful mother" of Freiberg had five pregnancies in the seven years from 1859 to 1866 and was besieged by the demands of her babies as well as the stress of poverty and inadequate housing. There is no evidence of her tuberculosis during this period, though we know that she went to Roznau several times.

In 1864 and again in 1866 the family moved their few belongings to other streets in the same district. It was not until 1875, when Freud was a nineteen-year-old university student, that they were able to find a larger apartment, at 3 Kaiser-Josef Strasse. In all these places, Anna reported, "no matter how crowded our quarters, Sigmund always had a room to himself" (Bernays, 1973, p. 141).

When Sigmund turned six he was not sent to a public primary school, as was the norm in Vienna. There are different stories about how he learned enough to pass the examination for the Gymnasium. His sister Anna gives two versions. In her memoirs she wrote: "My oldest brother was altogether the pride of the family. My mother taught him at home throughout the primary school years, so that, when he entered the Gymnasium at the age of ten, he set foot in school for the first time in his life" (Bernays, c. 1930, p. 7). But in the commentary she wrote for The American Mercury after the death of her brother, Anna said: "My father taught him privately until he entered high school. . . . My father, a self-taught scholar, was really brilliant" (Bernays, 1973, pp. 141–42). In the curriculum vitae submitted with his application for a scholarship to study with Charcot in Paris, Freud himself wrote: "I received my first instruction at home, then attended a private primary school. In the autumn of 1865 I entered the Leopoldstädter Real- und Obergymnasium" (E. Freud et al., 1985, p. 61). The only fact for which we have tangible evidence is that he entered the Gymnasium in 1865, at the age of nine and a half, while the family was living at 1 Pfeffergassestrasse, in the Second District.

It may be that all three versions are correct—that is, that both parents taught him and that he attended some private place of teaching that his sister did not mention. Perhaps he attended some private institution for Jewish boys, as had been the tradition of the shtetl. His father wrote in his dedication of the Philippson Bible that the young Sigmund had been enjoined to read the Bible "in the seventh of the years of your life." In 1935 Freud acknowledged how significant his early exposure to the Bible had been for him: "My deep engrossment in the Bible story (almost as soon as I had learnt the art of reading) had, as I recognized much later, an enduring effect upon the direction of my interest" (1925a, p. 8 [sentence added for second edition]).

On June 20, 1865, just before Sigmund entered public school, his uncle Joseph Freud, forty years old, and one Osias Weich were arrested for possession of counterfeit Russian rubles. The police, warned by an alert merchant, arranged for a meeting between Joseph Freud and a buyer. Joseph was found to be in possession of a significant sum of falsified rubles, and an additional 259 falsified bills were found in a search of his home. The *Neue Freie Presse*, a daily newspaper read by most Viennese, printed all the details of the arrest and trial. A document sent by the minister of police to the foreign minister deserves full quotation:

> On June 20 of this year the Israelite Josef Freud was apprehended in the act of attempting to pass on a relatively large sum of counterfeit money, namely, 100 forged fifty-rouble notes. Altogether he was found in possession of 359 such notes with a nominal value of 17,950 roubles. From his own statement it appears that Josef Freud is an Israelite, married and the father of two children; he was born in Tysmenitz in the Stanislav district of Galicia, but has for a long time resided in Moldavia; married in 1849 at Jassy, he later traded in English ironware in Galatz. Since 1861, he has been resi-

dent in Vienna,[1] whence he has paid three visits to London, Manchester and Birmingham, has been to Leipzig, Breslau, etc., and maintained a large correspondence with foreign countries. His son-in-law, Adolf Kornhauser of Trencsin in Hungary, is suspected of complicity in Freud's offense, for which reason Kornhauser, too, has been apprehended.

Regarding the source of the notes, which he knew to be forgeries, Josef Freud stated during his first interrogation that he obtained them from one Osias Weich from Czernowitz—whom he claims to have met in Galatz—during the latter's stay in Vienna last year. . . . There are indications that the forgeries originated in England, as may be surmised from letters of a very suspicious nature, written by two sons of the brother of Josef Freud, now in England. One of these letters states that they, the brother's two sons,[2] have money like sand on a seashore, that, since they are wise, clever, and circumspect, fortune could not but smile on them. In another letter they inquire whether the lucky star of the House of Freud had risen for him as well, and ask the recipient to find a banking house for the goods, one with larger, quicker and more profitable outlets. . . . The forgers of the fifty-rouble notes are based in England: the notes were first issued at the end of 1862 or the beginning of 1863; those responsible were Polish emigrants who printed and supervised the circulation of the notes for the benefit of rebellious, national causes. The actual circulation of the notes was placed almost exclusively in the hands of Israelites of Polish origin. (Gickl-

1. Joseph Freud moved to Vienna two years after his older brother Jakob arrived there with his whole family.
2. "The brother's two sons" could only be Emmanuel and Philipp because Abae, Jakob's other brother, had two sons who were not capable of writing letters. One was hydrocephalic, the other was insane and lived in Breslau (Krüll, 1986, table 3, p. 235).

horn, 1976, 39 ff., translated from the German in Krüll, 1986, pp. 164–65)

The letters from the brothers mentioned by the police have an optimistic and fantastic quality, similar to Jakob's dreams and plans. Philipp Freud had a disposition like his father's. Sigmund remembered him as very fond of puns and practical jokes (1887–1904, October 15, 1897).

Joseph's trial and sentencing to ten years in prison took place in February 1866 and were also reported in the *Neue Freie Presse*. Thirty-one years later, almost on the anniversary of the sentencing—perhaps spurred by Joseph's imminent death, which occurred on March 5, 1897—Sigmund Freud mentioned to Fliess the dream of "The Uncle with the Yellow Beard" (1900). Freud made no reference to his uncle's health at the time. The second sentence of the dream reads "I had a great feeling of affection for him" (p. 137). Later, in his associations to the face in the dream, he recalled: "My uncle did in fact have a face like that, elongated and framed in a handsome fair beard" (p. 138). Freud felt great resistance to analyzing this dream but did succeed in interpreting it. The occasion for the dream was his frustrated wish, and that of a colleague, to be promoted to professor. Here is what he has to say about it: "'R. *was my uncle.*' What could that mean? I never had more than one uncle—Uncle Joseph.[3] There was an unhappy story attached to him. Once— more than thirty years ago,—in his eagerness to make money, he allowed himself to be involved in a transaction of a kind that is severely punished by the law, and he was in fact punished for it. My father, whose hair turned grey from grief in a few days,

---

3. In a footnote Freud clarified that he had known "five of my uncles, and loved and honored one of them" (1900, p. 138), implying that this was Uncle Joseph. Joseph was the uncle Freud knew well as a child because he visited frequently and kept in touch with the family in Manchester.

used always to say that uncle Josef was not a bad man but only a simpleton" (1900, p. 138).

The authorities apparently did not connect the incident to Jakob Freud. It is difficult to ascertain how much, if anything, Jakob knew about his brother's illegal activities and the suspected complicity of his sons. Jakob's daughter Anna Freud Bernays writes: "By an earlier marriage father had two sons, but by the time that we of the second family were born, these boys were grown up and lived in Manchester, England, *where father had business interests* (1973, p. 141; my italics). If Jakob was a party to these activities, this could have been an additional reason for the family's move to Vienna.

The intensity of the stress suffered by the family is evident from Jakob's overnight graying hair and by Freud's dream thirty years later. For Sigmund, aged ten at the time, the impossible-to-ignore newspaper reports, the public exposure of family members, local and in England, the undeniable criminal behavior of his uncle, and his father's suffering must have been a shock and an embarrassment. The adult males who were supposed to act as role models—his uncle, his brothers in England, and perhaps his own father—were now convicted or suspected of wrongdoing. The family had to deal with the shame of public exposure and the unavoidable suspicion aroused by the newspaper reports about the Manchester connection. Sigmund had to come to terms with a father who had "lost all his means" and an uncle who "in his eagerness to make money" had, as a publicly recognized swindler, stained the family name.

Soon after this event, Freud learned of the episode of his father's unheroic behavior when a Christian knocked his cap into the mud. Sigmund wanted a strong, heroic father to match Jakob's imposing physical appearance. What he heard was the story of a meek man. He felt disillusioned with his father and rejected his lesson. He valued the heroic path of Hannibal and Napoleon. As an adult, Freud gave clear demonstrations of his identification with Hannibal. His son Martin (1957) describes Sigmund's behavior when his progress was blocked by a group of ten men "armed with sticks and umbrellas" and shouting anti-Semitic abuse: "Father, swinging his stick, charged the hostile crowd, which gave way before him and promptly dispersed, allowing him a free passage" (p. 71).

In much earlier days the courageous man who refused to identify with his father had been greatly impressed with him. He attributed the same attitude to all boys, but he was talking about himself: "A little boy is bound to love and admire his father, who seems to him the most powerful, the kindest and the wisest creature in the world" (1914b, p. 243). During his oedipal phase young Sigmund had seen that powerful man lose all his money. He saw him struggling with poverty. The admired father became weak and powerless. A change came upon his attitude toward his father:

> In the second half of childhood a change sets in in the boy's relation to his father—*a change whose importance cannot be exaggerated.* From his nursery the boy begins to cast his eyes upon the world outside. And he cannot fail now to make discoveries which undermine his original opinion of his father. . . . He finds that his father is no longer the mightiest, wisest and richest of beings; he grows dissatisfied with him, he learns to criticize him and to estimate his place in society; and then, as a rule, *he makes him pay heavily for the disappointment* that has been caused by him. (p. 244, my italics)

At Gymnasium, Freud was always at the top of the class. He "enjoyed special privileges there, and had scarcely ever to be examined in class" (1925a, p. 8). His brilliance and superior fund of knowledge were evident to his teachers. At home his parents and their children continued to live "in very limited circumstances." Everyday life, as described by Freud's sister Anna (Bernays, 1973) and in his correspondence with Eduard Silberstein (1871–81), reveals a close-knit nuclear family that "saw very little" of their "conventional relatives." Jakob was not an authoritarian father:

> He would discuss with us children, specially Sigmund, all manner of questions and problems. We called these sessions "the family council." When the youngest son was born, father took Sigmund aside to consult him on the name to be given to the boy. I remember how Sigmund enthusiastically chose Alexander, basing his selection on Alexander's generosity and prowess as a general, and how he recited the whole story of the Macedonian's triumph in support of his choice. His choice of name was accepted. (Bernays, 1973, p. 142)

Sigmund's only full-blood brother was not going to follow his father's example of a submissive Jew. He would be not a slave but the greatest of conquerors.

The episode shows that Sigmund was special in his family in spite of his youth. His mother in particular "hoped great things of her first born and treasured early incidents which gave body to her hope" (Bernays, 1973, p. 140). Like the biblical Joseph, Sigmund was the favorite of his mother and the special child, the counselor and helper, to his father. He assumed and was given the role of guide and adviser to his five sisters. He supervised their reading, counseled them on all sorts of matters, and helped them with their lessons. He also demanded that they stop playing the piano because it disturbed his studies; he even threatened to leave the house if his wish was not obeyed. His mother, "who was very musical" and wanted her eldest daughter to study the piano, had to comply. The dream of the biblical

Joseph that "the sun, the moon, and eleven stars were bowing down to me" (Genesis 37:9) had become an everyday household reality.

The "catastrophe" highlighted the difference between Sigmund and the biblical Joseph: Jacob, the biblical patriarch, was economically comfortable while Freud's father was painfully poor. Jakob Freud, however, did not lose his paternal authority; he insisted that his children, including his brilliant son, fulfill the commandment to honor one's father. He was tender and affectionate with Sigmund, admired his intelligence, but would not tolerate criticism. Wittels (1924) documents Jakob's reaction to an instance of a son's altercation with his own father:

> The pianist M. R. recently told me the following story: "It must have been in the seventies when my father and I met Freud senior one day in the street. At the moment I was arguing with my father about something. Freud senior laughingly reproved me: 'What, do you contradict your father? My Sigmund's little toe is cleverer than my head, but he would never dare to contradict me!'" (p. 60)

The Sigmund who "would never dare" was in his late teens or early twenties.

The family celebrated Passover, and Jakob presided over the seder. Judith Bernays Heller (1973) describes how as a young child, in the early 1890s, she "was greatly impressed by the way my grandfather recited the ritual, and the fact that he knew it by heart amazed me" (p. 336). At the age of twenty-one, in a letter to Eduard Silberstein, Freud described the new year celebration on September 7, 1877: "Today all the world is preparing for the High Holiday; I am told we are to have a leap year. There is much cooking and baking going on at home and the only result will be that I shall have a worse night's sleep than usual. I remember with pleasure that the whole spectacle passed me by last year in Trieste. . . . We young people who have half-left our families and have not yet found a new one are in fact singularly unsuited to the enjoyment of the holidays" (1871–81, pp. 166–67). Freud reduced the seder to a "spectacle." By that time he was well on the way to becoming a "godless Jew."

In the summer of 1875 Freud went to England for seven and a half weeks to visit his half-brothers, Emmanuel and Philipp. He found them and England much to his liking. He could see that his brothers were economically stable and well educated, and he fantasized in a letter to Silberstein about joining them one day (1871–81, September 9, 1875). The visit had other implications. According to the disguised autobiographical description in "Screen Memories" (1899): "I believe that my father and my uncle [his half-brother Emmanuel] had concocted a plan by which I was to change the abstruse subject of my studies for one of more practical value, settle down, after my studies were completed, in the place where my uncle lived, and marry my cousin. . . . I must sometimes have reflected that my father had meant well in planning this marriage for me, *to make good the loss in which the original catastrophe had involved my whole existence*" (p. 314, my italics).

The visit deeply affected Jakob's son: "My relationship with my father was changed by a visit to England" (1901, p. 219). Obviously Freud compared his improvident father with his "uncle" and himself with his early childhood playmate and rival, his nephew John. He could see that John did not have to confront poverty because he had a father who was able to provide for him. It was only after his father's death that Freud could acknowledge to himself the fantasy of "how different things would have been if I had been born the son not of my father but of my brother" (1901, pp. 219–20).

In April 1882, when he was almost twenty-six years old,

Freud met Martha Bernays, a friend of his sisters, and fell passionately in love. By June 17 the couple was secretly engaged. They began to write every day and to prepare themselves for the long wait until they would have enough money to marry. Their letters are a moving and painful document of Freud's extreme poverty. He is always counting florins, struggling to make ends meet. It is clear that by age twenty-six he was largely responsible for the support of his mother and siblings. The letter to Martha of May 26, 1885, illustrates this point: "My American [patient] . . . won't produce more than 120 florins. Of this sum at least half will have to be put aside for Mother" (1960, p. 147). The purchase of a new tie, a pair of trousers, or a coat required careful calculation. Freud was frequently thinking about whom to borrow from, who could rescue him at the last minute. He wrote to Martha on June 19, 1884: "Could you imagine me having a thousand gulden in the drawer and letting Rosa and Dolfi go hungry? At least half of it I would give to them" (p. 114).

The need to divide his earnings meant that Sigmund's marriage had to be postponed for four years, until September 13, 1886. There is no documentation of Jakob's response to his son's personal sacrifice. The data we have testify only that Sigmund had now become not only the guide and counselor of his siblings but also their financial savior. The roles of father and son had been reversed. Freud, like the biblical Joseph, was feeding his "starving" siblings and parents.

Little is known about the father-son relationship throughout this period or about Freud's early life as a married man until his thirty-fifth birthday, when his father gave him what remained of his Philippson Bible,[4] newly bound in leather and with a handwritten Hebrew inscription rich in meaning and message.

4. Anna Freud, in a September 24, 1979, letter to Théo Pfrimmer, described the book as an incomplete volume, which starts in the middle. The order of

In selecting Sigmund over his eight other living children, Jakob Freud was repeating the behavior of Jacob the Jewish patriarch: "Then Israel [Jacob] said to Joseph, 'Behold, I am about to die, but God will be with you and will bring you again to the land of your fathers. Moreover, I have given to you rather than to your brothers one mountain slope which I took from the hands of the Amorites" (Genesis 48:21–22). The "mountain slope" was Sechem, the place the Lord had given to Abram with the words, "To your descendants I will give this land" (Genesis 12:6–7).

Jakob's choice of Sigmund to receive the Philippson Bible as his personal gift and inheritance indicated not only that he favored Sigmund over his other children but also that he was making him the heir to something precious that had been his personal possession since 1848. Copies of the Philippson Bible were available; Jakob could have bought one instead of giving Sigmund his own. In fact, at a later date, Freud bought a copy of the three-volume edition.

In choosing Sigmund's thirty-fifth birthday as the occasion for this special gift, Jakob was adhering to a central European Jewish tradition that viewed the thirty-fifth year as the transition from youth to middle age, an entrance into manly maturity (Roback, 1957, pp. 95–96). Sigmund had just finished writing his first book, On Aphasia. On May 2, 1891, four days before his birthday, he wrote to Fliess: "In a few weeks I shall afford myself the pleasure of sending you a small book [ein Heft] on aphasia for which I myself have a great deal of warm feel-

---

the biblical books in this copy of the Philippson is as follows: "2 Samuel 11–24, pp. 423–86; 1 and 2 Kings, pp. 488–672; and the five books of Moses, pp. 1–966" (Pfrimmer, 1982, p. 14). That there are missing books supports the assumption that Jakob bought the bible not in complete volumes but in the early fascicle edition, properly numbered and ready to be bound when each volume was complete (see Chap. 5).

ing. In it I am very impudent [sehr frech], cross swords with your friend Wernicke, with Lichtheim and Grashey, and even scratch the high and mighty idol [hochthronenden Götzen] Meynert" (1887–1904, p. 28). Unlike Jakob, Sigmund was not a meek Jew. In his maturity he went to the battlefield of science to fence with heroes and gods. His father had his Jewish book; Sigmund, in turn, had his "small book" and knew that he would write many more, to topple the powerful and mighty, including the God of his father.

chapter four

Jakob, Man and Father

What kind of man was Jakob? What kind of father was he to his son? His 1847 passport, as we have seen, reports "figure slim, face oval, hair blond, eyes brown, nose turned up" (Gicklhorn, 1976, from a copy taken by J. Sajner, 1981). Although Sigmund was slightly shorter than his father, he described himself in an unpublished letter to Martha dated July 19, 1883, as "the duplicate of his father physically and to some extent mentally" (Jones, 1953, p. 2). Judith Bernays Heller, who as a child spent time with Jakob and Amalie, described her grandfather:

> Tall and broad, with a long beard, he was very kind and gentle, and humorous in the bargain. . . . He lived somewhat aloof from the others in the family, reading a great deal—German and Hebrew (not Yiddish)—and seeing his own friends away from home. He would come home for meals, but took no real part in the general talk of others. . . . I liked, too, to hear the stories he would tell about my mother, who, as eldest daughter, seemed to have been his pet; he held her up to me as an example to follow. . . . But what I think struck me most about my maternal grandfather was how, in the midst of this rather emotional household, with its three young women who sometimes did not get along with one another, and their mother, who was usually troubled and anxious—probably with financial worries—he remained quiet and imperturbable, not indifferent, but not disturbed, never out of temper and never raising his voice. (1973, pp. 335–36)

Jakob's "pet" daughter, Anna, saw him as a "happy optimist," "brilliant," and a nature lover, and said that his motto was "to think morally and to act morally" (Sittlich denken und moralish handeln; Bernays, c. 1930, p. 5). Freud's eldest son, Martin, who was seven when Jakob died, described his grandfather as tall and broad shouldered (1957, p. 10) and remembered him with great fondness: "I can recall him quite clearly, because he was a frequent visitor to our Vienna flat then in the Berggasse. Every member of my family loved Jakob and treated him with great respect. . . . He was terribly nice with us children. He brought us small presents and he used to tell us stories, mostly with a little twinkle in his great brown eyes, as if he wanted to say: 'Isn't everything we are doing and saying here a great joke?'" (1957, p. 10).

His son Sigmund described him in letters to Fliess as "an interesting human being, *very happy within himself*" (1887–1904, July 15, 1896, my italics), a "peculiar mixture of deep wisdom and fantastic light-heartedness" (November 2, 1896) who "retained his beautiful composure to the end" (February 6, 1899). Jones said that he was capable of "relapsing into a state of fatalistic helplessness and even childishness" (1953, p. 157). Freud portrayed his father as a smoker like himself: "My model in this was my father who was a heavy smoker and remained one until his 81st year" (quoted by Schur, 1972, p. 62, from the answer to a questionnaire sent to Freud).

Only Martha was privy to Sigmund's anger and frustration with his father. To her he described Jakob as "often grouchy" or "the greatest optimist" (1960, letter of August, 14, 1882), "full of projects, still hoping," while he was unable to provide for his family. Freud described his own shame at having to borrow money to support himself and the family (January 10, 1884), his worry if he were to use his money for himself about "letting Rosa and Dolfi go hungry" (June 19, 1884, quoted by Jones, 1953, p. 150), his intense fury and "revolutionary thoughts" because his sister Mitzi had to work as a governess (October 19, 1885). The situation was so extreme that "once, when he was invited out to lunch, he related how hard he found it to eat roast meat with the knowledge of how hungry his sisters were" (Jones, 1953, p. 159). Freud's contained frustration and rage at his father's incompetence in taking care of the family contrast sharply with his devoted concern to share equitably whatever money he had with his mother and sisters.

On August 17, 1884, Freud described himself to Martha as "a human being who is still young and yet has never felt young." On February 2, 1886, he wrote to her from Paris: "I believe people see something alien in me and the real reason for this is that in my youth I *was never young* and now that I am entering the age of maturity I cannot mature properly" (1960, my italics). The description suggests a man who as a child could not feel reliably assured of his parent's protection. Jakob must have failed him in a fundamental way.

The historical facts present Jakob Freud as a man incapable of functioning on his own in the commercial and business world. After moving to Vienna, he had no documented commercial or other remunerative activity; he was never able to provide adequately for his large family. He "often received financial assistance from his wife's family" (Jones, 1953, p. 17), which might have created a complex dynamic, given the scant ten years' difference between Jakob Freud and his father-in-law. In view of Jakob's lack of a known profession, and particularly after Joseph Freud's arrest and conviction, Sigmund must have wondered whether the entire family, including his father and his half-brothers in England, was involved in illegal activities. What is known is that as soon as Sigmund was able to earn money he felt the compelling obligation to share it with his family. His father could not provide for them. All Jakob had were fantastic dreams about making money.

From the composite picture, Jakob Freud appears as an intelligent, humorous, good-hearted, benign father and delightful grandfather who lived in an optimistic and impractical world of his own, where he found private satisfaction and happiness. The quarrels and suffering of his family did not seem to disturb his inner contentment. His improvidence did not faze him. He was not the typical authoritarian father but an affectionate, democratic, lighthearted—indeed, maternal—figure full of feeling for his children. As an adult in the world he was an optimistic dreamer, unable to master the complexities of business and finances. It is possible to conclude, as did his grandchildren, that Jakob Freud was a most enticing father for a young child. His good humor, his love of stories, the twinkle in his large brown eyes, his calmness and expressive affection reveal a tender and motherly man who adored small children and was adored by them. What he could not be was a provider and a model for a prepuberal boy, adolescent, or a young man. He himself did not know how to be a man of the world.

In spite of his obvious failure as a provider, Jakob demanded respect. As we have seen, he would not tolerate criticism from his children. He also required that some issues not be mentioned. Freud respected this prohibition and even repeated it with his mother by pretending that some deceased relatives were still alive so as not to upset her (see Chapter 11). Freud's own past remained closed to his children. Jones (1955) reported: "He never spoke with his children about his youth and early years; most of the knowledge they have of it has come from the present work. The topic, though not expressly proscribed, seemed to be taboo, and they never raised it" (pp. 408–9).

To speak with his children about these forbidden matters must have meant breaking the prohibition against describing the deep and prolonged suffering caused by his father's incompetence, the "catastrophe," and its never-ending effects, which deprived Sigmund of his youth. In spite of his intensely ambivalent feelings for his father, Freud never complained overtly about Jakob, never revealed his father's past, and, as far as we know, never questioned his father about his previous life. It is only in a dream—about the "communication from the town council of my birth place" that Freud alludes to these secrets (1900, p. 435–36). Like Goethe before him, Freud, the great revealer, became the great concealer of his father's private life and failures. His biographers were to be as helpless in relation to the father as Freud wished they would be about him (1960, letter to Martha, April 28, 1885).

There is no question that Jakob, born to an Orthodox Jewish family, had joined the followers of Moses Mendelssohn and the Philippson brothers, abandoning certain ritualistic practices and substituting the German of the Empire for the Yiddish of the shtetl. Like the Philippsons and their followers, he "wanted to raze 'the Ghetto of the mind,' to transilluminate the substance of the Scriptures and the Talmud with the vision and the wisdom of the *Aufklärung* [Enlightenment]; . . . but not to the point of abandoning the belief that the Jews were God's chosen people to whom he had revealed the moral law" (Kallen, 1990, p. 249). The plea to his son in the dedication of the Philippson Bible reflects this ideal, the wish that Sigmund, with his admirable intelligence, would become the new Jew, master of the modern sciences and of the Scriptures given by God to the chosen people.

How could Sigmund hear this plea from a father whose "catastrophe" had affected his entire life and whose improvidence deprived him of the experience of being young? How could he accept his role as Jakob's favorite when this required that he rescue his father's children and wife from starving, even postponing his own marriage for years? On the other hand, how could he not accept his role as the savior of the family when there was no one else to do it? How could he reject Jakob's obvious tender affection and lightheartedness when he had such fond memories of him from his early life, the time when he needed protection against "terrifying helplessness"? Could he reject him because of Jakob's financial incompetence and slavish behavior in front of scornful Christians? Freud had only one option: he had to close his eyes, not just his father's eyes, as the dream commanded him to do the night after his father's funeral.

As a growing child Sigmund had no adequate male models. His half-brothers, Emmanuel and Philipp, had disappeared from his life when he was three and a half years old. He had minimal contact with his uncles, with the exception of his favorite uncle, Joseph, who turned out to be an international delinquent, a man described in court as an experienced liar (Krüll, p. 272, note 40). His father was no model, either as a breadwinner or as a man capable of defending himself. Freud's ambivalence and sense of loneliness might have been unbearable had he not had the remarkable ability to identify with biblical and historical figures and create his own models of what a true man should be. These models—Joseph, Moses, Alexander, Hannibal—were courageous, adventurous, successful, and radically different from his father.

What did it mean to son and father that Jakob had selected Sigmund to be the favorite child and asked him to become the new Jew of the Aufklärung? And why did his father choose him from the day he was born as the special child of the family? As suggested earlier, Jakob seemed unable to function adequately without the help of others; his "fantastic lightheartedness," which made him the delight of children, reveals a man who, in spite of his impressive physical figure, his knowledge, and "wisdom," was fundamentally childish and unable to fully grasp the harsh realities of commercial or even familial life. He lived undisturbed in his private world, with his Bible and his Talmud, where he found the source of a happiness that kept him going.

By the time Sigmund was born, Jakob himself had lost many of his supports: at least one wife, his grandfather Siskind Hoffmann, and, two months before Sigmund's birth, his own father, Shlomo. It is possible to conjecture that, bereaved and wishing for a new beginning with Amalie, he consciously and unconsciously invested his son, named after his father, with feelings that belonged to his father as well as with optimistic dreams for the future of the new generation of Jews, who were to be the new masters of the sciences and the true heralds of the religious idea to the world. Jakob and Amalie expected that Sigmund would be a great man and treasured every folk prophecy that confirmed the hope. At the deeper layers of his psychic makeup, Jakob must also have transferred onto his son the longings awakened by his own "most poignant" paternal loss. His attachment to his son had a depth of feeling and need that went beyond an ordinary attachment. Sigmund became an idealized and overcathected image of the son he had to be. As a result, Jakob attended to him tenderly, sharing his humor, his exciting stories, his personal wisdom, and, in due time, introducing him to the Jewish Bible and the fantastically interesting illustrations of the Philippson Bible. The message was there: this child was to be, like the biblical Joseph, his great pride and consolation.

From early childhood Sigmund assumed the role of leader of the family, guiding his sisters' reading and social activities, naming his father's last son, born when Freud himself was aged ten, and being the most consulted member of the family council. It is clear that Jakob delegated to young Sigmund many of his own duties as a father. Later, when Freud was in his midtwenties, Jakob placed a good share of the economic responsibility for the household in his son's hands; ultimately he, his wife, and their unmarried daughter Dolfi depended entirely on Sigmund.

Sigmund accepted his duty with manly seriousness and grew accustomed to being the one to give the orders. This was the case to such an extent that he even threatened to abandon the family if they did not do as he wished (as with the piano playing of his sisters). In addition, he did not consult any member of the family, not even his brother Alexander, then aged thirty, about the funeral arrangements for Jakob. He assumed his responsibility as a father substitute with full moral integrity and caring devotion. He felt the burden, however, of being the special one, the one who owed it to his father and mother to be their support and consolation. The reversal of roles appears clearly in Freud's November 2, 1896, letter to Fliess, in which he says that he understood his father very well; nowhere does he indicate that his father understood him. Deep down he knew that the assigned role did not allow him to be a child.

In the privacy of his heart, particularly after his trip to England, he thought about "how different things would have been if I had been born the son not of my father but of my brother [Emmanuel]" (1901, pp. 219–20). He discovered his "suppressed fantasy" when he mistakenly wrote Hasdrubal, the name of Hannibal's brother, instead of Hamilcar, Hannibal's father. The echoes of the shame evoked by his father's meekness before the taunting Christian were still at work in him. He considered Emmanuel "strict," implying that he was capable of exercising the parental function (p. 227).

The duty to be the new Jew brought him to a great conflict. He found that as soon as he was able to be critical and judicious, he could not believe in the existence of God. He tried as hard as he could to forget the Bible stories, the Hebrew lessons, the teachings of his father, the family seders—and he succeeded for a while in avoiding anything that smelled of religion or of piety. He wrote to the members of the B'nai B'rith Lodge in 1926: "I was always an unbeliever, have been brought up without religion, but not without respect for the so-called 'ethical' demands of human civilization" (1960, p. 366). The sentence fails to mention the bible that his father gave him and begged him to read. Some repression had taken place. In the end, however, he could not repress it all. His deep emotional connection to his father's early teachings and his father's bible were there waiting until his urgent need for the "protective" presence of his father—once ambivalently loved and now dead—was reawakened.

chapter five

The Dedication and Freud's Response

The dedication Jakob wrote in the copy of the Philippson Bible he presented to his son (fig. 5.1) was in Hebrew, and it was composed of "a carefully constructed mosaic of phrases, most of them from the Bible, but at least one from the Talmud" (Ostow, 1989, pp. 485–86). With only a few minor differences, Ostow (1989) and Rice (1990) have traced each phrase to the same biblical source. Relying on their findings, I indicate below the book, chapter, and versicle to which each line of the dedication is related. Here is Ostow's translation, with the source phrase in italics and the biblical reference in parentheses:

1. Son (who is) *dear to me*, Shlomo, (Jeremiah 31:20)
2. In the seventh year of your life *the spirit of the Lord began to move you*, (Judges 13:25)
3. And spoke to you saying, "Go, read the Book that I have written"
4. And springs of *reason, knowledge and understanding* will be broken open for you. (Weekday Liturgy: Shmoneh Esray)
5. This Book of Books is a spring which *the sages dug*
6. And (from it) the *legislators* learned knowledge and judgment. (Numbers 21:18)
7. *The vision of the Almighty* you saw and you heard and you ventured (Numbers 24:4)
8. And you *soared on the wings of the wind*. (Psalm 18:11)

5.1 Dedication page in the Philippson Bible. Freud Museum

9. And since then this book was *hidden* like the *fragments of the tables* (Talmud: Baba Bathra 14a–b)
10. *In an ark with me.* (Deuteronomy 32:34)
11. On the day on which your thirty-fifth year was completed
12. I provided it with new leather binding
13. And I called it *"Spring up, o well—sing to it"* (Numbers 21:17)
14. And I dedicate it *in your name as a token of remembrance* (Isaiah 26:8)
15. And as a remembrance of love, from your father
16. Who loves you with an *eternal love.* Jakob son of Shlomo Freud. (Jeremiah 31:3)
17. In Vienna, the capital city, 29 of Nissan, 5651, 6 May 1891.

Rice (1990) adds to Ostow's biblical referents Genesis 47:28 for line 2, Exodus 32:32 for the quotation in line 3, Genesis 7:11 for line 4, and Numbers 4:10 for line 12.

Jakob's moving dedication follows the pattern of the inscriptions on the page where Shlomo Freud's death and Sig[is]mund's birth are registered. In both instances the three generations are linked to one another in a symmetrical manner: Shlomo, Jakob, Shlomo Sigmund. In the inscription, however, the linkage appears in reversed order. The father, who is a son, writes to his son about the Book of Books. Jakob wants to remind his son Shlomo Sigmund of the voice of God by placing in quotation marks a paraphrase of Exodus, 32:32: "*Go read the Book that I have written.*" In Exodus, Moses asks God to forgive the Israelites' sin of forgetting about God and making idols of gold for themselves, or otherwise to blot Moses out of God's book. God responds: "Whoever has sinned against me, him will

I blot out of my book" (32:34).[1] The book God and Moses speak of is not the Bible but the book of life, in which the names of God's worshipers are recorded while the names of idolaters are stricken out. God, whose Book of Books was yet to be written in Moses' time, asks for exclusive and faithful service from all his followers. The God of Moses and of Jakob Freud is a living being who writes, commands, and decides on the destiny of humankind. Jakob, in alluding to Exodus 32:32, makes a double reference to the need to read the Book of Books and the need to be inscribed by God in the book of life.

Study of the quotations in their biblical context suggests Jakob's probable meaning in addressing them to his son. The first line, "Son (who is) dear to me," depicts another son in need of repentance. In the preceding versicles (Jeremiah 31:18–19), the Lord hears Ephraim "bemoaning":

Bring me back that I may be restored,
for thou are the Lord my God.
For after I had turned away I repented . . .
I was ashamed, and I was confounded,
because I bore the disgrace of my youth.[2]

The Lord reflects (Jeremiah 31:20):

Is E'phraim my dear son?
Is he my darling child?
For as often as I speak against him,

1. The Hebrew Bible differentiates three types of books: the book of life, where the names of the living are inscribed, the book of divine decrees, and the book of remembrance (*The JPS Torah Commentary: Exodus.* [5751/1991], p. 209). Jon D. Levenson, Albert A. List Professor of Jewish Studies, Harvard Divinity School, graciously provided this source of information.
2. All biblical quotations are from the New Oxford Annotated Bible unless otherwise specified.

I do remember him still.
Therefore my heart yearns for him;
I will surely have mercy on him,
says the Lord.

Jakob's opening line suggests a loving invitation to Sigmund to leave behind his youthful rejection of God and return to him in maturity.

In line 2, Sigmund is reminded that in his childhood, in his seventh year, he was acquainted with "the spirit of the Lord" and was "moved" by it. The line, which is from Judges 13:25, depends on the preceding line to clarify its meaning: "And the woman [wife of Mano'ah] bore a son, and called his name Samson; and the boy grew, and the Lord blessed him. And the spirit of the Lord began to stir in him in Ma'hanehdan [an encampment of Dan[3]], between Zorah and Esh'ta-ol." Samson's extraordinary physical strength derived from the hair on his head. His wife, Delilah, cut his hair and thus sapped his strength so that he was captured by the Philistines, who gouged out his eyes and imprisoned him. Samson's hair grew again and with it his strength returned. When the Philistines brought him to the place where they planned to sacrifice him to their god, he prayed to the Lord to let him avenge the loss of his eyes. He grasped the two middle pillars upon which the house rested and leaned the full force of his arms against them. The pillars

3. In his September 21, 1897, letter to Fliess (eight years after the dedication) announcing the end of the seduction theory, Freud makes an allusion to the biblical passage: "It is strange, too, that my feeling of shame appeared—for which, after all, there could well be occasion. Of course I shall not tell it in Dan, nor speak of it in Askelon, in the land of the Philistines, but in your eyes and my own, I have more the feeling of victory than a defeat (which is surely not right)" (Freud, 1887–1904, p. 265). Yerushalmi (1991) notes that "Dan" is a slip; the correct word is Gath (p. 73).

fell and the house collapsed upon the Philistines, killing them all, at the price of Samson's own life.

Freud, too, had extraordinary power and was expected by his family to become a great man. According to Jakob's dedication, however, he needed to return to the Lord to obtain the "knowledge, discernment and wisdom" invoked by the Jewish daily prayer in its silent blessings. In context, the quotation (Jeremiah 3:12–15) enjoins:

> Return, faithless Israel, says the Lord.
> I will not look on you in anger,
> for I am merciful. . . .
> Only acknowledge your guilt,
> that you rebelled against the Lord your God . . .
> and that you have not obeyed my voice,
> says the Lord. . . .
> And I will give you shepherds after my own heart, who
>   will feed you with knowledge and understanding.

Any Jew who recites the eighteen silent blessings of the everyday prayer knows this passage well. There is no evidence to whether or not Jakob taught Sigmund to say this prayer (see Chapter 8).

Lines 4 and 5 refer to a time recounted in Numbers 21:16–18, when Moses and his people were in the wilderness and needed water:

> And from there they continued to Beer, that is the well of which the Lord said to Moses, "Gather the people together, and I will give them water." Then Israel sang this song [an ancient poetic fragment]:

> "Spring up, O well!—Sing to it!—
> the well which the princes dug,
> which the nobles of the people delved,
> with the scepter and with their staves."

Jakob compares the book to the well "the sages dug," as a source of knowledge and justice for Jewish rulers.

Line 7 refers to a moment of conversion to the true God of Israel. Balaam, a masterful curser, was asked by the princes of Moab to curse their oncoming enemy, the Israelites, but God intervened (Numbers 24:2–5):

> And Balaam lifted up his eyes, and saw Israel encamping tribe by tribe. And the Spirit of God came upon him, and he took up his discourse, and said,

> The oracle of Balaam the son of Be'or,
> the oracle of the man whose eye is opened,
> the oracle of him who hears the words of God,
> who sees the vision of the Almighty,
> falling down, but having his eyes uncovered:
> how fair are your tents, O Jacob,
> your encampments, O Israel!

The invitation to convert, to hear God, to see the Almighty, to dwell in the fair tents of Jacob the patriarch and of Jakob the believer and father, is clear and direct to anyone familiar with the story of Balaam, which is not only a biblical text but also a well-known story in its own right.

Line 8, "And you soared on the wings of the wind," comes from the description of God's intervention to deliver David from the sword of his enemies and from Saul (Psalm 18:10–11). The imagery pictures God in a tremendous thunderstorm:

> He bowed the heavens, and came down;
> thick darkness was under his feet.
> He rode on a cherub, and flew;
> he came swiftly upon the wings of the wind.

The entire psalm is a song of gratitude for God's deliverance of David from his enemies and a reiteration of David's promise that "For this I will extol thee, O Lord, among the nations, and sing praise to that name." The overall theme of this powerful psalm is God's loyalty to those who call upon him. He is the God who exalted David over his adversaries (18:48) and who "shows steadfast love to his anointed, to David and his descendants for ever" (18:50). This line in the dedication seems intended to remind Sigmund that God is with him, ready to do battle for him.

Lines 9 and 10 then make concrete reference to the broken book (the Philippson Bible), which Jakob, following a Talmudic tradition,[4] compares to the first set of the tables of the law, broken by Moses. These tables were placed in the Ark of the Covenant together with the new ones (Deuteronomy 10:1–3):

> At that time the Lord said to me, 'Hew two tables of stone like the first, and come up to me on the mountain, and make an ark of wood. And I will write on the tables the words that were on the first tables which you broke, and you shall put them on the ark.' So I made an ark of acacia wood, and hewed two tables of stone like the first, and went up the mountain with the two tables in my hand.

Jakob describes to Sigmund how he had kept the book in the same way that the Ark had kept the tables of the law. He implicitly suggests that the book, like Moses' tables, had been "broken," or at least discarded, by his son (Ostow, 1989, p. 487).[5] Jakob had collected the various fascicles of the bible, put

4. Ostow traces this comparison to the Talmud: Baba Bathra 14a–b.
5. Later in life Freud became obsessed with Michelangelo's statue of Moses in the church of San Pietro in Vincoli in Rome. He wanted to understand Moses' restraint of his anger as depicted by the artist.

them together, and had them covered in new leather (lines 11 and 12); he was now giving his adult son a second opportunity, as God gave Moses a second set of tables and a second chance.

At this moment, Jakob repeats (in line 13) the ancient song the Israelites had sung when the Lord gave them water at the well of Beer in the wilderness: "Spring up, O well!—sing to it!" This is the second time in the dedication that Jakob compares the Bible to a God-given well of much needed water, offered to his son "as a remembrance, as a reminder of love." The waters of the well from which the words of the Lord have guided the sages represent the best love Jakob has to offer his son.

The final line, "From your father who loves you with eternal love," comes from Jeremiah 31:3. The preceding versicles 1–2 are needed for clearer understanding:

> "At that time, says the Lord, I will be the God of all the
>   families of Israel, and they shall be my people."
> Thus says the Lord:
> "The people who survive the sword
> found grace in the wilderness;
> when Israel sought for rest,
> the Lord appeared to him [me] from afar.
> I have loved you with an everlasting love;
> therefore I have continued my faithfulness to you."

Jakob seems to be reminding his son that he loves him as God loves Israel, his people, and that, like God, Jakob has continued to be faithful to him.

This is what Jakob, the son of Shlomo Freud, from the Orthodox shtetl of Tismenitz, had to say to his son Shlomo, "in the capital city of Vienna," to commemorate his entrance into maturity. The message is subtle and poetic, an invitation and a plea from a father who knows every versicle of the Book and uses them to urge his son to read the Book again. It offers, in its deep biblical structure, repeated reminders of God's fidelity to and patience with his people, including hot-tempered Moses. Jakob, like the Lord with the tables of the law, gave the book to his son a second time. The giving—gentle, suggestive, and non-threatening—conveyed a promise of everlasting love.

Jakob had written "an original *midrash*, that is, an exegetical homily, in which the fountain is a metaphor for the Torah" (Ostow, 1989, p. 487). He linked the biblical contents to Sigmund's situation, promising that if he turned back to the Bible, he would find in it "knowledge and understanding." The dedication reveals Jakob as "a master of Scripture and of midrashic interpretation. He appropriates phrases and verses from the text of the scripture and employs them for his own purposes. . . . Such pastiches were commonly composed by eighteenth- and nineteenth-century Jews educated in the tradition" (pp. 488–89).

Jakob, the man his son portrayed as a liberal Jew who supposedly brought him up without a true religious education, insisted in his seventy-fifth year that his son return to learning from the Book—and not only to the reading of the Book the Lord had written but to the Lord himself, whose faithfulness and desires for the repentance of Ephraim, the "precious son," prompt him to say: "My heart yearns for him."

Freud claimed not to understand Hebrew. This dedication, however, makes that claim extremely doubtful. Why would Jakob, who made a point of having "councils" with his children and discussing all kinds of subjects with them, write a dedication so full of feeling and meaning that his son could not read, much less grasp the allusions to the biblical text, the source of its significance? We must conclude that Freud could indeed read the Hebrew text.

The bible has another handwritten text, the translation of the dedication into English. Ernst Freud (1956) commented:

"The first and last lines [were] written in the shaky hand of Jakob Freud himself. . . . That the language of the translation should be English is most likely explained by the fact that it was made by one of Jakob's sons from his first marriage" (quoted by Rice, 1990, p. 1). In fact, Rice adds, "no one knows when it was translated or whether one of Sigmund's half-brothers might have come from England for the birthday" (p. 7).

The dedication provides a portrait of Jakob that no others, with the exception of his granddaughter Judith Bernays Heller, have matched. Jakob appears as a true believer, a Jew who took the Bible as the word of the Lord and the fountain of "knowledge, discernment, and wisdom." He treated the Book with the reverence that God requested for the tables of the law. The dedication also reveals the depth of feeling the father had for his favorite child. The tender beginning, "my precious son," and the intensely affectionate ending, reminding Sigmund that his father loved him "with eternal love," disclose the deep bond that Jakob had with his son. The dedication as a whole reveals Jakob's poetic, nuanced intelligence.

Freud never documented in words his reaction to his father's gift and plea. He responded with his life work and his personal stance. His writings on the origin of religions claim that God is no more than a childhood creation stemming from an exalted vision of the father. Any mature adult should know better than to put his trust in such infantile invention. Freud the man did not believe in the existence of such a paternal God. Whenever he wrote about the subject, privately or publicly, he defined himself as "a godless Jew," a man who had no personal use for God or religion. The father's plea went unheard; the biblical well could not be a spring of refreshing waters for Sigmund, the son.

It was not until 1935, in a sentence added to his *Autobiographical Study* of 1925, that Freud could acknowledge that his "deep engrossment in the Bible story" as a young child "had an enduring effect upon the direction of my interest" (p. 8). It was, however, the "Bible story" that he acknowledged, not the Book written by God and given to him by his father as a source of knowledge and wisdom. The gift had become so irrelevant that his children were not aware of its existence. Ernst Freud described how he came upon it:

> In the last year of my father's life, shortly after his library had been reestablished in his new Hampstead house in London, he was working at his desk while I was rummaging through the shelves. By chance, I came across an insignificant-looking volume bound in black canvas, which I found to be a bible. Actually, it contained parts of the Philippson Bible (in Hebrew and German with a fair number of illustrations), an edition which had been very popular on the Continent about the middle of the last century. . . . What immediately aroused my interest was the discovery of several Hebrew inscriptions on the outer pages. . . . My father, noticing my enthusiasm, presented me with the book. (1956, pp. 6–7)

The Bible had once more gone from the hands of a father to the hands of a son. This time, however, it made its passage silently, without message or meaning.

Four months after his thirty-fifth birthday, in September 1891, Freud moved to 19 Berggasse, in the Ninth District. He came upon the apartment on one of his walks, inspected it, and promptly signed the lease. He reported to Martha that he had found the ideal apartment. She found the neighborhood poor, the building dark, and the space limited, but, as was her custom, she did not complain (Clark, 1980, p. 112). They were to remain in that building for forty-five years, until they were forced to leave Vienna to escape the Nazis' "final solution." The year after Freud's move to Berggasse, his parents and his sister

Dolfi must have moved nearby because in 1892 Jakob's address is listed as 14 Grüne Thorgasse, also in the Ninth District (Lehmann, 1859, quoted by Krüll, 1986, p. 262). He still lived there at the time of his death.

Freud's financial stability had improved, but he still felt the burden of being in charge of the whole family, as he wrote to Fliess on August 16, 1895 (1887–1904): "Between the 22nd and 24th I shall travel to Venice with my little brother [Alexander] and therefore I regret that I cannot simultaneously be in Oberhof. . . . My motive for coming to this decision, since I had to make one, was my concern for the young man who together with me carries the responsibility for two old people and so many women and children. . . . I am very eager to bind him closer to me while we are actively pursuing the possibility of finding a husband for our only sister who is not yet provided for." Freud appears here as the universal provider for his family, concerned with everything from economic support, to finding a husband for his sister, to caring for the well-being of his "little brother," who was twenty-nine years old at the time.

In June 1896 Jakob was very ill, as Freud reported in his June 30 letter to Flies. In his July 15 letter he used the past tense: "The old's man condition, by the way, does not depress me. . . . He was an interesting human being, very happy within himself" (my italics). Freud's use of the past tense suggests that to him his father was already dead. The remark "very happy within himself" reveals his perception that Jakob enjoyed a private happiness, originating in a source apart from the shared life of the family.

Freud was not aware of the feelings that were to come upon him after his father's death on October 23. He made all the funeral arrangements but arrived late for the ceremony, because, he said, he had been kept waiting at the barbershop. The family was offended by the austerity of the funeral itself, as well as by Sigmund's lateness and his lame excuse for it. The night after the funeral Freud had a dream, which he reported to Fliess in his November 2 letter. The letter merits repetition here because it has so many revealing references to his relationship with his father. It begins:

Dear Wilhelm,

I find it so difficult to write just now that I have put off for a long time thanking you for the moving words in your letter. By one of those dark pathways behind the official consciousness the old man's death has affected me deeply. I valued him highly, understood him very well, and with his peculiar mixture of deep wisdom and fantastic light-heartedness he had a significant effect on my life [er hatte viel in meinem Leben gemacht]. By the time he died, his life had long been over, but in [my] inner self the whole past has been reawakened by this event. I now feel quite uprooted. . . .

I must tell you about a nice dream I had the night after the funeral.[6] I was in a place where I read a sign:

You are requested
to close the eyes.

I immediately recognized the location of the barbershop I visit every day. On the day of the funeral I was kept waiting and therefore arrived a little late at the house of mourning. At that time my family was displeased with me because I had arranged for the funeral to be quiet and simple, which they later agreed was quite justified. They were also somewhat offended by my lateness. The sentence on the sign has a double meaning: one should do one's duty to the dead (an apology as though I had not done it and were in need of leniency), and the actual duty itself. The dream thus stems

6. In chapter 6 of *The Interpretation of Dreams* Freud changes the date to: "During the night before my father's funeral."

from the inclination to self-reproach that regularly sets in among the survivors. [my italics]

There is a striking contrast between Freud's acknowledgment of having been affected deeply and the lighthearted way in which he treats the dream, calling it "nice" even while recognizing that it has to do with survivor guilt. Furthermore, he plays down his lateness, ignoring the fact that under strict Jewish law it is sacrilegious to cut one's hair at the time of a relative's death;[7] thus his visit to the barber itself, aside from his lateness, might have offended some Orthodox friends of the family. He even claims that the funeral arrangements were justified. In *The Interpretation of Dreams* he described how: "I had chosen the simplest possible ritual for the funeral, for I knew my father's own views on such ceremonies. But some other members of the family were not sympathetic to such puritanical simplicity and thought we should be disgraced in the eyes of those who attended the funeral. Hence one of the versions: 'You are requested to close an eye', i.e. to 'wink at' or 'overlook'" (1900, p. 318).

In 1900 Freud seemed content to interpret the dream at its social level. But in the letter to Fliess he spoke of reproaches and guilt and the need for leniency. It is tempting to conclude that the so-called puritanical simplicity of Jakob's funeral—an affront in the eyes of some to Freud's duty as the son of a Jewish father who had urged him to learn from the Book—was a reflection of Freud's absolute intolerance of religious ceremonies rather than of his father's wishes.

What was the "duty" he might not have fulfilled? Both *The Interpretation of Dreams* and the letter to Fliess are so ambiguous in their description that it is impossible to know what kind of fu-

7. Personal communication from Evelyne Schwaber, M.D. Male relatives are also supposed to refrain from shaving for thirty days.

neral he arranged for his father. Even more striking is the explanation that Freud, a man who scrutinized every human motive, offered for his own lateness. This externalization (the barber kept him waiting), the reaction formation of calling the dream "nice," and the use of the past tense (he "*was* an interesting human being") five months before his father's death were symptomatic manifestations of his contradictory emotions about losing his father. They heralded the storm of conflicting feelings, the uprootedness, the overpowering effect that his father's death was to have on him for the rest of his life (Schur, 1972, p. 109). He was to remain in the grip of tremendous ambivalence for years to come, becoming the great conquistador of the unconscious in his efforts to master his inner storm. At the time, however, when the "whole past had been reawakened," he had first "to close the eyes." To see all there was to see was more than he could bear. He had to keep himself going in a hypomanic mood by avoiding the unavoidable, as indicated by his remark to Fliess in the December 4 letter: "My bad time has run its course in typical fashion; I am fully occupied, with every hour taken, and *am not in the least interested in life after death*" (my italics).

On November 22, barely a month after Jakob's death, Freud rented new quarters at 19 Berggasse, decorating them with the "Florentine statues," which he found to be an "extraordinary invigoration." It was the beginning of the antiquities collection. By May 16, he reported to Fliess that he was feeling the need for an "audience": "Let me go on taking advantage of you as a kindly disposed audience. Without such an audience I really cannot work."

The work had to do with dreams. Like the biblical Joseph, Freud seemed to have known that his future depended on the interpretation of dreams: "I have felt impelled to start working on the dream [book]. . . . I have been looking into the literature and feel like the Celtic imp: 'Oh, how glad I am that no one, no one knows. . . .' No one even suspects that the dream is not nonsense but wish fulfillment." Freud, who in late adolescence had decided to become a physician so as to unveil the secrets of nature, was now compelled by the psychic commotion caused by his father's death to carry out the unrelenting search for the secrets of dreams and his own infantile past. The search had the same complexity of contrary needs and wishes that Freud had detected in Goethe: "Goethe was not only, as a poet, a great self-revealer, but also, in spite of the abundance of autobiographical records, a careful concealer" (1930b, p. 212). Hanns Sachs (1944) reports that Freud once said, pointing to the three shelves in his library holding the complete works of Goethe: "All this was used by him as a means of self-concealment" (p. 105).

The allusion to himself is clear. Freud promised himself to explore it all, to shake open the doors of the underworld (*Acheronta movebo*). As he demonstrated to others, however, the censoring power of internalized parental prohibitions and superego demands about family dynamics required that he conceal as much as he unveiled. Krüll (1986) concluded that his motive for concealment was that "Jacob had placed a taboo on the discovery of the real answers" to the family's dark secrets (p. 178). This interpretation seems accurate but too narrow. It does justice neither to Freud's commitment to intellectual and scientific honesty nor to the complexity of his mind.

In 1908, in the preface to the second edition of *The Interpretation of Dreams*, Freud revealed his full awareness of his motive in writing the dream book and carrying out his self-analysis: "It was, I found, a portion of my own self-analysis, my reaction to my father's death."

Freud believed that the mother has less to offer the growing child than the father does. In his conception of the origin of religious ideas, fathers provide the link with gods: "They are illusions, fulfillments of the oldest, strongest and most urgent wishes of mankind. The secret of their strength lies in the strength of those wishes. As we already know, *the terrifying impression of helplessness in childhood aroused the need for protection—for protection through love—which was provided by the father;* and the recognition that this helplessness lasts throughout life made it necessary *to cling to the existence of the father,* but this time a more powerful one. Thus the benevolent rule of a divine Providence allays our fear of the dangers of life" (1927, p. 30, my italics).

Freud tried not "to cling to the existence of the father" by not thinking about the afterlife. No one knew better than he how much he needed the paternal presence to protect him against the "terrifying helplessness of childhood." Two questions arise from Freud's description: what was in his case the "terrifying helplessness," and why could he not find protection in his mother as well as in his father? Detailed examination of his parents' characters as well as the life events of his childhood offers some answers to these questions (see Chapters 11 and 12).

Freud, having rejected the God his father had offered as a substitute for Jakob himself, was therefore unable to cling to his father in the shape of a God. He could, however, cling to him in other shapes, because he needed Jakob's presence and, as he said to Fliess, he needed an audience. As he tried endlessly to answer the riddles of human life and to unveil the secrets of the mind, he continued to wrestle with his intensely contradictory feelings about his father. He also brought him back, as I hope to demonstrate, in his collection of antiquities. Bringing Jakob back in this manner hid as much as it revealed about his conflicted but psychologically indispensable relation to a deeply disappointing father whose love protected him against obscure childhood terrors.

Freud's Childhood Impressions from the Philippson Bible

*What someone thinks he remembers from his childhood is not
a matter of indifference; as a rule the residual memories—
which he himself does not understand—cloak priceless pieces
of evidence about the most important features in his mental
development.* Freud, 1910, p. 84

In preceding chapters I have described the
concrete and psychical circumstances between Freud and his father at the time
when Freud received the Philippson Bible
as a special gift. Now I shall discuss the circumstances in which young Freud found
himself when Jakob first introduced the
Bible to him. The dedication indicates that
Sigmund was seven years old at the time.

What was his life like up to the age
of seven? A complex one, to say the least.
He had three mothering figures: his own
mother, Amalie: his nanny, Monika Zajik
(or perhaps Resi Wittek, as Krüll suggests,
1986, p. 119), and his "Aunt" Maria, wife
of his half-brother Emmanuel, who lived
nearby. Their son, John, his half-nephew,
was nine months Sigmund's senior, and their daughter, Pauline,
six months his junior. Several episodes described in *The Interpretation of Dreams* show how close the families were. Regarding John, Freud writes: "Until the end of my third year we had
been inseparable. We had loved each other and fought with
each other; . . . this childhood relationship . . . had a determin-

ing influence on all my subsequent relations with contemporaries" (1900, p. 424).

When he was twenty-three months old, Sigmund had lost his first sibling, Julius, who died at the age of six months of a "bowel infection" (Krüll, 1986, p. 135). Julius's death also marked Sigmund for life, as he disclosed to Fliess in an October 3, 1897, letter: "I greeted my one-year-younger brother (who died after a few months) with adverse wishes and genuine childhood jealousy; . . . his death left the germ of [self-]reproaches in me" (1887–1904, p. 268). Much as Freud talked later in life about his rivalry with Julius, he must also have been attached to his little brother.[1]

There were three significant adult male figures in his life, all closely related. First, there was his impressive-looking father, at that point an economically comfortable wool merchant. Second was his half-brother Emmanuel, twenty-three years his senior, the father of two, who lived with his family two blocks away on the other side of the town's plaza. Finally, there was his half-brother Philipp, who lived across the street. Philipp, the same age as Freud's mother, seemed to be closely involved in the affairs of the family; it was he, for example, who called the police to denounce Sigmund's nanny for stealing and who explained things to little Sigmund. Emmanuel and Philipp, two adult men, called Jakob, Sigmund's father, "father"; Sigmund's playmate and nephew John called him "grandfather." It must have been very hard for the young Sigmund to sort out these complex and bewildering relationships.

Then he lost them all. First, his nanny disappeared abruptly and mysteriously early in 1859, during his mother's confine-

1. Martin Freud (1957) relates the story of how his father reacted to his own son Walter, who as a young boy put himself in danger of being killed: "Father said in effect that there was not the slightest sense in becoming attached to a boy who must sooner or later kill himself in dangerous escapades" (p. 193).

ment with Anna. Freud was thirty-one months old and was facing the arrival of a new competitor eight months after the death of the first rival, Julius. Sigmund was told that his nanny had been sent to prison for stealing from him. That somehow made him an accomplice to her crime,[2] for, as he wrote to Fliess on October 15, 1897, "she induced me to steal zehners [coins] and give them to her." Little Sigmund feared losing his mother as he had lost his nanny. In the same letter to Fliess he described

> a scene . . . which in the course of twenty-five years has occasionally emerged in my conscious memory without my understanding it. My mother was nowhere to be found; I was crying in despair. My brother Philipp (twenty years older than I) unlocked a wardrobe [Kasten] for me, and when I did not find my mother inside it either, I cried even more until, slender and beautiful, she came through the door. . . . I was afraid she had vanished from me, just as the old woman had a short time before. So I must have heard that the old woman had been locked up and therefore must have believed that my mother had been locked up too. (1887–1904, pp. 271–72)

Philipp, "who had taken his father's place as the child rival [and] . . . had the lost nurse 'boxed up,'" was at the center of little Sigmund's despair. He "was full of mistrust and anxiety that his mother's inside might conceal more children" and suspected that Philipp "had in some way introduced the recently born baby into his mother's inside" (1901, p. 51, note 2). The matter touched on Freud's relationship with Jakob, who was father to both Philipp and Sigmund. In the young child's mind there were two fathers, one young, the age of his mother, placing babies in her, and the other, the older father.

2. Freud must have remembered this episode when his Uncle Joseph was sentenced for circulating counterfeit rubles.

Jakob, Amalie, Freud, and baby Anna moved to Vienna. Philipp, Emmanuel, Maria, and the children went to England. Sigmund was not to see them again until his first trip to England when he was in his late teens. He was three and a half years old and his life was already marked by death (Julius), loss (his nanny), and lasting separation (the rest of his family). He must also have been affected by his parents' grief over the earlier death of Shlomo Freud and the death of his mother's brother Julius Nathansohn. As though these losses were not terrible enough, he had to leave forever the town of his birth, so rich in sensual pleasures, for the Leopoldstrasse ghetto in Vienna's suburbs. The days of the "happy child" from Freiberg were over (1960, p. 408). This was the last time Sigmund could describe himself as a "happy child." After the move, he wrote in the crypto-autobiographical essay "Screen Memories" (1899), "Long and difficult years followed, of which, as it seems to me, nothing was worth remembering. I never felt really comfortable in the town. I believe now that I was never free from a longing for the beautiful woods near our home, in which (as one of the memories from those days tells me) I used to run off from my father, almost before I had learnt to walk" (pp. 312–13).

The contrast between these memories is sharp. Unrelenting poverty, city congestion, and the limited nuclear family had replaced economic comfort, open air, and a lively extended family. Jakob Freud, who had made the decision to move, was solely responsible for these changes.

Of those long years of which "nothing is worth remembering," Sigmund nevertheless retained a few significant visual memories. In *The Psychopathology of Everyday Life* (1901), Freud describes people who are, according to Charcot's categorization, *visuels* or *auditifs* in their manner of recalling. Freud points out that in his own case, "the earliest childhood memories are the only ones of a visual character: they are regular scenes worked out in plastic form, comparable only to representations on the stage. In these scenes of childhood, whether in fact they prove to be true or falsified, what one sees invariably includes oneself as a child, with a child's shape and clothes" (p. 47). Obviously, Freud is speaking of consciously recalled memories, which he clearly says are screen memories developed over time, with many psychic revisions. Unconsciously, he remembered much more than these few vignettes in an equally significant "plastic form."

Freud's first conscious recollection, recounted in *The Interpretation of Dreams*, has to do with a book and his father: "It had once amused my father to hand over a book with *coloured plates* (an account of a journey through Persia) for me and my eldest sister to destroy. Not easy to justify from the educational point of view! I had been five years old at the time and my sister not yet three; and the picture of the two of us blissfully pulling the book to pieces (leaf by leaf, like an *artichoke*, I found myself saying) was almost the only plastic memory I retained from that period of my life" (p. 172). Freud connects his having become "a book worm" and a "bibliophile" to this screen memory.

The recollection appeared in his analysis of the dream of "The Botanical Monograph." Freud interprets the dream, like the "Irma's Injection" dream, as "in the nature of self-justification," as "a plea on behalf of my rights." In both cases, he asserted, "what I was insisting was: 'I may allow myself to do this'" (1900, p. 173). The dream and the interpretation convey the dialectic between lax permissiveness and the compelling need to plead for what one justly deserves. Freud had the dream on March 10, 1898 (Grinstein, 1980), eighteen months after his father's death. The dilemma presented in the dream could indicate the tension between the childhood wishes of the five-year-old Sigmund and his suppressed protestations to his father.

The detailed analysis of the dream connects it to childhood and adolescent sexual wishes and to present-day wishes for fame and acknowledgment. In discussing the dream, Freud also remembered how, as a teenager, having already "*developed a passion for collecting and owning books,*" he overcharged his account at the bookseller. "'My father had scarcely taken it as an excuse that my inclination might have chosen a worse outlet" (pp. 172–73, my italics). Freud, the collector of books, was cleverly defending his passion in front of a disapproving father. The book in "The Botanical Monograph" dream is of a special kind, with colored plates. As he elaborates on his associations to the dream, Freud describes how as a medical student he was "enthralled" by the colored plates of medical monographs.

Freud's first recollection from his childhood years in Vienna is of playing with his sister and a book. The next memory, from the age of seven or eight, would plague Freud to the end of his days. He could not forget it; it became embedded in his character structure, as a thorn in his side:

> When I was seven or eight years old . . . one evening before going to sleep I disregarded the rules which modesty lays down and obeyed the call of nature in my parents' bedroom while they were present. In the course of his reprimand, my father let fall the words: "The boy will come to nothing." This must have been a frightful blow to my ambition, for references to this scene are still constantly recurring in my dreams and are always linked with an enumeration of my achievements and successes, as though I want to say: "You see, I *have* come to something." (1900, p. 216)

Several of Freud's dreams and their associations bring out revengeful, humiliating, mocking images and fantasies related to his father, father substitutes, or rivals. The attempt to reverse the humiliation of that fateful evening colors Freud's affects and wishes in most of them. Why did Jakob's rebuke cut such a deep wound in Sigmund's heart? He gives no clues except that it confronted his ambitions. Remarks like Jakob's often slip from the mouths of frustrated parents. In Sigmund's case, the deeper and more lasting frustration was his. He had already experienced the "catastrophe" of Jakob's losing his business, disappointing his son in a profound and irretrievable way. Freud modulated his intense dissatisfaction by attributing disillusionment about the father to all boys during the second half of childhood: "The boy begins to cast his eyes upon the world outside. And he cannot fail now to make discoveries which undermine his original high opinion of his father and which expedite his detachment from his first ideal. He finds that his father is no longer the mightiest, wisest and richest of beings; he grows dissatisfied with him, he learns to criticize him and *to estimate his place in society*; and then, as a rule, he makes him pay heavily for the disappointment that *has been caused by him*" (1914b, p. 244, my italics). Sigmund had learned that the father he once thought mighty could scarcely feed the family and that his place in society was among the lowest. To be told that he too, in his father's appraisal, could come to nothing must have been truly horrifying, a thought more frightful than any other because his father had demonstrated that it was possible to come to nothing. Freud, as a child, an adolescent, and an adult, did everything he could to truly "come to something."

With his sharp intelligence and his subtle emotional perceptiveness, he understood very early that he could "come to something" by learning from books. His becoming a "book worm" stemmed from the compelling need to overcome a profound childhood trauma. The actual childhood disenchantment with his father could never be ameliorated, because as a provider his father was never able to redeem himself. There was no provident father to idealize or even respect at any age.

It was in the context of this bitter disillusionment, and at the time of his first encounters with other books, that the seven-year-old Sigmund was introduced to the Book of Books, the Philippson Bible. The Bible described the relationship between God, the creator of the whole world, and the people he had chosen as his own. This God, outspoken and expressive, constantly manifests his wishes in relation to all things, but most directly to human beings. The Bible presented the child Freud with the stories, among many others, of Abraham, Jacob, Joseph, and Moses, the great leader who sealed the unending covenant between God and the people of Israel. Freud himself reports that both Jakob and Amalie talked to him about these stories.

A third memory from his boyhood reveals an oral biblical tradition in the family:

> When I was six years old and was given my first lessons by my mother, I was expected to believe that we were all made of earth and must therefore return to earth. This did not suit me and I expressed doubts of the doctrine. My mother thereupon rubbed the palms of her hands together—just as she did in making dumplings, except that there was no dough between them—and showed me the blackish scales of *epidermis* produced by the friction as a proof that we were made of earth. My astonishment at this ocular demonstration knew no bounds and I acquiesced in the belief which I was later to hear expressed in the words: "*Du bist der Natur einen Tod schuldig.*" (1900, p. 205)

Freud was obviously rebelling against God's strong words after Adam's disobedience, "you are dust and to dust you shall return" (Genesis 4:19). The quotation in German is, as Jones points out in his footnote, "a reminiscence of Prince Hal's remark to Falstaff in 1 *Henry IV*,v. 1: 'Thou owest God a death.'" (See Chapter 11 for the substitution of Nature for God.)

Curiously enough, both of Freud's two direct references to his early biblical knowledge relate to death. The second concerns a dream that includes Freud's only explicit reference to the illustrations of the Philippson Bible. The last dream reported in The Interpretation of Dreams, it serves to illustrate the sexual source of "anxiety-dreams dreamt by young people." The full quotation is indispensable to do justice to the complexity of Freud's childhood psychic experience:

> It is a dozen years since I myself had a true anxiety-dream. But I remember one from my seventh or eighth year, which I submitted to interpretation some thirty years later. It was a very vivid one, and in it I saw my beloved mother, with a peculiarly peaceful, sleeping expression on her features, being carried into the room by two (or three) people with birds' beaks and laid upon the bed. I awoke in tears and screaming, and interrupted my parents' sleep. The strangely draped and unnaturally tall figures with birds' beaks were derived from the illustrations to Philippson's Bible.[3] I fancy they must have been gods with falcons' heads from an ancient Egyptian funerary relief. Besides this, the analysis brought to mind an ill-mannered boy, a son of a concierge, who used to play with us on the grass in front of the house when we were children, and who I am inclined to think was called Philipp. It seems to me that it was from this boy that I first heard the vulgar term for sexual intercourse [vögeln, from Vogel, the ordinary word for bird], instead of which educated people always use a Latin word, "to copulate," and which was clearly enough indicated by the choice of the falcons' heads. I must have guessed the sexual signif-

3. All authors trace the illustration to the hearse accompanying the commentaries to 2 Samuel 3:31–35. The page is among those not found in the bound volume given to Freud by his father. Its absence suggests that the page was lost after Freud saw it as a child (see fig. 6.2).

icance of the word from the face of my young instructor, who was well acquainted with the facts of life. The expression on my mother's features in the dream was copied from the view I had had of my grandfather a few days before his death as he lay snoring in a coma. The interpretation carried out in the dream by the "secondary revision" must therefore have been that my mother was dying; the funerary relief fitted in with this. I awoke in anxiety, which did not cease till I had woken my parents up. I remember that I suddenly grew calm when I saw my mother's face, as though I had needed to be reassured that she was not dead. But this "secondary" interpretation of the dream had already been made under the influence of the anxiety that had developed. I was not anxious because I had dreamt that my mother was dying; but I interpreted the dream in that sense in my preconscious revision of it because I was already under the influence of the anxiety. The anxiety can be traced back, when repression is taken into account, to an obscure and evidently sexual craving that had found appropriate expression in the visual content of the dream. (pp. 583–84)

This complex dream has been the subject of many interpretations. Grinstein (1980) concurs with Freud in interpreting the dream as related to anxiety over sexual and aggressive wishes— in particular, Absalom's sexual relations with the concubines of his father, David, in the presence of David's men, who finally kill him, causing his father bitter grief. He concludes: "no clearer presentation of the father-son conflict can be imagined" (p. 455) and surmises that "Freud was afraid not only that parental coitus would result in his mother's death but that his Oedipal feelings would result in his own castration" (p. 458).

Anzieu (1986) goes so far as to say that Freud's analysis of the childhood dream, undertaken as an adult, during the mourning of his father's death, was a way of "completing the discovery which would refute his father's curse once and for all and bring him the symbolic possession of his beloved mother" (p. 308). Rosenfeld (1956) studied the dream for what it reveals symbolically about the man who had entered the realm of self-knowledge that "had for thousands of years been ascribed to God or gods" (p. 98) and whose revolutionary discoveries in that realm led him to begin collecting antiquities.

This rich and vivid dream has many layers of meaning. Three points are of particular interest here. First, the dating of the dream is incorrect. Freud's maternal grandfather, Jacob Nathansohn, died on October 3, 1865, when Sigmund was nine and a half years old. He was seven or eight when he was being taught that we are dust and to dust we return. He probably confused the memory of the intolerable lesson with the reality of his grandfather's going into the ground. Second, the imagery of the dream does originate in the Philippson Bible illustration of "gods with falcons' heads from an ancient funerary relief."

6.1 Egyptian ferryboat. From a sculpture depicting the netherworld (*Todtengericht*). Philippson Bible, vol. 2, p. 459

6.2 Hearse.
From a bas-
relief in Thebes.
Philippson
Bible, vol. 2,
p. 394

Bahre. Von einem Basrelief in Theben.

The bible has two illustrations that portray funerary reliefs. One, showing an Egyptian ferryboat (fig. 6.1), illustrates the commentary to versicles 17–18 of 2 Samuel 19. The text describes the aftermath of Absalom's death, when the people went to David to ask him to cross back from the river and become their king again: "Ziba the servant of the house of Saul, with his fifteen sons and his twenty servants, rushed down to the Jordan before the king [David], and they crossed the ford to bring over the king's household, and to do this with pleasure." Philippson's comment is not about this dramatic story but about the ferries used in antiquity to navigate seas and rivers.

The second illustration (fig. 6.2), to accompany 2 Samuel 3:31–35, gives graphic form to the story about the treacherous killing of Abner, David's general: "Then David said to Jo'ab and to all the people who were with him, 'Rend your clothes, and gird on sackcloth, and mourn before Abner.' And King David followed the bier. They buried Abner at Hebron; and the king lifted up his voice and wept at the grave of Abner; and all the people wept." Philippson's commentary describes the funeral and the bier in the sculpture as illustrative art without concern for the biblical story itself.

Nine-year-old Sigmund must have just attended his grandfather Jacob Nathansohn's funeral after seeing him comatose in bed. If the dream occurred a few days after his maternal grandfather's death, it took place when the family was still in acute mourning, sitting shiva and receiving condolences from their friends and neighbors in the Leopoldstadt Jewish ghetto where the Nathansohns had lived for years.[4] Sigmund must have seen his grandfather buried, as Abner was, with the people, especially his mother, weeping, following the funeral bier. He must have seen the mourning clothes and the rabbi and his assistants clothed in long robes. As far as we know, Jacob Nathansohn was the first immediate relative that Sigmund knew after Julius who died. Sensitive as Sigmund was to death and loss (Schur, 1972), it is impossible to think that the dream imagery functions only to disguise sexual matters. He must have been thinking about, or trying to forget about, the afterlife, as he was much later when his father died. The ferryboat carrying the dead to their judgment seems a clear enough allusion to the last judgment. It is in that ferryboat illustration that the people with birds' beaks appear.

The third point of interest is the adult Freud's lack of associations to the biblical illustrations in analyzing this very significant dream. This failure to investigate the meaning of the Philippson Bible illustrations in his dream indicates defensive avoidance. As soon as he says that the illustrations were derived from the bible and that "they must have been gods with falcon heads from an ancient Egyptian funerary relief," he drops the subject. Freud associates to Philipp, the concierge's son who gave him sexual lessons in childhood, and considers only the sexual meaning of the falcon heads. The Philippson Bible, however, could scarcely be an indifferent selection from his unconscious imagery. There is the direct connection among the three Philipps—who are sons: Philipp his half-brother, the suspected

4. Amalie Freud was the only one of Jacob's four surviving children who lived in Austria. Jacob helped the Freud family during their economic difficulties.

maker of babies in his mother's womb; Philipp-son, the Bible translator; and, Philipp, the concierge's son. All three directly or indirectly connect sex with death and disappearance. The images that prevailed in the manifest dream were those taken from the Philippson Bible, the one he had known as a child, later given to him by his father six years before his death. Freud's conclusion leaves out the obvious significance of death anxiety and substitutes a sexual one: "The anxiety can be traced back, when repression is taken into account, to an obscure and evidently sexual craving that had found appropriate expression in the visual content of the dream" (1900, p. 584).

Following Freud's own theories about dreams, the questions emerge: What about the day residues—the death of his grandfather, whose name was also Jacob, and the funeral? Why select death and mortuary images from the bible to sexually represent a mother who taught him lessons about death from it? Could a dead mother be a substitute for a dead Jakob, grandfatherfather as Sigmund knew him to be? All this suggests that the adult self-analyzing Freud could not deal with the imagery of the bible in relation to death and loss and analyze why he had used it. He had to remain in the well-known territory of sexual desire and oedipal competition. Death and the bible continued to be repressed.

Further, his analysis of the "Open-air Closet" dream— which he had in late July or early August of 1898, close to the time of the analysis of the childhood anxiety dream—elaborates on its literary sources in Swift's *Gulliver's Travels*, in Rabelais's *Gargantua*, and in C. F. Meyer's *Die Leiden eines Knaben* (A boy's sorrows). There is a striking difference between Freud's treatment of the Philippson Bible illustrations and his discussion of literary works as a source of imagery and dream associations. The conclusion imposes itself: there was no significant repression to be lifted with regard to the literary sources. There was, however, a repression that he could not overcome in analyzing—in adulthood, after his father's death—the images originating in the Bible, so charged were they with the feelings of his filial history.

Two issues must be addressed. The first is Freud's visual ability to use the biblical illustrations in the dream. The second is his motive for ignoring the psychic function of such images as the manifest content of the dream.

The visual ability to use the images from the Philippson Bible unconsciously suggests that the images, deeply invested with emotions, had been registered and had become available for psychic functions, such as dreaming. In spite of his disclaimer in the quotation above, where he asserts that his memories are no longer plastic, there is evidence that Freud possessed sharp visual perception and memory. For example, in his August 23, 1883, letter to Martha he describes his intense pleasure in reading *Don Quixote* and studying the details of Doré's illustrations:

> They are superb only when the artist approaches his subject from the fantastic angle: when for instance he picks out a few words of the tavern-keeper's wife to show how a wretched little knight has cut in half six giants with one blow of his sword, the lower halves of the bodies still standing while the upper halves roll in the dust. . . . He is good wherever the text lends itself to caricature, for instance when the ghosts bewitch the knight and lock him up in a cage. It's enough to make one die with laughter. (1960, p. 46)

The description is so graphic and vivid, the pleasure so obvious, that it allows the conclusion that Freud's visual imagination and memory were very significant traits of his character. Ginsburg and Ginsburg (1987) have discovered additional illustrated books that Freud read as a child: Wilhelm Busch's humorous and satirical compositions and Alfred E. Brehm's *Animal*

Life with Illustrations, which Freud won as a school prize at the age of eleven. They conclude that "such visual stimuli from Freud's pre-adolescent period were stockpiled and reanimated in subsequent memories and mental attitudes" and "continued to come alive for him and assert themselves in his daily life" (pp. 469, 484). Freud was and remained a visuel.

His vivid visual imagination and his pleasure in it find further confirmation later in the same letter to Martha: "I can well imagine how magnificent his illustrations for *Orlando Furioso* must be, material that would seem to be made for Doré, and even several things out of the Bible, especially legendary and heroic scenes."[5] This is one of the very rare occasions, perhaps the only one, in which Freud indicates that he is acquainted with biblical "legendary and heroic scenes"—before the comment added to his autobiography in 1935.

I have noted that several of the figures in Freud's original copy of the Philippson Bible—illustrations of Egyptian soldiers, a pyramid, Persian and Oriental men, plants and some animals—had been colored in. There is every indication that Freud himself colored them as a child. In 1848, the handwritten date on the Bible, Philipp, Jakob's youngest son at the time, was fourteen, too old for such amusements. Neither Freud's siblings nor his children were acquainted with the home Bible. The manner of coloring suggests that it was done by a child who had the capacity to remain within the margins of the figure—that is, a child of seven or eight. There are also two lead pencil scribbles made by a child who could hardly hold a pencil. The coloring and scribbles suggest that a lenient Jakob let his child play with the book. As mentioned above, Jakob once allowed Sigmund and Anna to pull the pages out of an illustrated book.

5. An edition of the Philippson Bible, without the commentary and illustrated by Doré, was published in 1874.

What happened to Freud's capacity for the registration, enjoyment, and recollection of graphic images when it came to the copiously illustrated Philippson Bible? This is the fundamental question for this chapter. The question converges with the earlier query about Freud's motives in 1897–98, when, in analyzing the childhood anxiety dream, he avoided exploring the psychic functions of the biblical images.

Two conclusions emerge. The first is that Freud's early childhood ambivalence toward his father—based partly on normal oedipal rivalry but mostly on the terrible suffering and disillusionment of the "great catastrophe"—prompted him to repress any conscious use of the Philippson illustrations. That ambivalence dominated his life from latency onward and deeply colored the mourning of his father's death. After Jakob's death, the images returned and remained with him to the very last minute of his life, compelling him to re-create them by collecting and surrounding himself with archaeological objects, many of which were direct replicas of the Philippson Bible illustrations.

Freud returned to the images for a reason. As we have seen, Jakob Freud was full of fun, with a "peculiar mixture of deep wisdom and fantastic light-heartedness." How did Jakob teach Sigmund during his latency and prepuberal periods the "legendary and heroic scenes" so abundant and dramatic in the Bible? With his flair for the poetic and profoundly inspiring use of biblical language, so evident in the dedication of the bible, Jakob must have been an exciting and engaging teacher, capable of bringing the biblical narratives to life. Father and child were in this respect a most compatible pair. Imaginative, inquisitive, capable of being "enthralled" by the illustrations and the complexities of the texts, they must have shared the pleasure of contemplating the exotic biblical characters and lands. The satisfactions of this shared learning must have been deep. Sigmund must have found his father's detailed knowledge of the book admirable, perhaps even awesome. Freud recognized his father's "deep wisdom," carried generation after generation by the scholarly readers and interpreters of the Book of God. He saw in his father's inscription the unforgettable generational link between Shlomo and Shlomo Sigmund. He witnessed Jakob's careful documentation of his son's entrance into the covenant of the Jewish people. Yes, Jakob, the man who studied and taught the Bible, was indeed a respectable, impressive, and very exciting father.

But Sigmund also saw the other Jakob—the incompetent businessman full of empty dreams, the improvident father, the dweller in the poor and crowded quarters of the Leopoldstrasse ghetto, the man who had removed Sigmund from the "happy" town of Freiberg. To add insult to injury, there was the Jakob who had announced that he, Sigmund, would "come to nothing." This narcissistic summation of wounds overwhelmed the child. An ambivalent internal split developed in relation to his father, which, in the end, became a profound character trait. His best friend and protector was also his worst enemy, whose actions had brought much suffering to his life and had deprived him of a childhood.

The everyday suffering and his father's unforgettable insult invoked the talion. His father had disappointed him deeply in the two aspects most precious to him: as an improvident father fallen from exalted idealization and as the destroyer of his compensatory self-idealization to become "something." In his limited capacity for ambivalent but deeply needed revenge, he could injure his father in what was most precious to him: he rejected his father's Bible and the God it offered. This rejection, which will be elaborated in Chapter 12, seems to have occurred at the end of adolescence. Jakob's dedication indicates that he understood Sigmund's rejection of his Bible very well, if not his motives.

Freud, the adult son of Jakob, could reject the Bible and refuse to read it; he could repress the exciting texts and illustrations. He could not, however, make images and stories already registered within him disappear. Consciously suppressed or unconsciously repressed as they were, they could not be erased from his memory. As he himself would later say: "in the unconscious nothing can be brought to an end, nothing is past or forgotten" (1900, p. 577).

chapter seven

The Philippson Bible and Freud's Antiquities Collection

What kind of book was this Philippson Bible that Sigmund Freud, the book lover, apparently refused to read? It was a work of love by Ludwig Philippson, the rabbi of Magdeburg, and his older brother Phoebus, a doctor of medicine, the oldest children of Moses Philippson (1775–1814). Moses's father, a Polish peddler who spoke only Yiddish, wanted his son to become

a rabbi and, after the child had learned some basic Hebrew from a local kheyder, hired private Hebrew teachers and later sent Moses to the yeshiva at Halberstad. From Halberstad, Moses went to Frankfurt, where he became a teacher of Hebrew, religion, and arithmetic at a private Jewish school. After his marriage Moses started to translate and publish biblical texts in Hebrew and German. He also published a periodical, *Der neuer Sammler* (The New Compiler), and a Hebrew-German and German-Hebrew dictionary. In the midst of this intense activity he contracted typhus and died, on April 20, 1814, aged thirty-nine; Phoebus was seven years old and Ludwig three.

Moses Philippson was a man at the dawn of the Haskala who dedicated his efforts "to overcom[ing] the inertia, ignorance, and religious formalism of the Jews of his period" (J. Philippson, 1962, p. 98). His children, especially Ludwig (1811–89), took it upon themselves to perpetuate their father's ideals. After an elementary education at his father's school, Ludwig joined Phoebus (1807–70) in Halle, where he attended the *Frankesche Stiftunge Gymnasium*, studied Latin and Greek privately, wrote poetry, and was tutored in medical subjects by his brother. At the age of sixteen, he published a metrical translation of several of the Minor Prophets. Soon he moved to Berlin to study the classics, which he mastered to the point of winning a writing competition in Latin.

In 1833, having obtained a doctorate in philology from the University of Berlin, Ludwig was invited to give a sermon to a Jewish community near Magdeburg. His preaching so impressed the congregation that he was appointed their *Prediger* (preacher). This provided him with a regular income and an opportunity to pursue his profound desire "to regenerate Judaism without breaking with the past" (J. Philippson, 1962, p. 104). Ludwig Philippson's freedom of spirit is perhaps best shown in his approach to his congregation: "He preached in German, because he knew that otherwise he could not reach his congregation; he wanted them to sing in German to be sure they knew what they sang. He needed the organ to make the service more attractive. He introduced confirmation for both sexes to make the women feel they were an integral part of the community. But he insisted on certain traditional forms in Hebrew during the service, and thought circumcision indispensable" (p. 105).

Following in his father's mission to persuade all German Jews to become integrated into the modern world while remaining faithful to the God of the covenant, Ludwig founded the newspaper *Allgemeine Zeitung des Judentums,* which he edited from 1837 to his death in 1889. It became "the mouthpiece of German Jewry" (p. 105). He also "dreamt of a world that would accept Judaism as the only possible creed" (p. 106). Still, he regarded himself as a true German and remained a patriot to the end.

Philippson wrote and lectured prolifically about biblical and religious subjects, but by far his most significant work was the translation of the Jewish Bible into German and its publication in a Hebrew-German edition with his own voluminous commentaries. Ludwig began the translation in 1838 and completed it in 1854 (p. 106).[1] Phoebus translated and commented on the books of Joshua, Judges, Samuel, and Kings.

The first edition was in three volumes, each of them published in installments, in the form of paginated fascicles (Lieferungen) ready to be bound together when a volume was completed. In August 1839 the First Book of Moses appeared, with an introductory note by Ludwig Philippson. It also contained a note from the publisher, Baumgärtner's Buchhandlung of Leipzig, inviting the reader to subscribe to the series and promising "prompt continuation of the work." Subsequent printings presented other biblical books section by section.

The publication continued uninterrupted. The first volume was completed in 1841 and reprinted in 1844. In 1847 an edition of the complete first volume, containing the Five Books of Moses without the commentary and in German, was produced for use as a school textbook. Johanna Philippson (1962), Ludwig's granddaughter, reports that this "cheap edition . . . was distributed in large numbers to counteract the activities of Protestant missionaries among the Jews." A notice from the publisher on the back of the book indicates that the first volume had been completed and bound and that publication of the thirty fascicles of the second volume was proceeding in installments.

The first part of volume 2, translated by Phoebus Philippson

1. There is some confusion about the dates. According to Allan D. Satin, of the Hebrew Union College in Cincinnati, the first three-volume edition was completed and published in 1853. J. Philippson does not seem fully reliable in this matter.

and consisting of the Books of Joshua, Judges, Samuel, and Kings, was published in 1841. The second part of volume 2, which included the Prophets, appeared some time later. There is a bound edition dated 1848, which may be the date of completion.

The bound volume that Jakob gave Sigmund includes the entire first volume and portions of the second—all of 1 Kings; 2 Kings from 18 to 28:35; and 2 Samuel from 11:17 to the end (24:25)—representing pages 423–86 and 488–672. Page 394 of volume 2, with the illustration of a hearse to which Freud seemed to refer in his childhood anxiety dream, is not included in the bound volume. There are two possibilities: either that illustration is not connected to Freud's childhood dream or, by the time Jakob had the book bound in 1891, many fascicles had been lost. I favor the second interpretation, based on Freud's frequent quotation from memory of versicles pertaining to the missing pages.

The third volume was completed in 1854. The work went through several editions subsequently, but only the 1841–54 and 1858–59 editions were published in the three-volume format. The complete three-volume edition contains a total of 3,820 pages. Jakob Freud's copy has 1,215 pages. The page indicating the edition is missing, but it seems likely that it was one of the early editions, probably the one published in 1841.

Later in life Freud bought a copy of the three-volume 1858 edition. The set had belonged to a Rabbi Adolf Altmann, who had underlined and annotated the Book of Esther in preparing a study of the Purim festival. Rabbi Altmann died in 1944, so it is unlikely that he was the first owner of this set. There is no evidence of when Freud bought the 1858 edition or for what purpose. He did not need it in preparation for *Moses and Monotheism* (1939) because his father's edition contained the complete text of the Five Books of Moses.

חמשה חומשי תורה,

Der Pentateuch.

Die

fünf Bücher Moscheh.

Enthaltend:

Den heiligen Urtext,

die deutsche Uebertragung,

die

allgemeine, ausführliche Erläuterung nebst Einleitung mit vielen
englischen Holzschnitten.

Herausgegeben

von

Dr. Ludwig Philippson.

7.1 Title page of
the Pentateuch,
Philippson
Bible

The Philippson Bible is a handsome, perfectly printed, and
beautifully illustrated work. The title page of the Pentateuch
(fig. 7.1) describes the contents: "The original holy text, the
German translation, and general comprehensive explanatory
notes together with an introduction and many English wood
engravings." A typical page (fig. 7.2) has the Hebrew text on the
right, the German translation on the left, with running heads
consisting of the book name and number in the respective languages. Extensive German commentaries on particular versicles
of the text appear as footnotes.

Gechasi, dem Knaben des Mannes Gottes, sprechend: Erzähle mir doch alle Großthaten, die
Elischa gethan. 5. Und es geschah, er erzählte
eben dem Könige, wie er den Todten lebendig
gemacht, siehe, da schrie das Weib, deren Sohn
er lebendig gemacht, zum Könige um ihr Haus
und um ihr Feld, und Gechasi sprach: Mein Herr
König, das ist das Weib, und das ihr Sohn,
den Elischa lebendig gemacht. 6. Und der König
befragte das Weib, und sie erzählte ihm, und
der König gab ihr einen Hämling mit, sprechend:
Schaffe ihr alles wieder, was ihr gehört, und
allen Ertrag des Feldes, von dem Tage an, da
sie das Land verließ, bis jetzt. 7. Und Elischa
kam gen Dammesek, und Benhadab, der König
von Aram, war krank. Und es wurde ihm
berichtet, also: Der Mann Gottes ist hierher
gekommen. 8. Da sprach der König zu Chasahel:
Nimm mit dir ein Geschenk und gehe dem Mann
Gottes entgegen und befrage den Ewigen durch
ihn, sprechend: werde ich genesen von dieser
Krankheit? 9. Und Chasael ging ihm entgegen
und nahm ein Geschenk mit sich und allerlei Gut
von Dammesek, eine Last von vierzig Kameelen, und
trat vor ihn, und sprach: Dein Sohn Benhadab,
der König von Aram, sendet mich zu dir, sprechend: werde ich genesen von dieser Krankheit?

אֵת כָּל־הַגְּדֹלוֹת אֲשֶׁר־עָשָׂה אֱלִישָׁע:
(ה) וַיְהִי הוּא מְסַפֵּר לַמֶּלֶךְ אֵת־אֲשֶׁר
הֶחֱיָה אֶת־הַמֵּת וְהִנֵּה הָאִשָּׁה אֲשֶׁר־
הֶחֱיָה אֶת־בְּנָהּ צֹעֶקֶת אֶל־הַמֶּלֶךְ עַל־
בֵּיתָהּ וְעַל־שָׂדָהּ וַיֹּאמֶר גֵּחֲזִי אֲדֹנִי
הַמֶּלֶךְ זֹאת הָאִשָּׁה וְזֶה־בְּנָהּ אֲשֶׁר־
הֶחֱיָה אֱלִישָׁע: (ו) וַיִּשְׁאַל הַמֶּלֶךְ לָאִשָּׁה
וַתְּסַפֶּר־לוֹ וַיִּתֶּן־לָהּ הַמֶּלֶךְ סָרִיס אֶחָד
לֵאמֹר הָשֵׁיב אֶת־כָּל־אֲשֶׁר־לָהּ וְאֵת כָּל־
תְּבוּאֹת הַשָּׂדֶה מִיּוֹם עָזְבָה אֶת־הָאָרֶץ
וְעַד־עָתָּה: (ז) וַיָּבֹא אֱלִישָׁע דַּמֶּשֶׂק
וּבֶן־הֲדַד מֶלֶךְ־אֲרָם חֹלֶה וַיֻּגַּד־לוֹ לֵאמֹר
בָּא אִישׁ הָאֱלֹהִים עַד־הֵנָּה: (ח) וַיֹּאמֶר
הַמֶּלֶךְ אֶל־חֲזָהאֵל קַח בְּיָדְךָ מִנְחָה וְלֵךְ
לִקְרַאת אִישׁ הָאֱלֹהִים וְדָרַשְׁתָּ אֶת־יְהוָה
מֵאוֹתוֹ לֵאמֹר הַאֶחְיֶה מֵחֳלִי זֶה: (ט)
וַיֵּלֶךְ חֲזָאֵל לִקְרָאתוֹ וַיִּקַּח מִנְחָה בְיָדוֹ
וְכָל־טוּב דַּמֶּשֶׂק מַשָּׂא אַרְבָּעִים גָּמָל
וַיָּבֹא וַיַּעֲמֹד לְפָנָיו וַיֹּאמֶר בִּנְךָ בֶן־הֲדַד
מֶלֶךְ־אֲרָם שְׁלָחַנִי אֵלֶיךָ לֵאמֹר הַאֶחְיֶה

v. 6. הה' בלא מפיק.

genannt wird, will man auf die frühere Zeit dieser Begebenheit schließen, denn Gechasi sei nach seinem Vergehen vom Propheten gewiß entfernt worden. Letzteres ist höchst wahrscheinlich, allein dennoch kann er hier noch, in Bezug auf seine frühere Stellung, dieses Epitheton beibehalten haben. Der König läßt sich auch nur frühere Thaten des Propheten erzählen, was die Krankheit Gechasi's nicht verhinderte, da nur der Kontakt Aussätziger verboten war. Vielleicht fand das Gespräch statt in einem der k. Gärten außerhalb der Stadt. — 6. סריסים Verschnittene, Eunuchen, die durch eine Zerstörung der Zeugungsorgane zum Beischlaf oder wenigstens fruchtbaren Konkubitus unfähig gemacht worden sind. Dergleichen wurden schon in den frühesten Zeiten an den orientalischen Höfen, besonders zur Bewachung des Harems, gehalten (vgl. Esth. 2, 3.). Indeß bezeichnet das Wort auch im Allgemeinen Hofbediente (s. Anm. zu 1 M. 37, 36.). — 7. 12) Elischa verkündet Chasael zum König von Aram. Vgl. 1 Kön. 19, 15. Dort wird die Salbung Chasael's schon Elijahu befohlen. Dieser hat es also seinem Nachfolger überlassen. Abarb. weist auf 1 K. 21, 29. hin, wo die Bestrafung des Hauses Achab aufgeschoben wird, daher auch Elijahu die Salbung Chasael's, der ein Werkzeug zur Bestrafung der Israeliten werden sollte, unterlassen mußte. — Eine förmliche Salbung Ch.'s nimmt aber Elischa nicht vor, sondern weist denselben auf seine Bestimmung hin. — 9. Das Geschenk muß sehr werthvoll gewesen sein, obgleich nicht jedes Kameel seine volle Ladung getragen haben mag, da es eine gewöhnliche Praxis im Orient ist, aus Prahlerei eine weit größere Menge Lastthiere und Menschen zum Transport eines Geschenkes anzustellen, als nothwendig wäre. Das Gewicht einer Kameellast ist nach Umständen verschieden. Burckhardt sagt, daß die Last eines arabischen

7.2 A typical page of the Philippson Bible, vol. 2

The third volume offers a forty-four-page essay on the Bible as a whole, presenting the biblical authors in the context of the history of the Jewish people and in a chronology based on the Gregorian calendar. The Books of Moses are preceded by a thirty-page introduction; all other books have brief preliminary notes.

The French scholar Théo Pfrimmer has carried out an exhaustive study of the Philippson Bible. His observations about the brothers' style of translation, presented in his book *Freud, lecteur de la Bible* (1982), reveals their efforts to remain faithful to the original Hebrew, including its rhythm and metric structure. The aim of the commentaries is to "let the Bible speak for itself" (p. 234; translations from this work are mine) in delivering its essential messages: that God is the eternal, immutable being, the creator of man in his own image, and that nature is also the work of God's creation.

Ludwig and Phoebus drew on all contemporary knowledge to illustrate the points made in the text, providing what Pfrimmer calls a "cultural commentary" that "informs, reasons, [and] suggests reflection in order to convince" (pp. 226–27). "There is a very acute sense of the history and the historicity of the Jewish people and of human beings in general. It [the commentary] is very concerned with biblical anthropology, comparative anthropology, history of religions and of mythologies, the sciences of nature and medicine" (p. 216).

Pfrimmer notes "a contrast . . . that is striking and almost constant: the commentaries on documentary, historical, geographical, and botanical [topics], and on human costumes are most abundant. On the other hand, certain specifically spiritual pages, such as, for example, Solomon's prayer (Kings 8, 19–29),[2] go totally without a commentary" (p. 220).

2. Pfrimmer is correct in citing the chapter but not the versicles. Solomon's prayer is in versicles 23–53.

The Philippson brothers demonstrated a profound respect for exegesis by reviewing the most significant available interpretations of scriptural passages by Jewish and Christian philosophers, theologians, and others (p. 219). They quoted both classical and modern works in several languages—Arabic, Syrian, Ethiopian, Egyptian, Greek, Latin, French, and English—as well as Hebrew and German.

As interpreters of the biblical text they showed the reader that "it is always necessary to consider a multitude of factors," to regard a problem from many angles (p. 260). Pfrimmer concluded that Freud learned from his early reading of the Bible that "one must bring to action all the available resources of the intelligence and of an encyclopedic knowledge to grasp the meaning of a text; it is necessary to attend to every detail because its meaning may be determined in multiple modes" (p. 214).

The reader of the Philippson Bible and its commentary could transcend the boundaries of the culturally closed ghetto. The whole world with all its marvels was available in the pages of the sacred text for the pious or the scholarly Jewish reader to enjoy. To the seven-year-old Sigmund, who lived in the Orthodox ghetto and did not yet attend public school, the astonishing illustrations of the Philippson Bible as well as the text must have suggested the existence of a wider and fascinating world. Figures 7.3–7.7 are examples of the illustrations Freud saw as a child, perhaps before he himself was able to read.

What effect did Freud's "deep engrossment in the Bible story" have on his imagination and on the development of his conception of the world? He could not have failed to register the imagery, particularly as he colored in some of the illustrations. What was the influence of biblical teachings, and in particular those conveyed by the illustrations of his father's bible, on the formation of his mind? Is there any evidence that they provided any psychic services for him?

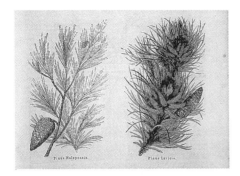

7.3 Botanical illustration, Philippson Bible, vol. 2, p. 1,240

His father, as is shown by the dedication he wrote, knew the biblical text by heart. And his mother could provide appalling domestic evidence that the Bible's assurance of "dust to dust" was literally true. Vienna was a Catholic city, and people often quoted the Scriptures. Freud had studied the Bible and Hebrew grammar in elementary private school, and the religious cur-

Gräberhöhlen in den Felsen von Wady Mousa im Gebirge Seir, nach Laborde.

7.4 Ruins. Philippson Bible, vol. 1, p. 108

Anſicht von den Ruinen des alten Epheſus.

7.5 Landscape with ruins. Philippson Bible, vol. 3, p. 684

riculum of the Gymnasium he attended for eight years was "built around the Bible" (Rainey, 1975, p. 45).

The title page of the Philippson Bible, as we have seen, promises "many English wood engravings." The actual count amounts to 685 illustrations—744 if the double figures are counted twice. Selected by the publisher, Baumgärtner, many of them from collections of the British Museum, they complement the text but often add their own messages as well. Each of them is an apt illustration of a biblical description and of Philippson's commentary about a particular object, animal, plant, city, inhabitant of a foreign land, and so on. The captions, often lengthy, frequently offer a historical, cultural, or scientific overview of what is known about the particular subject.

The illustrations in the Philippson Bible must have engaged Freud's curiosity and esthetic sense. As his complex, lively dreams and his rich metaphorical writing style attest, he was

Ruinen von Tyrus.

Seeküste zwischen Sidon und Tyrus.

7.6 Landscapes with ruins. Philippson Bible, vol. 2, p. 101

7.7 Ancient coins. Philippson Bible, vol. 2, p. 1,320

gifted both as a child and as an adult with a vivid visual imagination. In his foreword to Patrick Mahony's book *Freud as a Writer* (1982), George H. Pollock observed that "Freud's mode of thinking and intelligence were predominantly verbal. In his writings, as with the spoken word, he captured the attention and the imagination of his audience, visually rounding out his lectures, essays, and monographs with the excellent use of imagery, metaphor, analogy, parallels, and models for purposes of explanation and illustration, and drawing upon his prodigious memory and thorough classical education" (p. x).

What happened to that marvelous command of imagery and "prodigious memory" where the illustrations of the Philippson Bible were concerned? We have seen that except for his description of a childhood anxiety-dream at the time of the death of his maternal grandfather, which drew on a biblical illustration, Freud never mentioned the illustrations of the bible. Freud's own theories must provide an explanation for this astonishing fact.

A mighty conflict must have called for a powerful repression of memories connected to those days of his early life, of which he said "nothing was worth remembering" (1899, p. 312). The images he saw together with his father were not allowed into his conscious awareness. His own conclusions about Leonardo apply as well to him: "What someone thinks he remembers from his childhood is not a matter of indifference; as a rule the residual memories—which he himself does not understand—cloak priceless pieces of evidence about the most important features in his mental development" (1910, p. 84).

In "Remembering, repeating and working-through" (1912), Freud established the relation between the compulsion to repeat and the act of remembering the actual past. The relation obtains in real life as well as in treatment: "As long as the patient is in the treatment he cannot escape from his compulsion to repeat; and in the end we understand that this is his way of remembering" (p. 150). In "Beyond the Pleasure Principle" (1920) Freud confirmed that the patient cannot remember repressed unconscious material and is "obliged to repeat [it] . . . as a contemporary experience" (p. 18). The motive for the compulsion to repeat and the inability to recall an aspect of the past is the ego's effort "to avoid the unpleasure which would be produced by the liberation of the repressed" (p. 20).

The compulsion to repeat it in the absence of conscious memory not only protects against such unpleasure but may, in fact, bring a pleasure of its own. Freud's compulsion to collect antiquities and to decorate his office and study with archaeological pieces similar to the illustrations in the Philippson Bible must be considered a way of repeating an experience without remembering it. The "remembering" was not of residual memories, as in Leonardo's case, but was in the actual compulsive act of seeking out unconsciously recognized objects. (This psychodynamic process of refinding childhood objects without recognizing them is discussed in Chapter 12.)

Freud's purchases of archaeological objects did not follow

the explicit plan of a collector. A study of the objects he collected suggests that he followed an unconscious plan based on
replicating as actual archaeological objects those he had seen
pictured in the Philippson Bible. Both the Philippson Bible and
Freud the collector were biased in favor of Egypt. Of the 685
engravings in the Philippson Bible, 211 (31 percent) depict
Egypt and 93 (14 percent) Israel (Pfrimmer, 1982, pp. 220,
372–73). The Philippson Bible also contains illustrations originating in 29 other identified countries and a few unidentified
ones. Rome follows Egypt and Israel with 64 objects, Persia
with 48, Greece with 41, and Syria with 22. Some 42 additional
illustrations originate in the Middle East, but the specific country is not identified. Other countries, including faraway China,
are represented by one or a few objects. There is no doubt, however, that Egyptian objects predominate over all others.

The Philippson Bible's illustrations offered young Freud a
broad view of many other nations, other peoples and landscapes. It showed him the glory of nations, marvelous worlds
beyond the land of "milk and honey." The child exposed to this
pictorial universe became the man with boundless curiosity,
particularly about the relations between those complex and rival neighboring lands, Israel and Egypt. Egypt won in him. In
a letter to Fliess on August 27, 1899, for instance, he called The
Interpretation of Dreams "the Egyptian dream book" (my italics).[3] He
might have called it the book of Joseph the Israelite, son of
Jacob, who interpreted dreams in the court of Pharaoh.

Freud's collection of antiquities became largely Egyptian.[4]

3. "What would you think of ten days in Rome at Easter (the two of us, of
course) if all goes well, if I can afford it, and have not been locked up, lynched,
or boycotted on account of the Egyptian dream book?" (Freud, 1887–1904,
p. 368).
4. The Freud Museum has not catalogued the collection, but there is no doubt
that Egyptian objects are the most numerous.

Later in his life, Moses became for him an Egyptian prince and monotheism an Egyptian invention imported by Moses, not the result of the God of Israel's self-revelation and covenant with his people. Freud, with his habit of reversing facts or phrases, had made the heathen Egypt the God-giver to the tribes of Israel. What he could not reverse was his repressed childhood memories. And what he could not remember of the book that he and his father had shared in his boyhood he felt compelled to buy in the antiquary's shop.

The evidence to support these assertions is visual. It can be seen by comparing the pictures in the bible with the objects in Freud's collection of antiquities. The illustrations make the point by their sheer numbers, but for brevity's sake I have chosen from among the objects shown in the exhibition sponsored by the Freud Museum.

Freud had several ancient seals, for example. Figure 7.8 shows a Babylonian cylinder seal from the nineteenth or eighteenth century B.C. and a Mesopotamian, Sumerian seal (Early Dynastic III), c. 2500 B.C., from his collection; for comparison, it shows an illustration from the Philippson Bible (1 Kings 21) depicting two cylinders and their impressions. In both cases the impressions show human figures in long robes.

Freud bought a beautiful small bronze of Isis suckling the infant Horus, dated about 664–525 B.C. The Philippson Bible has an illustration of the Babylonian buried pictures (Zechariah 21) portraying a mother holding her child in the same manner that Isis holds hers. Both are shown in figure 7.9.

The collection has a donation stele from the Ptolemaic Period in Egypt, dated 301 B.C. The bible (2 Chronicles 34) has an engraving of "Sarbout-el Cadem; an ancient burying place in Idumea." A stele there shows Egyptian figures whose short-skirted attire and hairdress resemble those of the figures on the

Alte Siegel.

7.8 Cylinder seals
in Freud's collec-
tion and as pic-
tured in the
Philippson Bible,
vol. 2, p. 592

stele in the collection. The form of the steles is identical. Both
are shown in figure 7.10.

Freud bought a small heart scarab from Egypt, dated to the
New Kingdom, 1540–1190 B.C. In 2 Moses [Exodus] 8, the
bible has a small woodcut of a "Blatta Aegyptiaca. A colossal

beetle from Egypt." The two pieces, shown in figure 7.11, are very similar.

The collection of antiquities contains several mummified figures in the round, made of stone, wood, pottery, glass, bronze, or faience. These figures, known as shabtis, were used to substitute for the dead in funeral locales. Freud owned several of them. The Philippson Bible has an illustration (5 Moses [Deuteronomy] 4) of five shabtis in frontal and profile postures. They are shown in figure 7.12, along with some from Freud's collection.

The collection contains a terracotta Mycenaean stirrup jar, from c. 1300–1200 B.C. The Philippson Bible has an illustration (Ezekiel 24) of several pieces of "Old Egyptian cooking ware." One of the jars is very similar to the one in the Freud Museum, as can be seen in figure 7.13.

Freud's collection includes many vessels from different periods. Figure 7.14 shows an Athenian black-figure lekythos from c. 500–480 B.C. and another from c. 490–470 B.C., along

Babylonische eingegrabene Bilder.

7.9 Isis in Freud's collection and Babylonian buried pictures in Philippson Bible, vol. 2, p. 784

7.10 Steles in Freud's collection and as pictured in the Philippson Bible, vol. 3, p. 1,164

Sarbout-el-Cadem; ein altes Gräberfeld in Idumäa. Nach Coffat.

with three illustrations from the Philippson Bible. The first, from 4 Moses [Numbers] 31, depicts "the purification of the returned warriors and their captured property." The second, from 4 Moses 7, portrays "the offerings of the Turks." The third is a full-page illustration in 2 Samuel 8 of "containers for domestic use and for decoration, from Egyptian sculptures."

Freud's antiquities include an Etruscan engraved mirror, made of bronze, from the late fourth or early third century B.C. The Philippson Bible (Job 37:18) has an illustration of many

Blatta aegyptiaca. Ein koloſſaler Käfer
aus der ägypt. Sammlung des Britiſchen
Muſeum's.

7.11 Scarabs in
Freud's collection
and in the Philipp-
son Bible, vol. 1,
p. 340

ancient metal mirrors, among them one in the center of the figure almost identical to the one Freud bought. The mirrors illustrate the question, among many, that Elihu addresses to Job:
"Can you, like him, spread out the skies, hard as a molten mirror?" The mirrors are shown in figure 7.15.

Freud had a small Chinese camel, an early Tang–style twen-
tieth-century forgery. The Philippson Bible has two camel illustrations. The first, from 1 Moses 12:16, illustrates the animals that Abraham had in Egypt: "ox, he-ass and camel in
Syria." The second engraving belongs to 2 Kings 8 and depicts
"loaded camels." All three are shown in figure 7.16.

A comparison of the illustrations shown in this chapter,
most of which appear in the bound bible that Jakob gave his
son, should demonstrate the striking similarity between the

Hölzerne Götzenbilder von bemalten Sykomorholz.

7.12 Shabtis in Freud's collection and in the Philippson
Bible, vol. 1, p. 873

7.13 Jars in Freud's
collection and in the
Philippson Bible,
vol. 1, p. 340

Alt-ägyptisches Kochgeschirre.

Philippson Bible illustrations and the objects with which Freud
filled his office and study. Moreover, many of the fifty-odd
prints on the walls of his study resemble the sites depicted in
the Philippson engravings. Figure 1.3, for example, shows the
door to the study from the office. The overview of both rooms
and their compact collection of objects reveals the similarity of

7.14 Vessels in
Freud's collection
and in the Philippson
Bible, vol. 1, p. 826;
vol. 1, p. 716; and
vol. 2, p. 416

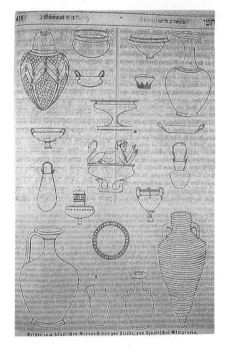

Reinigung des zurückgekehrten Kriegers und seiner Beute. — Nach Melville.

Gaben der Fürsten. — T. Landseer.

7.15 Mirrors in Freud's collection and
in the Philippson Bible, vol. 2,
p. 598

the whole office to the Philippson Bible illustration of the Temple of Denderah in Egypt (fig. 7.17), which accompanies the text of Ezekiel 8:7–9, in volume 2 of the Philippson Bible. There the Egyptian temple was used to illustrate "the great abomination" of the people who had driven the Lord far from his sanctuary and had come to worship "all the idols of the house of Is-

7.16 Camels in
Freud's collection
and in the
Philippson Bible,
vol. 1, p. 57;
vol. 2, p. 629

Der Ochs, das Kamel und der Esel in Syrien.

Beladene Kameele.

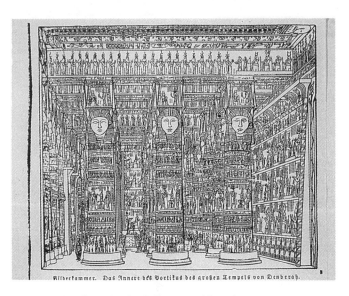

Silberkammer. Das Innere des Portikus des großen Tempels von Denderah.

7.17 Temple of Denderah. Philippson Bible, vol. 2, p. 1,164

rael" (8:3–11). Freud's arrangement of his office has a similar division of space and a comparable abundance of objects in every available space. It also shares a most significant detail with the Philippson illustration. At the top of each column in the temple there is a large Egyptian figure with hair around the face. In Freud's consulting room, at the left of the entrance to his study, higher than all other objects, there is a framed picture of the Egyptian Sphinx of Giza.[5] The door next to it places it in a location similar to that of the sphinx located next to the open space between columns in the Temple of Denderah.

5. The print bears the legend "'Sphinx,' Original Etching by H. Ulbrich, 1906." Erica Davies, director of the Freud Museum in London, provided this information.

Freud had seen in the form of the Egyptian gods the forbidden divinities no Jew could ever make or worship in the Philippson Bible illustration of Deuteronomy 4:15–31 (fig. 7.18). He had also read a selection of the Prophets during his Gymnasium religious studies. If he read Ezekiel, he must have known how insistent the prophet was in reminding Israel of the preeminence of the Lord God. Freud's study, however, became a private chamber where "the great abomination" of Denderah was consciously or unconsciously renewed. There was no room either in Freud's psychic life or in his analytic chambers for any remembrance of the God of Israel. The gods of the abomination of Israel were his working companions and audience.

The analytic question raised earlier has to do with remembering and repeating. Freud's collection of antiquities, the objects he selected, his compulsive need to acquire them, and the manner in which they were arranged suggest that what Freud could not remember of his terrible boyhood days, his father, and his father's Bible was unconsciously recalled in his choice of archaeological pieces. He could not "remember" the biblical illustrations that invited his awakening to the world as a child. Instead, Freud surrounded himself with the childhood imagery, the art functioning almost as living objects to accompany him on his lonely journey. If Ezekiel had come to visit Freud's office-temple, he would have said once again: "So I went and saw; and there, portrayed upon the wall round about, were all kinds of creeping things, and loathsome beasts, and all the idols of the house of Israel" (8:10).

Sigmund, whose entrance into God's covenant was registered in the Philippson Bible, had committed, to his iconoclastic pleasure, "the great abomination" against a God he had rejected long ago.

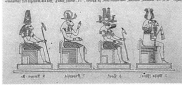

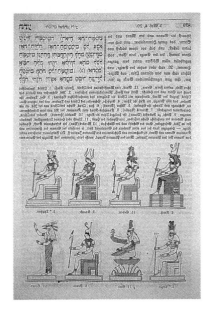

7.18 Egyptian gods.
Philippson Bible, vol. 1,
pp. 869, 870, 871

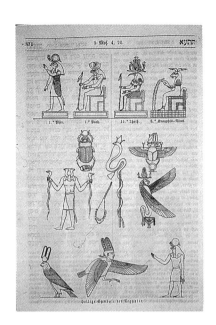

1.° Phre.   1.° Pooh.   11.° Thoth.   S.° Knouphis-Nilus.

Heilige Symbole der Aegypter.

Shlomo Sigismund Freud entered the Jewish Covenant with the Lord and people of Israel on May 13, 1856, according to his father's entries in the family bible and the Register of Copies of Entries of Persons of Different Faith in Freiberg.[1] There was a very small community for him to join in the Czech town, where Jews constituted only 2.9 percent of a population of less than five thousand. The nearest synagogue was in Neu Tischein, seven miles away (Sajner, 1968, p. 168). Virtually nothing is known of the religious practices of the family in those days except that Jakob had written in the Gedenkblatt of his bible "Freiberg, 1 of November [1]848," suggesting that he bought the bible there, after he left Tismenitz, where his Orthodox relatives lived. The Philippson Bible certainly was not acceptable to Orthodox Jews.

The parish church of Mariae Geburt to which Sigmund's nanny took him was located in the center of town and dominated the landscape. The church features a central altar and ten lateral altars and chapels, with paintings of Mary Magdalene and Saints Joseph, Urban, Vandelins, and Isidore. In a side chapel a painting of Saint Joseph by Johann Jakob Ulrich forms the central figure of the tablet *Schewedenbild* (Swedish painting), surrounded by

1. Josef Sajner photocopied several documents pertaining to the Freud family. His findings appear in his 1968 paper.

smaller figures commemorating the horrors of the Swedish war. Joseph appears as an affectionate father, standing relaxed on a small cloud, holding a blooming lily in his right hand and tenderly supporting the baby Jesus on his left arm. The infant hugs his father's neck and intently gazes up at him (E. Freud et al., 1985, p. 49 and notes). Sigmund must have noted that the Catholic house of God was a very different place from any he knew.

Freud lost his nanny around the time of his sister Anna's birth, on December 31, 1858; he was two years and seven months old. He retained no conscious recollection of his visits to the church, but he must have been very much impressed by the experience, judging by his mother's response in 1897 to his questions about his nurse in the course of his self-analysis: "'Of course,' she said, 'an elderly person, very clever, she was always carrying you off to some church; when you returned home you preached and told us all about God Almighty'" (1887–1904, p. 271). Freud believed that: "I must have understood Czech in my earliest childhood, for I was born in a small town in Moravia which has a Slav population. A Czech nursery rhyme, which I heard in my seventeenth year,[2] printed itself on my memory so easily that I can repeat it to this day, though I have no notion what it means" (1900, p. 196).[3] Czech was the language spoken by his nurse and the rest of the churchgoing population, and he must have "preached" to his family in the same language.

Amalie's description of her son's preaching reveals much about Freud's earliest religious experience. It suggests, first,

2. This was the time of his visit to the Fluss family in Freiberg, where he again heard Czech spoken in the town.
3. Amati-Mehler et al. (1993) have described in detail the emotional consequences of forgetting a language linked to early experiences with a beloved person. Some affects are inaccessible in a language different from the original.

that before the age of three, Sigmund had formed some representation of God; second, that the representation was connected to his nurse, the Catholic Church, and the Czech language; third, that he found something exciting about "der liebte Gott" because he "preached" to his parents "all about God"; fourth, that he must have identified with the priest preaching from the high pulpit to the attentive congregation;[4] and fifth, that his parents accepted his being taken to church, which shows that they were relaxed about the Jewish laws. No Orthodox Jewish family would have tolerated it.

Sigmund's grief at the loss of his nanny was deep and lasting. It left him vulnerable to separation and loss. Moreover, if God was linked in his mind to his nanny, her abrupt loss must have affected the way he conceived of God. The loss also deprived him of the excitement of going to church and attending the services. Freiberg had few other attractions. At church he was exposed to the music of the organ and the church choir as well as to the smell of burning incense and candles and the majesty of the large and highly decorated building. He was never to return to church services, but he was left with a compelling and "deeply neurotic" longing to go to Rome, as he confessed to Fliess in his letter of December 3, 1897. Grinstein (1980, pp. 76, 91) and Krüll (1986, p. 120) suggest—correctly, it seems to me—that this expresses the unconscious desire to return to Freiberg. Goldsmith (1992) believes that Freud's fascination with Michelangelo's sculpture *Moses* in Rome demonstrates, among other psychodynamics, "the resurgence of affects relating predominantly to preoedipal maternal loss and conflict, and defenses against those affects" (p. 268).

A few months after the loss of his nanny, the family left Freiberg for good. The train trip to Vienna left an indelible im-

4. Perhaps this is his earliest identification with such leaders as Joseph, Moses, Hannibal, and others.

pression on young Sigmund. His interpretive fantasizing during the trip linked what he was seeing with the stories of hell he must have been told and the pictures he must have seen on his visits to the Church of Mariae Geburt. In his letter to Fliess he notes: "Breslau also plays a role in my childhood memories. At the age of three years I passed through the station when we moved from Freiberg to Leipzig, and the gas flames which I saw for the first time reminded me of spirits burning in hell" (1887–1904, p. 285). The word "reminded" suggests that Freud had already seen or heard about those burning in hell. The experience connected the nurse to his religious experience and to sexuality in the context of traveling with his mother.

The "prime originator" of his sexuality, Freud told Fliess, "was an ugly, elderly, but clever woman [his mother's words], who told me a great deal about God Almighty and hell; . . . later (between two and two and a half years) my libido toward *matrem* was awakened, namely, on the occasion of a journey with her from Leipzig to Vienna, during which we must have spent the night together and there must have been an opportunity of seeing her *nudam*" (1887–1904, p. 269).

Young Freud's sexual excitement in relation to his mother reveals much about his longing for his "prime originator." He knew that his first sexual mother, the nanny, was at the foundation of his psychic life, as he said later in the same letter: "I have not yet grasped anything at all of the scenes themselves which lie at the bottom of the story. If they come to light and I succeed in resolving my own hysteria, then I shall be grateful to the memory of the old woman who provided me at such an early age with the means for living and going on living [Leben und Weiterleben]." The last sentence portrays a child who clings literally for dear life to his nurse, a woman who offers him sexual and religious excitement, and a God who deserves to be preached. He lost the woman, the sexual excitement, and the churchgoing all at once. After the loss, he saw in the flames of burning chimneys the sorrows of hellish spirits.

These were his first experiences with the "dear Lord." At the age of seven, in 1863, Freud mentions God in his first documented letter, addressed to Emmanuel in England: "I and my dear parents and sisters are thank God well" (E. Freud et al., 1985, p. 57). Whether this letter was dictated by his parents, who had taught him to write, or was of his own inspiration, the fact is that it mentions God as deserving of gratitude for the family's well-being. Even if he used the term as a standard expression, he still used it. Besides, at seven he was being introduced to the Philippson Bible and coloring some of its figures. It was during those days that he put to his mother the question about people dying and returning to dust. His "amazement" at his mother's powerful demonstration of having "dust" in her hands must have proved to him that, no matter how disagreeable the biblical idea was, he must believe it.

As soon as he learned to read he became deeply involved with the Philippson Bible. He could have learned the rudiments of Hebrew at the private Jewish Volkschule in which he was enrolled (Rainey, 1975, p. 39). Just before entering the Leopoldstädter Gymnasium at the age of nine and a half, Freud had the dream of his mother's dying, which he associated with the illustrations of the Philippson Bible. At the Gymnasium, religion was a required part of the curriculum, but only two hours a week were allotted to this subject, which made it difficult to study anything in depth. Rainey describes the educational policy of the time:

> During Freud's school years religious education was compulsory in the schools of Austria, both public and private. This requirement extended from the first year of the Volkschule through the last year of the Gymnasium. The

"ideas" of "religion" and "morality" were considered by the government authorities to be the "focal point" of the student's general education. Schools were expected to develop a student's "piety" (Frömmigkeit) as well as academic skills. A student received a grade for religion just as he did for his other subjects. (p. 36)

Jewish students followed their own special curriculum under the guidance of public instructors supervised by the Kultusgemeinde (religious community):

The study of the Hebrew Bible formed the core of the curriculum in both the Volkschule and the Gymnasium. This was regarded as the indispensable way toward a "personal encounter" with the "spirit of Judaism." Particular emphasis was placed upon the Pentateuch. Biblical study was supplemented by lessons in Jewish history and liturgical practices. There was also a small amount of doctrinal study from a Lehrbuch, or textbook, on doctrine. Parents were expected to supplement the instruction at home. (p. 37)

The Bible used in Hebrew religious classes was Jakob Aurbach's Small Bible for School and Home (1858), which contained selected biblical passages with a few clarifications (p. 45). Freud, of course, had the Philippson Bible, with its illustrations and notes, at home. The Lehrbuch was written by Leopold Breuer, the father of Josef Breuer, coauthor with Freud of Studies on Hysteria. Rainey describes Breuer's perspective:

"Religion is faith in God and the worship of God." Faith in God is innate to human nature and it is intimately connected with man's higher spiritual and moral nature. "No people on earth have been without some faith in God." . . . Primitive people are "superstitious." Their conceptions of God and forms of worship are "childish." . . . As man's reason develops he formulates a "religion of reason." His perception of the order and purpose of "nature" and his own inner consciousness of the "laws of morality" lead him to acknowledge the existence of a being who has created the universe and the "laws of morality." (pp. 47–48)

Breuer insisted that the knowledge of reason does not suffice to form a true and adequate knowledge of God; rather, this requires revelation, direct instruction from God. God's progressive revelation came in turn to Adam, Noah, Abraham, and Moses. "The essential core of this revelation is contained in the Torah, which was written by Moses" (p. 48).

The study of the Hebrew language was included in the curriculum of the Gymnasium to facilitate students' understanding of the Scriptures, prayer services, and the community of Jews. Rainey quotes Freud's teacher Samuel Hammerschlag about the great importance of Hebrew as "the only means through which he [the Jew] remains conscious of his connection with his brothers in faith and his own religious particularity" (p. 38). The limited time allotted for all religious studies made mastery of Hebrew and the Scriptures impossible to achieve. This, however, does not explain Freud's declaration of his ignorance of Hebrew in his 1925 letter to the editor of the Jewish Press Center in Zurich.

Rainey (1975) examined the curriculum of religious studies for private Jewish Volkschulen during the period 1862 to 1864. He presents the program for the first class: "Hebrew language and Religion: reading in Hebrew; important portions of selected prayers are translated. The pupils are drilled in the reading of daily, Sabbath, and festival prayers in order that they may be able to participate in the public services of worship. Bible in the original text. First Book of Moses, Chapters 1 and 2" (p. 40).

The curriculum for the Gymnasium for the first three years

included Hebrew grammar, together with the translation of prayers. The study of the Bible included the Pentateuch, some Psalms, Samuel, Kings, Judges, Proverbs, some of the Prophets, and passages from the Book of Job. In addition, the students learned Jewish history from the Babylonian exile to the end of the seventeenth century (Rainey, 1975, pp. 44–45). We know, therefore, that Freud had studied Hebrew grammar and Hebrew translation for at least three years. Surprisingly, it seems that he did not achieve elementary mastery of the language, although we know that during his school years he taught himself to write and speak Spanish, with the use of a dictionary. However rudimentary his Hebrew lessons may have been, it appears that he could have learned the language if he had wanted to. Also, Freud became a close friend of Hammerschlag. Rainey (1975) describes the religion teacher's educational stance:

> He was fond of drawing links between Jewish tradition and modern European culture. . . . He regarded the concepts of "a free, autonomous personality" and "innate human rights," two of the fundamental affirmations of the Enlightenment, as firmly rooted in the Jewish prophetic tradition. For him, Judaism was not a religion of authoritarian doctrine but [one] of free and open inquiry. His pedagogical technique was consciously modeled on that of Pestalozzi. He endeavored to confront his students with the "concrete material" of the Bible and to guide them in "abstracting" for themselves its essential concepts. (p. 43)

Freud's relationship with Hammerschlag was not subject to his notorious need to alienate his best friends. Aware of Freud's poverty, Hammerschlag gave him gifts of money, his own or sums others had given him to distribute to people in need. In a January 10, 1884, letter to Martha, Freud poignantly contrasts his encounter with his improvident and dreamy father in the street and Hammerschlag's giving him fifty florins. Freud was always welcome in Hammerschlag's home. He relished the family's warmth and generosity and visited them when he felt emotionally depleted, as described in a letter to Martha of November 15, 1883: "Today it is a holiday and I have done no work whatsoever, in order to refresh myself. The weather is quite horrible; this evening I think I will go and see Hammerschlag. I am so weary that it will do me good if someone is friendly to me" (1960).

When Hammerschlag died, in November 1904, Freud (1903–4) wrote an obituary published in the *Neue Freie Presse*: "Those of his pupils who were later allowed to seek him out in his own home gained a paternally solicitous friend in him and were able to perceive that sympathetic kindness was the fundamental characteristic of his nature" (pp. 255–56). Such closeness to a beloved teacher suggests that Freud's "extremely behindhand" knowledge of Hebrew was not the result of the failure of "free-thinking religious instructors" to teach him properly. Had he wanted to master Hebrew, he had in Hammerschlag the best resource available. The conclusion follows that Freud was not interested in mastering the language or in benefiting from the teaching he did receive—or that he was disingenuous in reporting that he did not know Hebrew. This possibility looms even larger when we note that "in the last year of the Gymnasium he received the highest possible marks in religion" as well as in the final graduation examination (Gicklhorn, 1965, p. 24, quoted by Rainey, 1975).

Freud's first series of published letters, addressed to his fellow student Eduard Silberstein and to his Freiberg friend Emil Fluss, come from his Gymnasium years. The letters to Fluss describe his first visit to Freiberg, at the age of sixteen, and contain three references to God. The first, dated September 18, 1872, says: "I am writing to you, as promised, to tell you about my journey from my old home town. But God knows what whirlwind blew me so fast from Freiberg to Vienna!" (1969, p. 419). Historians have discovered that the "whirlwind" was Gisela Fluss, his friend's younger sister, with whom Freud had fallen in love. The next reference (February 7, 1873) provides the first documented indication of his religious doubts. Freud is talking about Emil's new girlfriend: "You find Ottilie. Truly, any more such strokes of Providence could convince even me of the inscrutable workings of a divine power."

The next reference (May 1, 1873) is about praying: "The next time you feel a 'burning' desire for something, pray to God 'Grant me this or that,' and add 'but not too soon'" (p. 424). In his letter of September 18, 1872, he made no specific reference to God but described to Fluss his contempt for a particular type of religious Jew whom he met on his return trip from Freiberg to Vienna:

This Jew talked in the same way as I have heard thousands of others talk before, even in Freiberg. His very face seemed familiar—he was typical. So was the boy with whom he discussed religion. He was cut from the cloth from which fate makes swindlers when the time is ripe: cunning, mendacious, kept by his adoring relatives in the belief that he is a great talent, but unprincipled and without character. . . . I have had enough of this lot. In the course of the conversation I learned that Madame Jewess and family hailed from Meseritsch: the proper compost heap for this sort of weed. (p. 420)

Freud's contempt is intense. Obviously, he wants to put distance between himself and the pious, mendacious swindlers who adore a boy only to transform him into a cunning Jew like themselves. Was he also thinking about his jailed uncle Joseph and his pious yet suspect half-brothers in England? Clearly, he wanted nothing to do with their hypocrisy and immorality. God, in the three instances in which Freud mentions him, seems to be suspected equally of false providential claims and nonresponse to prayers. The undisguised sarcasm about God and religion unveil the adolescent Freud's contempt for the mendacity of those Jews and of God.

The correspondence with Eduard Silberstein began in 1871, when both boys were fifteen, and continued until 1881. The letters reveal a typical adolescent friendship between two gifted, aspiring, and spirited young men. Issues of identity (Freud changed his signature from Sigismund to Sigmund), of relations with the female sex (cryptically called "principles"), of literary and career ambitions, of the idiosyncrasies of parents, and of religion and belief characterized Freud's rich and ironic reflections. The correspondence is cast in the mode of secrecy. Freud makes his request: "I trust you do not show my letters to anyone, if they should ask to see them, because I want to be able to write with complete candor and about whatever comes into my head" (1871–81, p. 24).

To enforce their pact of secret sharing they wrote in self-taught Spanish and in the personae of two characters from Cervantes's "Colloquy of the Dogs" (in *Novelas Ejemplares,* 1613). Cipión (Freud) and Berganza (Silberstein) are twin dogs that meet one night in Valladolid. These animals were conceived as human children and transformed into dogs by a malicious witch. The only human trait they are allowed to retain is the capacity to speak. On the night of their first encounter, the only scene actually presented in Cervantes, Berganza tells the story of his life to Cipión, who agrees to reciprocate the following night. Berganza describes all the flaws he has observed in people—greed, malice, cruelty, and disloyalty. Cipión, the wise listener, observes, comments, is ironic, makes fun of things, reflects deeply, pontificates, and murmurs. Of the Freud-

Silberstein correspondence only the words of Cipión (Freud) remain; the letters of Berganza (Silberstein) are lost.

Freud's rich and varied comments include fifty-four references to God and nine biblical references. They cover the correspondence only from July 1873 to April 1875, the years of Freud's late adolescence (seventeen to nineteen), when he had to decide whether God existed or not.

The first reference, dated July 11, 1873, is a playful paraphrase of Genesis 24:2–3, where Abraham directs his servant to find a wife for Isaac, his son. It presents an "allegory" to Berganza, suggesting that he must marry, as did Eliezer, a maiden from "the land of my fathers," as "the Lord hath bidden." Cipión-Freud agreed with the Lord.

In the letter of July 24, 1873, Freud lamented the loss by the post office of a book on stenography and a letter that Freud had sent to Silberstein:

If the letter is lost it cannot be replaced. And just this letter, oh, jealous fate! You see, this letter contained a short essay, a biblical study with modern themes, something I cannot write again and of which I am as proud as of my nose or my maturity. It would have refreshed you like balm; one could not tell it was concocted in my den. It was so sensitive, so biblically naive and forceful, so melancholy and so gay—it's the very devil that it's been lost, it grieves me.

The missing letter had not been found by August 2, and Freud—who signed the letter not Cipión but Sigmund—was desolate: "It is in vain that you try to console me upon the loss of my biblical study; I have not suffered a similar loss for years. The disaster is in no way mitigated by the fact that you do not know what you have missed, for it was intended for your perusal." The "biblically naive" and "sensitive" study, as Freud himself described it, is the only scriptural writing by Freud until he wrote *Moses and Monotheism* at the end of his life. It is curious that Freud, with his remarkable memory, could not write it again. Emotional factors must have been at work.

In the next letter, dated August 6, Sigmund continued to bemoan the loss:

> I am beginning to share Herodotus's view of the malevolence of fate.[5] Why couldn't ten of my other scribblings have been lost, and the one incomparable [letter] be saved! How much elevating thought would you not have found in it, especially in respect of this instruction to you. Don't speak to me of substitutes. If the sun should explode one day and we should dwell in darkness, what substitute could you find for it? If the sea dried up and the heavenly sources, what substitute for water would you prescribe? So don't speak to me of substitutes; it is irretrievably lost and will never return (1871–81, p. 32).

Although this letter contained no direct biblical quotations, it made allusions to the Book of Job: "I dare not go on lest I write a chapter of Job, mutatis mutandis." It also made reference to "Jeremiads," "my salvation," and "the Resurrection."

Freud graduated from the Gymnasium in the spring of 1873. The curriculum indicates that in the eighth class he read "selected passages from the Book of Job" (Rainey, 1975, p. 43). The style and dramatic power of God's interrogation of Job shape the content and form of Sigmund's interrogation of his friend. The other references to Job in his letters suggest that the Book of Job, with its majestic references to the might of nature, made a powerful impression on him. Compare Freud's questioning of Silberstein with God's in Job 39:33–35:

> Do you know the ordinances of heavens?
> Can you establish their rule on the earth?

5. This is Freud's first reference to the dangers of fate.

Can you lift up your voice to the clouds, that a flood of
    waters may cover you?
Can you send forth lightnings, that they may go and say to
    you, "Here we are"?

This verse is the one Sigmund referred to in his "Egyptian darkness" experience, in the August 16 letter: "Yesterday, when I
had to suffer an Egyptian darkness for an hour because I could
not lay hands on flint or matches and because, as the Book of
Job puts it, I cannot send lightnings to make light for me." Sigmund identified with Job's powerlessness.

The fourth biblical reference appears at the end of the August 22, 1874, letter: "wishing you as much prosperity as can
be attained in the familiar 120 years." (Here Freud draws on
Genesis 6:3: "his days shall be a hundred and twenty years.")
The fifth reference, in the November 8, 1874, letter, is to Genesis 21:19. Freud was commenting on the "arid stuff" that Silberstein studied at the university: "If there be any refreshing
well in that desert, or an angel to proffer languishing Ishmael
a cool source, then do let me know and I shall cease marveling
at your classes." A few lines further down Freud referred to
himself for the first time as "the godless medical man and empiricist," while reporting that he was attending Professor
Brentano's classes about the existence of God.

The sixth mention of the Bible is in a much lighter tone, referring to Freud's efforts to persuade his sisters Anna and Rosa
to write to Silberstein: "I have in accordance with the biblical
saying 'For thou shalt heap coals of fire upon his head,' Ps. 33.
12, done my outmost to persuade the young ladies to write"
(December 6, 1874).[6] On December 11, 1874, Sigmund re-

6. Freud's reference is wrong. Psalm 33:12 reads: "Blessed is the nation whose
God is the Lord, the people he has chosen for his heritage." It is Proverbs 25:22
that says: "You will heap coals of fire on his [your enemy's] head."

sponded to the "gloomy" mood that had afflicted Silberstein: "I, for one, would feel unable to join you and sing the second part in Jeremiah's lamentations." Freud had probably read chapters 7, 22, 25, and 29 of Jeremiah in his second year at the Gymnasium (Rainey, 1975, p. 44).

The next reference, once again from the Book of Job, appears in the January 30, 1875, letter. Freud placed himself in the role of God as he reported to Silberstein his future plans for secret walks with his friend, "perhaps with principles" (girls), as well as the demise of the journal he and three friends had started:

> When I was a child, I firmly believed in the envy of the "so-called gods" and would take great care not to speak of the fulfillment of a precious wish lest it invoke the very opposite. But today the world looks brighter and I need not be afraid to consider possible something that, to my greatest joy, promises to come true. With so happy a prospect I may allow to mix an obituary; the journal founded by the three, and later four, of us, namely myself, Paneth, Loewy Emmanuel, Lipinier, has passed peacefully into the keeping of the Lord.
>
> It was I who delivered the death blow; it had been ailing for a long time and I took pity on its suffering. I gave it life and I have taken its life away, so blessed be my name, for ever and ever, Amen.

Job 1:21 describes Job's worship: "the Lord gave, and the Lord has taken away; blessed be the name of the Lord." Freud's playful and ironic irreverence, after declaring that he has lost the fear of the gods, reveals that he had turned a corner; he declares the Old Testament God nonexistent and appoints himself the minor god of the life and death of the journal. He does admit, however, that he once "firmly believed in the envy of the gods."

The last biblical reference in his letters to Silberstein is superficial and literary. Freud wrote on April 28, 1875, about a future walk with Silberstein in Vienna, "the land of milk and honey." The allusion is to Exodus 3:8, where the Lord promised Moses to lead the Israelites to "a land flowing with milk and honey."

The biblical citations document the evolution Sigmund was undergoing between the ages of seventeen and nineteen, from the first solemn injunction to his friend to select a Jewish wife in accordance with the commands of the Lord, through his desolate and dramatic lament at the loss of his biblical essay, to his self-appointed role as life- and death-giving god. He resorts to biblical quotes at first to convey strong feelings. Yet ultimately, he espouses a carefree irreverence in his parody of Job's worship of God, transformed into self-worship. A process of liberation had occurred. The biblical text retained its fullness of emotion for ironic effect, for self-referential and paradoxical recognition of past beliefs and deep concerns, but it commanded no longer. These citations document how deeply engrossed in biblical thinking Freud was in his late adolescence. They also reveal the moment when the adolescent Freud makes himself a minor god to replace God. They show firsthand the emotional and stylistic impact the biblical text had on Freud's everyday life and mode of thinking and writing. The biblical quotations convey intense personal feelings briefly and pointedly with minimal self-exposure.

Freud also announced the completion of his secondary education with references to God and kind Providence. He wrote to Silberstein: "I take the liberty of informing you herewith that, with God's help, I passed my examination yesterday, July 9, 1873, and that I was awarded a matriculation certificate with distinction." He had written to Fluss on June 16, 1873, reporting his success on the written part of the examination: "On occasions as important as these, kind Providence and the caprices of fortune always have a finger in the pie" (1969, p. 425). In these quotations Freud exhibits his marvelous stylistic trait of walking a fine line between investing a topic with serious meaning and undercutting that seriousness with subtle irony.

Freud and Silberstein enrolled in the University of Vienna as students of medicine and jurisprudence, respectively. In 1874 they attended Franz Brentano's philosophy classes for the first time. Freud took five full courses with Brentano, a former priest who had remained a believer. Brentano taught Aristotle, empirical psychology, and the proofs of the existence of God. Freud wrote to Silberstein on November 8, 1874: "I, the godless medical man and empiricist, am attending two courses in philosophy. . . . One of the courses—listen and marvel!—deals with the existence of God, and Prof. Brentano, who gives the lectures, is a splendid man, a scholar and philosopher, even though he deems it necessary to support the airy existence of God with his own expositions" (1871–81, pp. 70–71).

Freud and his friend Paneth wrote to Professor Brentano objecting to some of his ideas, and Brentano invited them to his home for further discussions. Freud was deeply impressed by the man and his knowledge. In a letter to Silberstein on March 7, 1875, he called Brentano a "remarkable man (a believer, a theologist(!) and a Darwinian and a damned clever fellow, a genius in fact), who is, in many respects, an ideal human being" (p. 95). Brentano's lectures and arguments about "the airy existence of God" posed the greatest challenge for Freud. He wrote to Silberstein on March 15:

> I have not escaped from his influence—I am not capable of refuting a simple theistic argument that constitutes the crown of his deliberations. . . . He demonstrates the existence of God with as little bias and as much precision as another may argue the advantage of the wave over the emission theory.

Needless to say, I am only a theist by necessity, and am honest enough to confess my helplessness in the face of his argument; however, I have no intention of surrendering so quickly or completely. Over the next few semesters, I intend to make a thorough study of his philosophy, and meanwhile reserve judgment and the choice between theism and materialism. For the time being, I have ceased to be a materialist and am not yet a theist. (pp. 104–5)

On March 27, Freud confided to Silberstein his continuous wrestling with Brentano's teaching: "Unfortunately, when we allow the God concept we start down a slippery path.[7] . . . Brentano cannot possibly be refuted before one has heard and studied him and plundered his stock of knowledge. So sharp a dialectician requires one to hone one's own wits on his before challenging him" (pp. 106–7). Freud laments his inability to refute Brentano's arguments: "The bad part of it, especially for me, lies in the fact that science of all things seems to demand the existence of God. . . . We are completely powerless in the face of attacks from that quarter" (April 11, 1875). Extant records do not indicate whether Freud ever managed to refute Brentano's arguments. In any case, his adolescent crisis highlights the internal tension between his emotional need not to believe in God and his teacher's compelling arguments demonstrating God's existence.

The remaining references to God in the Silberstein correspondence are a mixture of irony and playfulness. This point is best illustrated by Freud's explanation of why God took six days to create the world: "He wanted to show mankind that in any task it is essential to observe a rational order and a logical sequence of steps; had God created everything in a second, this

7. The expression is curious. Where could the slippery slope of the God concept lead Freud? Would he end up like the despicable mendacious boy in the train? How did he conceive of the danger of belief?

important lesson would have been lost on humanity in its strivings toward godliness" (August 13, 1874).

The published correspondence with Martha Bernays contains several colloquial references to God, such as "thank God" and "the dear Lord," but nothing of substance. Freud adamantly refused to have a religious ceremony at his wedding. He had recently attended the traditional marriage ceremony of his friend Paneth and wrote Martha "a letter of sixteen pages describing all the odious detail in a spirit of malign mockery" (Jones, 1953, p. 140). He could not altogether avoid the same fate, however, because Austrian law required a religious marriage ceremony. He had to memorize the Hebrew prayers and follow the ritual. Nevertheless, he did exercise some control over the celebration because "only eight relatives were present besides the immediate family" (p. 150). Moreover, from that moment on, he obliged Martha, who had been reared as an Orthodox Jew, to renounce all religious practices, including the lighting of the Sabbath candles. Gay (1987) reports an episode on a Friday afternoon in London in 1938 when Martha said to a visitor, "You must know that on Friday evenings Jewish women light candles for the approach of the Sabbath. But this monster—*Unmensch*—will not allow this, because he says that religion is a superstition" (p. 153). After his death she reestablished the ritual.

The rest of Freud's published letters reveal the same pattern: colloquial references to God in a mixture of playfulness and irony, but never irreverence or anger. His great anger was reserved for religious rituals. Jones (1957) presents a conversation with the mature Freud that vividly illustrates his manner of referring to God:

> I ventured to reprove him for his inclination to accept occult beliefs on flimsy evidence. . . . I then asked him where such

beliefs could halt: if one could believe in mental processes floating in the air, one could go on to a belief in angels. He closed the discussion at this point (about three in the morning) with the remark: "Quite so, even *der liebe Gott.*" This was said in a jocular tone as if agreeing with my *reductio ad absurdum* and with a quizzical look as if he were pleased at shocking me. But there was something searching also in his glance, and I went away not entirely happy lest there be some more serious undertone as well. (p. 381)

Freud remained an atheist to the last moment of his life. He was, however, an atheist who needed to explain religion, to unravel its emotional power over humankind, and to wrestle with the great leader of his people, Moses the man of God. This he did, creating, to his satisfaction, a comprehensive psychodynamic explanation for human belief in God (see Chapter 9).

Wrestling with religion seemed to be a continuation of Freud's difficulties in refuting Brentano's "scientific" proof of the existence of God. The depth of Freud's metaphysical investment is revealed in his April 2, 1896, letter to Fliess: "I hope you will lend me your ear for a few *metapsychological* questions as well. . . . As a young man I knew no longing other than for philosophical knowledge, and now I am about to fulfill it as I move from medicine to psychology" (1887–1904, p. 180). Thirty-one years later, Freud responded to Werner Achelis's discussion, in his book *The Problems of Dreams, a Philosophical Essay,* of Freud's theory of dreams: "You seem to be familiar with my attitude to philosophy (metaphysics). Other defects in my nature have certainly distressed me and made me feel humble; with metaphysics it is different—I not only have no talent for it but no respect for it either. In secret—one cannot say such things aloud—I believe that one day metaphysics will be condemned as a nuisance, as an abuse of thinking, as a survival from the period of the religious *Weltanschauung*" (1960, pp. 374–75). The youthful longing had been transformed into contempt. The rejected metaphysics had been replaced by his own creation, metapsychology. Metaphysics could prove God's existence, and Freud lacked the talent to refute Brentano's arguments. Metapsychology could prove that Brentano's God was humankind's creation of an imaginary protector.

Even when Freud exempted himself from the psychic need to have a religion or a God, he could not stop himself from thinking about religion. Some of the antiquities in his collection were imbued with "religious feelings" ranging from destruction to gratitude; with them he demonstrated the touch of playful irony he had reserved for "the dear Lord." For example, Freud relates in *The Psychopathology of Everyday Life* (1901) how he carried out a sacrificial act:

> One morning . . . I yielded to a sudden impulse and hurled one of my slippers from my foot at the wall, causing a beautiful little marble Venus to fall down from its bracket. As it broke into pieces, I quoted quite unmoved these lines from Busch:
>
> "Ach! die Venus ist perdü—
> Klickeradoms—von Medici!"
> ["Oh! the Venus! Lost is she!
> Klickeradoms! of Medici!"]
>
> This wild conduct and my calm acceptance of the damage are to be explained in terms of the situation at the time. One of my family [his daughter Mathilde] was gravely ill, and secretly I had already given up hope of her recovery. That morning I had learned that there had been a great improvement, and I know I had said to myself: "So she is going to live after all!" My attack of destructive fury served therefore

to express a feeling of gratitude to fate and allowed me to perform a "sacrificial act"—rather as if I had made a vow to sacrifice something or other as a thank-offering if she recovered her health! The choice of the Venus of Medici for this sacrifice was clearly only a gallant act of homage towards the convalescent; but even now it is a mystery to me how I made up my mind so quickly, aimed so accurately and avoided hitting anything else among the objects so close to it. (p. 169)

Freud's last known reference to religious concerns occurred on August 22, 1938, a month before his death, when, under the heading "Findings, Ideas, Problems," he wrote what seems to be his final comment on religion and mysticism: "Mysticism is the obscure self-perception of the realm outside the ego, of the id" (1941 [1938], p. 300).

chapter nine

Freud's Theories About Religion

On Easter Sunday 1886 Freud opened his private office for the practice of what would become psychoanalysis. The choice of date was no accident; it expressed Freud's love of defiance, aimed at mortal Viennese and their immortal God. His mother nonetheless "called down the blessing of the Almighty God on his endeavors" (Amalie Freud's letter of July 5, 1886, cited in Jones, 1953, p. 19). But the Almighty had to wait twenty-one

years, until 1907, before the "godless medical man" directly addressed the subject of religion.

A hint of what was to come appeared in *Jokes and Their Relation to the Unconscious* (1905a). Freud was referring to tendentious jokes, particularly those that are "not only Jewish anecdotes, [but] attack religious dogmas and even the belief in God" (p. 114). Freud recounted a story told about the German poet Heinrich Heine:

Heine is said to have made a definitely blasphemous joke on his death-bed. When a friendly priest reminded him of God's mercy and gave him hope that God would forgive his sins, he is said to have replied: "Bien sûr qu'il me pardonnera: c'est son métier." ["Of course he'll forgive me: that is his job."] . . . The force of the joke lies in its purpose. What it means to say is nothing else than: "Of course he'll forgive me. That's what he's there for, and that's the only reason I've taken him on (as one engages one's doctor or one's lawyer)." So in the dying man, as he lay there powerless, a consciousness stirred that he had created God and equipped him with power so as to make use of him when the occasion arose. What was supposed to be the created being revealed itself just before its annihilation as the creator. (pp. 114–15).

Heine's purported dying joke became Freud's theoretical program. He cited another anecdote in a paragraph he added in 1910 to The Psychopathology of Everyday Life (1901). At a social gathering someone had said "Tout comprendre c'est tout pardoner"; Freud retorted that pardons should be left to God and priests, and he added that he had thought of something even better. But he could not remember it after he said it. He withdrew from the company to try to retrieve it, in vain. What came to his mind instead was: "God created man in His own image" and the same idea in the reverse: "Man created God in his" (p. 19). A few lines later Freud commented wryly: "It is interesting that a screen-association was provided by a sentence in which the Deity is debased to the status of a human invention" (p. 20).

Debasing the deity became Freud's goal and proud achievement. In his paper "On Narcissism" (1914c), he took pleasure in linking his contribution to those of Copernicus and Darwin in that all three denied man his narcissistic wish to be at the center of the universe. The Bible, on the other hand, says that God assigns man dominion over "every living thing that moves upon the earth" (Genesis 1:28). Freud asserts that man cannot tolerate being displaced from his narcissistically assigned position; he resists seeing himself as a descendant of other animals. What Freud did not explicitly say in that essay was that he was not only dethroning man from his privileged position but was also demoting God from creator to the dispensable creation of man's unconscious.

At the end of his life, pressed by the terrible political conditions in Europe, Freud constructed another reversal of traditional views. He wrote to Arnold Zweig on September 30, 1934: "Faced with the new persecutions, one asks oneself again how the Jews have come to be what they are and why they have attracted this undying hatred. I soon discovered the formula: Moses created the Jews" (1970, p. 91). Freud's entire theory of religion stands bracketed between these two reversals of creation.

His first contribution to the understanding of religion appeared in his essay "Obsessive Actions and Religious Practices" (1907), which considers the similarities between obsession and religion. Freud concludes: "One might venture to regard obsessional neurosis as a pathological counterpart of the formation of a religion, and to describe the neurosis as an individual religiosity and religion as a universal obsessional neurosis" (p. 126).

What are the similarities that emboldened Freud to reach this sweeping conclusion? First, both phenomena are "ceremonial." For the obsessive, "any deviation from the ceremonial actions is visited by intolerable anxiety" (p. 118). For the religious person the sacred acts of ritual require fulfillment, are performed separatedly from other actions and must be carried to completion. In both cases, the actions are "significant in every detail" (p. 120), even though the obsessive person is not aware of this. In obsessive ritual, the meaning is private and is expressed through direct or symbolic representation, most frequently of sexual experiences. Although religious ritual is public and communal, its significance is also based on symbolic meaning (p. 119). Most believers perform the ritual without concern for its significance and, furthermore, are driven by unconscious motives.

Second, both kinds of rituals, according to Freud, are spurred by guilt. In the obsessive, this guilt is unconscious and "has its source in certain early mental events" (p. 123) revived in the present by contemporary provocations. Anxiety about feared punishment is connected with "the internal perception of the temptation" (an instinctual impulse). The ceremonial acts function to defend against it. Religious people protest that they are "miserable sinners" and use prayers, rituals, and invocations as protective measures against their own temptations (pp. 123–24). Religion, too, is based "on the suppression, the renunciation of certain instinctual impulses"—in particular, sexual strivings and social aggression.

This essay reveals much about Freud. First, it shows his unmatched ability to make analogies in sweeping strokes. Second, it reveals his ignorance of core aspects of religious experience. He focuses on ritual (which he abhorred), fear of punishment as a painful emotion, and the need for "protestations" and renunciation of instinct. He says nothing about religion's efforts to understand the universe, to relate to a transcendent reality, to acknowledge human limitations and fragility while wondering about mysteries exceeding the powers of the intellect. Freud shows a need to simplify religion, to reduce it to a symptom.

The essay also reveals that Freud wrote about religious persons while himself remaining an outsider to concrete religious experience, removed from the sources of religion. Freud described his situation in a letter to Romain Rolland in 1929 about Rolland's understanding of the "oceanic feeling" as the foundation of all religious experiences: "How remote from me are the worlds in which you move! To me mysticism is just as closed a book as music. I cannot imagine reading all the literature which, according to your letter, you have studied"[1] (1960, p. 389).

The following year, in December 1930, Freud described himself in the preface to the Hebrew translation of *Totem and Taboo*

1. Romain Rolland, who had received the 1915 Nobel Prize in literature, was immersed in the study of Oriental mysticism.

(1913b) as "completely estranged from the religion of his fathers—as well as from every other religion" (1913b, p. xv). The "godless Jew" who was compelled to understand the religion of others was, by his own confession, facing a personally "closed book." Perhaps his need to understand it, to explain it away, was his honest human effort to deal with the closed mystery. Freud hoped that *Totem and Taboo*, as he wrote in the preface to the Hebrew edition, would allow him to "be at one with his readers in the conviction that unprejudiced science cannot remain a stranger to the spirit of the new Jewry." Freud had, after all, internalized one of his father's ideals, as expressed in the Philippson Bible.

Freud's first known theorizing about religious belief appeared in 1910, in his essay "Leonardo da Vinci and a Memory of his Childhood." The wording suggests that Freud had formed the theory much earlier:

> Psychoanalysis has made us familiar with the intimate connection between the father-complex and belief in God; it has shown us that a personal God is, psychologically, nothing other than an exalted father, and it brings us evidence every day of how young people lose their religious beliefs as soon as their fathers' authority breaks down. Thus we recognize that the roots for the need for religion are in the parental complex; the almighty and just God, and kindly Nature,[2] appear to us as grand sublimations of father and mother, or rather as revivals and restorations of the young child's ideas of them. Biologically speaking, religiousness is to be traced to the small child's long-drawn-out helplessness and need for help; and when at a later date he perceives how truly for-

2. "Kindly Nature" is an infrequent expression in Freud. Most of his descriptions refer to the "terrifying" power of nature and the need to seek protection from her.

lorn and weak he is when confronted with the great forces of life, he feels his condition as he did in childhood, and attempts to deny his own despondency by a regressive revival of the forces which protected his infancy. The protection against neurotic illness, which religion vouchsafes to those who believe in it, is easily explained: it removes their parental complex, on which the sense of guilt in individuals as well as in the whole human race depends, and disposes of it, while the unbeliever has to grapple with it on his own.[3] (1910, p. 123)

To Freud, then, religious belief allows believers to handle despondency by denying their unsatisfied needs and exalting the father's internal representation to the rank of God. A few pages later Freud seems to retreat from his own view by referring to the early suffering of children: "We naturally feel hurt that a just God and a kindly providence do not protect us better from such influences [fate] during the most defenseless period of our lives" (p. 137). Immediately after these remarks, Freud adds a painful comment about the absence of parental protection. A child is the product of a blind and fateful biological event: "We are too ready to forget that in fact everything to do with our life is chance, from our origin out of the meeting of spermatozoon and ovum onwards—chance which nevertheless has a share in the law and necessity of nature, and which merely lacks any connection with our wishes and illusions" (p. 137).

Thus Freud started out by affirming the paternal protection afforded to children early in life but ended the essay with a pessimistic note about careless chance that deals out irrevocable and unavoidable pain. Parents possess only a limited capacity to

3. This last sentence was added in 1919. Freud himself was one of those who had to deal with a multiplicity of feelings without the help of "revived" parents.

shelter their offspring from the cruelties of fate. There is no God
or kindly nature. There is, however, the hurt of the unprotected
and the religious neurosis of those who believe themselves to
be protected by God. Such reasoning may serve as a displacement for the "hurt" of not being protected. If fate, not our parents, is responsible for our suffering, we have no right to complain. We must endure stoically, without tears and without
questioning unprotective parents.

Freud's first explicit theorizing about the sources of belief
and the unprotected condition of human beings remained the
core of all his subsequent writings on religion. Humans model
the God in their psyche after the "father in the flesh." Thus, God
is "an *exalted* father" (1910, p. 123; 1913b, p. 147; 1923, p. 85);
"a *transfiguration* of father" (1911, p. 51); "a *likeness* of father"
(1913b, p. 147); "a *sublimation* of father" (1918, p. 115); "a *surrogate* of father" (1918, p. 114); "a *substitute* for father" (1923,
pp. 85, 86); "a *copy* of father" (1923, p. 85); or God "really *is*
the father" (1933, p. 163).

Freud provided many clinical illustrations to support his
point. "Notes upon a Case of Obsessional Neurosis" (1909) describes the religious vicissitudes of the "Rat Man" as he wres-
tled with love and hatred for his father and his God. In "Psycho-analytic Notes on an Autobiographical Account of a Case
of Paranoia (Dementia Paranoides)" (1911) Freud suggested
that the father of Senate President Schreber, a very prominent
educator, was suitable "for transformation into a God in the affectionate memory of the son" (p. 51). In "From the History
of an Infantile Neurosis" (1918), Freud presents the treatment
of the "Wolf Man," with his compulsive prayers and his need
to say "God-swine" or "God-shit," or "to think of the Holy Trin-
ity whenever he saw three heaps of horse-dung or other excre-
ment lying in the road" (p. 17). The Wolf Man identified with

Christ, which "gave him a chance of sublimating his predominantly masochistic attitude towards his father" (p. 64). "He also rebelled against the passive character of Christ and against his ill-treatment by his Father" (p. 65). The Wolf Man's predicament was based on a deep erotic attachment to his father, which found in religion an apt means for its expression: "His extravagant love for his father, which had made the repression necessary, found its way at length to an ideal sublimation. As Christ, he could love his father, who was now called God, with a fervour which had sought in vain to discharge itself as long as his father had been a mortal" (p. 115).

The religious sublimation lasted for a while before it gave way to a new attachment: "As soon as the course of events presented him with a new father-surrogate, who threw his weight into the scale against religion, it was dropped and replaced by something else" (p. 117). Thus, the Wolf Man's vicissitudes of belief followed the path Freud had predicted: "young people lose their religious beliefs as soon as their father's authority breaks down" (1910, p. 123).

Like the Schreber case, "A Seventeenth-Century Demonological Neurosis" (1923) is based on historical data, not on reports by psychoanalytic patients. Freud studied the documents describing the miraculous release of the seventeenth-century painter Christoph Haizmann from a pact with the devil through the intervention of the Virgin Mary. The painter made the pact after the death of his father and when he was doubting his capacity to support himself. The pact promised that after nine years Christoph would belong in body and soul to the devil. The miraculous liberation occurred in September 1677, shortly before the deadline. Freud's study of the documents led him to conclude that Christoph's father was the source of his God and his devil:

We know that God is a father substitute . . . an exalted father . . . a copy of the father as he is seen and experienced in childhood. . . . We also know, from the secret life of the individual which analysis uncovers, that his relation to his father was perhaps ambivalent from the outset. . . . The same ambivalence governs the relations of mankind to its Deity. The unresolved conflict between, on the one hand, a longing for the father and, on the other, a fear of him and a son's defiance of him, has furnished us with an explanation of important characteristics of religion and decisive vicissitudes in it. . . . It does not need much analytic perspicacity to guess that God and the Devil were originally identical—were a single figure which was later split into two figures with opposite attributes. . . . Thus the father, it seems, is the individual prototype of both God and the Devil. (pp. 85–86)

Freud did not present other case histories to illustrate this theory about the formation of God and devil representations in the child's mind. He did not present clinical material about religion or about belief in God in his female cases, nor did he theorize about the formation of the God representation in little girls or address the role of the mother in the formation of the God representation. The father seemed to occupy most of the child's psychic space: "Of all the imagos of a childhood which, as a rule, is no longer remembered, none is more important for a youth or a man than that of his father. A little boy is bound to love and admire his father, who seems to him the most powerful, the kindest and the wisest creature in the world. God himself is after all only an exaltation of his picture of a father as he is represented in the mind of early childhood" (1914b, p. 243). The maternal absence from Freud's theory of religion requires interpretation.

At the next level of theorizing about religion, Freud established its historical and cultural foundations. In *Totem and Taboo* (1913b) he presented his historical reconstruction of how religion began. Departing from Darwin, Freud argued that "men originally lived in hordes, each under the domination of a single powerful, violent and jealous male" who had exclusive rights over the women of the group (1925a, p. 67). "One day the brothers who had been driven out [by this male] came together, killed and devoured their father, and so made an end to the patriarchal horde" (1913b, p. 141). The first totem meal, in which an animal substitutes for the devoured father, commemorated the original deed. Thus began the "social organization of moral restrictions and of religion" (p. 142). In the minds of his sons, the murdered father left behind a mnemic image that was inherited and transformed into the individual God of each believer (Rizzuto, 1979, pp. 13–41). Immediately after the murder, the image of the father was repressed. Soon it returned in symbolic displacement as the totem animal and, finally, in the creation of a paternal image of God: "A new creation such as this, derived from what constitutes the root of every form of religion—a longing for the father—might occur if in the process of time some fundamental change had taken place in man's relation to his father, and perhaps, too, in his relation to animals" (1913b, p. 148).

The individual developing child repeats the race's history. During the oedipal period, the desire for sole possession of the mother inspires in males strong wishes to destroy the father. Guilt follows and with it a need to repress the instinctual strivings and the murderous intentions toward the father. The paternal imago becomes internalized and is available for transformation into a God representation. The affectionate and ambivalent feelings associated with attachment to the father are now transferred to the Deity. The racial and individual processes of "creating" God once more leave out the mother. The individual longs only for the father and for his symbolic, sacrificial, and divine return.

The next theoretical essay, The Future of an Illusion (1927), begins by locating religion in the context of civilization as it helps humans to curb their instinctual wishes for "incest, cannibalism and lust for killing" (p. 10). Religion has made great contributions to the coercion of instinct and to civilization. Civilization is absolutely necessary to modulate the terrifying power of nature. Nature seems tolerant and "would let us do as we like." But "she has her own particularly effective method of restricting us. She destroys us—coldly, cruelly, relentlessly, as it seems to us, and possibly through the same things that cause satisfaction. It was precisely because of these dangers with which nature threatens us that we came together and created civilization . . . to defend us against nature" (p. 15).[4]

This is the same Freud who, at age seventeen, after hearing the essay on nature attributed to Goethe, changed his vocational direction from law to medicine in order to "eavesdrop on Nature" and extract her secrets. Now, at the age of seventy-one, having dedicated his life to listening to her whispers, he could speak from experience about her cruelty. Freud asked how mankind defends "against the superior powers of nature" in facing a life that "is hard to bear" (p. 16). This situation, he concluded, "calls for consolation." In his efforts to overcome the terrors of nature and helplessness, man reacts psychologically and creates gods by making "the forces of nature not simply into persons with whom he can associate as he would with his equals . . . but he gives them the character of the father.[5] He

4. Freud's tragic vision of human life (Schafer, 1970) finds its starkest description here.
5. There is a curious switching of gender in this sentence. "Kindly Nature" was once referred to as the maternal part of the parental couple. In all other

turns them into gods, following in this . . . not only an infantile prototype but a phylogenetic one" (p. 17).

The gods are charged with a threefold task: to exorcize the terrors of nature, to reconcile men to the cruelty of fate, and to compensate them for their sufferings (p. 18). The last task is not easy to fulfill, and it leads to the development of systems of morals to control the evils of civilization. Freud now claimed that moral precepts were of "divine" origin. Thus, in the course of time, the religious illusion promises higher purposes and a final good outcome. When monotheism arrived in history, a new revival of the relationship with the father came with it. "Now that God was a single person, man's relations to him could recover the intimacy and intensity of the child's relation to his father" (p. 19).

The final form of religious illusion came into being at this point and persists to the present time. The believer trusts that a superior being, God, orders everything for the best and that "over each of us there watches a benevolent Providence which is only seemingly stern and which will not suffer us to become a plaything of the overmighty and pitiless forces of nature" (p. 19). Freud considered it his duty to show the relation between the father complex and the helplessness of the child and adult (p. 23). Talking about early childhood, Freud mentioned for the first time the role of the mother and the child's attachment to her as the first love-object that satisfies its hunger and "its first protector against anxiety." But "the mother is soon replaced[6] by

references nature is female. When transformed into God, however, it models itself on the paternal imago.

6. Throughout his work Freud insisted on the significance of very early experiences. In his theorizing about religion he neglected to mention what happens to the memories of the "first protector" after the father replaces the mother.

the father, who retains that position for the rest of childhood" (p. 24). Regardless of the child's love, admiration, and ambivalence in regard to the father, he realizes that he needs the father for protection. The adult also recognizes this need. Freud concluded that religion stems from the recognition of one's helplessness and the turning to a divine father for protection (p. 24).

According to Freud, the evidence for religious belief does not stand the test of reason. Religious people can say only that religious teachings "deserve to be believed because they were already believed by our primal ancestors" and that "it is forbidden to raise the question of authentication" (p. 26). Thus religion suppresses the intellect and demands belief on the authority of elders. For Freud, however, analysis of the psychic origin of religious ideas led to his final conclusion: "They are illusions, fulfillment of the oldest, strongest and most urgent wishes of mankind. The secret of their strength lies in the strength of those wishes. As we already know, the terrifying impression of helplessness in childhood aroused the need for protection—for protection through love—which was provided by the father; and the recognition that this helplessness lasts throughout life made it necessary to cling to the existence of the father, but this time a more powerful one" (p. 31).

In Freud's view, reality and religion have little to do with each other in mankind's efforts to unveil the secrets of the universe; "scientific work is the only road which can lead us to the knowledge of reality outside ourselves" (p. 31). Freud still had to wrestle with Brentano's scientific proof of the existence of God. At this late date, Brentano's tight reasoning received a harsh response: "Where questions of religion are concerned, people are guilty of every possible sort of dishonesty and intellectual misdemeanour. Philosophers stretch the meaning of words. . . . They give the name of God to some vague abstraction. . . . They can pose before all the world as theists, as be-

lievers in God . . . notwithstanding that their God is now nothing more than an insubstantial shadow and no longer the
mighty personality of religious doctrines" (p. 32).

It is easy to recognize in these words Brentano's "airy" God.
This God, Freud insists, must be relinquished. Man must face
reality as it is. Undeniably, however, some people, particularly
those in whom "the sweet—or bittersweet—poison," religion,
has been instilled from childhood on, cannot face "the cruelties of reality" without it (p. 49). "They will have to admit to
themselves the full extent of their helplessness and their in-
significance in the machinery of the universe. . . . Men cannot
remain children forever; they must in the end go out into 'hostile life'" (p. 49). Freud sets himself up as an example of the
newly liberated man: "From that bondage I am, we are, free.
Since we are prepared to renounce a good part of our infantile
wishes, we can bear it if a few of our expectations turn out to
be illusions" (p. 54).

The book closes on a defyingly triumphant note: "No, our
science is no illusion. But an illusion would be to suppose that
what science cannot give us we can get elsewhere" (p. 56). The
ability to curb the terrifying power of nature has changed
hands, from God (father) to Freud, the eavesdropping scientist.
God has been replaced by reason: "Our[7] God, *Logos*, will fulfill
whichever of these wishes nature outside us allows, but he
would do it very gradually, only in the unforeseeable future, and
for a new generation of men. He promises no compensation for
us, who suffer grievously from life" (p. 54).

In summary, Freud claimed that human beings must be sto-

7. The expression "*our God*" places Freud, once more, in direct counterpoint
with "*their*" God. As he had said earlier, in *The Resistances to Psychoanalysis* (1925):
"To profess *belief* in this new theory called for a certain degree of readiness to
accept a situation of *solitary opposition*—a situation with which no one is more
familiar than a Jew (p. 222, my italics).

ical, renouncing their wishes for protection and consolation. They must stop clinging to their fathers and to God, his substitute. The best they can and must do is to face their fate and believe in science; that will make them true adults. The analyst, however, must ask why it is that clinging to the father, in whatever form, has become for Freud synonymous with infantile wishes. Is it possible to cling to a father as an adult; is there such a thing as mature clinging? Freud's solution for himself was a stark and stoic realism with no consolation but the pride of being able to accept suffering and terror without clinging to anyone.

In debunking all religions, Freud was exercising his capacity for defiance, his disposition "to gladly sacrifice my life for one great moment in history" (1960, p. 202). The writing of *The Future of an Illusion* was, for Freud, akin to one of those great moments in history when his passionate defiance once and for all destroyed the temple of his ancestors and all other places of worship.

Schur (1972) noted the connection in Freud's experience between death and the need to establish an internal center of control. Freud was obsessed with his death and that of others for most of his adult life. Schur (1972) reflects: "The formulation of the death-instinct concept [in 1920]—paradoxical as this may seem . . . prepared him for his belief in the supremacy of the ego, of the intellect, of Logos, the only force with which he could face *Ananke*.[8] It paved the way for *The Future of an Illusion* and for the formulation of a scientific *Weltanschauung*" (p. 332).

Freud's cancer had been diagnosed in April 1923, four years before he wrote *The Future of an Illusion*. He went to his first surgery without informing his family about the cancer or making any

8. This is the Greek word for necessity. Freud uses it to describe all the limitations nature and life impose on human beings confronting their omnipotent narcissism.

provisions for his aftercare. His wife and his daughter Anna were notified by telephone that he had had the operation and must remain in the hospital because of excessive bleeding (Jones, 1957, p. 90). Freud practiced what he preached: he could face the terrors of Fate alone, without complaining or asking for consolation. He described himself to Lou Andreas-Salomé, in his letter of July 30, 1915: "I cannot be an optimist, and I believe I differ from the pessimists only in that wicked, stupid, senseless things don't upset me, because I have accepted them from the beginning as part of what the World is made out of" (1960, p. 311).

The expression "from the beginning" suggests a modality of acceptance established in early childhood and supported perhaps by deeply painful experiences that persuaded him not to entrust himself to anyone's care. A 1918 letter to his respected friend and disciple, the Swiss pastor Oskar Pfister, a man Freud considered an optimist, revealed Freud's darkest view of his fellow men: "I have found little that is 'good' about human beings on the whole. In my experience most of them are trash, no matter whether they publicly subscribe to this or that ethical doctrine or none at all. . . . If we are to talk of ethics, I subscribe to a high ideal from which most human beings I have come across depart most lamentably" (Freud and Pfister, 1963, pp. 61–62).

If human beings are trash and theistic philosophers deceptive, if religious leaders demand belief on the basis of the testimony of their ancestors, religious belief can only be an exercise in self-deception. Freud instead developed an ideal that made him different and better than those despicable others. Freud's stance was one of deep disillusion. There is no one to trust, no one to lean on or to help us find the truth in our painful lives. The only consolation is in ourselves, in using the soft voice of the intellect.

Freud's last work on religion was *Moses and Monotheism: Three Essays* (1939). Writing the essays posed a difficult psychological task for him, and the resulting manuscript reveals the intense struggle he must have gone through in expressing his ideas.[9] The man who in 1930 won the Goethe Prize, given annually to "a personality of established achievement whose creative work is worthy of an honour dedicated to Goethe's memory" (J. Strachey, editor's note to Freud, 1930b, p. 206), seemed to have lost the mastery of his art. James Strachey in his editor's note comments: "What is perhaps likely to strike a reader first about *Moses and Monotheism* is a certain unorthodoxy, or even eccentricity, in its construction: three essays of greatly different length, two prefaces, both situated at the beginning of the third essay, and a third preface situated halfway through that same essay, constant recapitulations and repetitions—such irregularities are unknown elsewhere in Freud's writings" (1939, p. 4).

Freud's final essay, "Outline of Psycho-Analysis," published posthumously in 1940, reveals Freud in full possession of his literary and intellectual mastery. Strachey comments: "Nowhere else, perhaps, does his style reach a higher level of succinctness and lucidity" (p. 143). The explanation for this discrepancy must lie in the vicissitudes of psychic conflict.

Freud's conflict was with Moses. He developed an obsession with Moses that could only have arisen from the deep layers of his mind. On December 16, 1934, he wrote to Arnold Zweig: "The man and *what I wanted to make of him* pursue me everywhere" (1970, p. 98, my italics). Freud's psychic compulsion continued, as he told Zweig on June 13, 1935: "As far as my own productivity goes, it is like what happens in analysis. If a particular subject has been suppressed, nothing takes its place and the field of vision remains empty. So do I now remain *fixated on the Moses*,

9. Grubrich-Simitis (1991) notes the unusual number of corrections and the significant amount of rewriting in Freud's manuscript.

which has been laid aside and on which I can do no more" (p. 107, my italics).

In describing how he had written the essay, Freud presented his dilemma: "Actually it has been written twice: for the first time a few years ago in Vienna, where I did not think it would be possible to publish it. I determined to give it up; *but it tormented me like an unlaid ghost*"[10] (1939, p. 103, my italics). Why should the unlaid ghost of Moses torment Freud, fixate him as a suppressed subject does, and refuse to be shaken off? Why did Freud "want to make something of him"? The phrase has very profound child-father echoes coming from Freud, the child who was supposed to come to "nothing." He gave at least one clue in an earlier letter to Zweig (May 8, 1932), through a close paraphrase of the Philippson Bible. Zweig had visited Palestine, and Freud commented:

> How strange this tragically mad land you have visited must have seemed to you. Just think, this strip of our mother earth is connected with no other progress, no discovery or invention—the Phoenicians are said to have invented glass and the alphabet (both doubtful!), the island of Crete gave us Minoan art, Pergamon reminds us of parchment, Magnesia of the magnet and so on ad infinitum—but Palestine has never produced anything but religious, sacred frenzies, presumptuous attempts to overcome the outer world of appearance by means of the inner world of wishful thinking. (1970, p. 40)

Phoebus Philippson had written: "Die Juden selbst zeichneten sich nicht durch Erfindungen aus"—the Jews did not distinguish themselves through their discoveries. The Israelites

10. The allusion must refer to the ghost of Hamlet's murdered father. Freud's unlaid ghost not only gave him no rest but would ultimately bring to an end the Jewish lineage.

did not have their own tools to measure the sun when, in 2 Kings 20:9–11, they had to assess the changes in the shadows. The sign of the Lord was the miraculous reversal of the sun's shadow by ten steps on the dial. The miracle did happen, but Israel had no dial of its own to register it.

There could have been something in Palestine's inability to produce anything but "sacred frenzies" that reawakened painful childhood feelings in Freud. He had witnessed his father's inability to provide for his family while remaining "the greatest optimist of all" (1960, p. 22). Jakob had continued to read his Bible and his Talmud, as his private sacred frenzy. He also wanted his son to join him in this pursuit, as he suggested by his gift of the Philippson Bible.

Freud never documented in words his reaction to his father's plea. He responded with his life work and through his personal attitude toward religion and God—his conviction that God is a childhood creation originating in the child's exalted vision of his father. In *Moses and Monotheism*, Freud attempted to prove that not even the "sacred frenzies" were created by Jews. They were the gift of an Egyptian prince, Moses, whose God was a direct descendant of an Egyptian god, Aten.

Freud mentions his involvement with Moses for the first time in *The Interpretation of Dreams*, where he interprets a dream of Bismarck as a liberator facing rebellious subjects as an identification with Moses (1900, pp. 378–81). In September 1901, Freud overcame his inhibition to visit Rome and for the first time encountered Michelangelo's *Moses*. It was a fateful moment. He returned to see the statue again and again during that holiday and told Martha that he was planning to write about it (Gay, 1988, p. 314). He drew sketches of the way Moses holds the Tables of the Law and pondered for hours about the artist's intent in portraying the patriarch as self-possessed and restrained. He wrote a brief essay in 1913, "The *Moses* of

Michelangelo," which he published anonymously, as a layman, in Imago in 1914 and did not acknowledge as his until 1924. The essay admitted that "no piece of statuary has ever made a stronger impression on me than this" (1914a, p. 213). It seemed to Freud that Moses was depicted facing the worshipers of the Golden Calf, that he should have "dash[ed] the Tables to the earth and let loose his rage upon his faithless people" (p. 216). Freud's essential question was: "Did Michelangelo intend to create a 'timeless study of character and mood' in this Moses, or did he portray him at a particular moment of his life and, if so, at a highly significant one?" (p. 215).

Very early in life, Freud had seen a picture of a peaceful Moses: the first volume of the Philippson Bible had a full-page picture of Moses' upper body, leaning on a table, serenely holding a rod in his right hand and the Tables of the Law in his left hand. Freud's repression must have been deep for him to make no reference to a picture he must have seen many times in early childhood and again in his own 1858 edition of the bible.

He fantasized in front of the stone Moses: "I used to sit down in front of the statue in the expectation that I should now see how it would start up on its raised foot, dash the Tables of the Law to the ground and let fly its wrath. Nothing of the kind happened. Instead, the stone image became more and more transfixed, an almost oppressively solemn calm emanated from it, and I was obliged to realize that something was represented here that could stay without change; that this Moses would remain sitting like this in his wrath forever" (pp. 220–21).

Hours and years of pondering followed. Freud developed a "friendship" with the statue. In 1912 he wrote to Jones: "I envy you for seeing Rome so soon and so early in life. Bring my deepest devotion to Moses and write to me about him." Jones fully understood the nature of his task and wrote back: "My first pilgrimage the day of my arrival was to convey your greetings to

Moses, and I think he unbent a little from his haughtiness" (cited in Gay, 1988, pp. 314–15). That same year Freud "brought a small plaster cast of Moses home with him," presumably from Italy (Gay, 1988, p. 315).

Finally, after much pondering, Freud reached his own conclusion:

What we see before us is not the inception of a violent action but the remains of a movement that has already taken place. In his first transport of fury, Moses desired to act, to spring up and take vengeance and forget the Tables; but he has overcome the temptation, and he will now remain seated and still, in his frozen wrath and in his pain mingled with contempt. Nor will he throw away the Tables so that they will break on the stones, for it is on their especial account that he has controlled his anger; it was to preserve them that he kept his passion in check. . . . He remembered his mission and for its sake renounced an indulgence of his feelings. (1914a, pp. 229–30)

Freud could have been describing himself. The disclosure of his innermost passions to Martha in his February 2, 1886, letter forces the comparison:

Breuer told me that hidden under the surface of timidity there lay in me an extremely daring and fearless human being. I had always thought so, but never dared tell anyone. I have often felt as though I had inherited all the defiance and all the passions with which our ancestors defended their Temple and could gladly sacrifice my life for one great moment in history. And at the same time I always felt so helpless and incapable of expressing these ardent passions even by a word or a poem. So I have always *restrained myself*, and it is this, I think, which people must see in me. (1960, pp. 202–3, my italics)

What people saw in Freud—fierce defiance and restraint—Freud saw in Moses. Like Moses, Freud felt he had a "mission" and was determined to fulfill it, to lead people away from their contemptible condition of dishonesty. He wanted them to see that God was their own creation. He, too, had to control his wrath and contain "his pain mingled with contempt."[11] There is no doubt that Freud believed his mission was as important as Moses' and that he fully and explicitly identified with the patriarch. He wrote to Jung on January 17, 1909: "We are certainly getting ahead; if I am Moses, then you are Joshua and will take possession of the promised land of psychiatry, which I shall only glimpse from afar" (Freud and Jung, 1974, pp. 196–97).

Freud knew that he shared with the Moses of the statue the most profound commitment: "The giant frame with its tremendous physical power becomes only a concrete expression of the highest mental achievement that is possible to man, that of struggling successfully against an inward passion for the sake of a cause to which he had devoted himself" (1914a, p. 233).

The child whose father had predicted that he would "come to nothing" had restrained his rage, his inward passion, and made himself the new Moses. The Moses of the Bible, however, did not disturb Freud until 1934, when Moses' "unlaid ghost" began to "torment" and obsess him as a bewildering and unshakable presence. Freud was forced to start his confusing and consuming effort to make sense of the person of Moses himself. On September 30, 1934, Freud informed Arnold Zweig

11. Freud's wrath and contempt were already apparent in his description of the Galician Jewish parents on the train. His rage had deep roots in childhood losses, bitter disappointments, and the inability to express them. His kind father did not tolerate complaints.

about his discovery: "I have written something myself[12] and this, contrary to my original intention, took up so much of my time that everything else has been neglected." It was in this letter that Freud revealed his discovery of the source of centuries of anti-Semitism: "Moses created the Jews" (1970, p. 91).[13]

Freud was then seventy-eight years old and was suffering intensely from his advanced cancer. He knew that he was approaching death. He found himself once more dealing with suppressed rage. He wrote to Lou Andreas-Salomé on May 16, 1934: "I cannot agree with the eulogy of old age to which you give expression in your kind letter. For personal reasons, no doubt. I am glad that you adapt yourself to it so much better than I. But for that matter you are by no means so old and *you do not get so angry. The suppressed rage exhausts one or what is still left over of one's former ego*" (1966 [1972], p. 202, my italics).[14]

Seven years earlier, in a letter of December 11, 1927, Freud had explained to Andreas-Salomé the source of his wrath at that time: "You don't want to come to the aid of the Almighty either. But my wrath was not so much directed against him as against the gracious Providence and moral-world order for which he is, to be sure, responsible. Nor do I pursue by any means all illusions, but why should I cling precisely to the one which makes such mock of reason?" (1966 [1972], p. 172).

It is only natural that in dealing with his own suppressed rage at "gracious Providence," Freud turned again to the admired Moses, who had suppressed his wrath for the sake of his mission. The biblical description of the story of Moses and the Jews

12. "Moses an Egyptian?" This essay later became part of *Moses and Monotheism*.
13. Freud's explanations are not sufficient. Even if Moses did "create" the Jewish people, persecution would not necessarily follow.
14. Freud completed the essay "The Man Moses, a Historical Novel" in the summer of 1934. He could have begun writing it at the time of this letter. He certainly was thinking about it.

did not satisfy him. What displeased him most was God's intervention in history. It was not God who chose the Jews, he insisted, but Moses. This "discovery" did away once and for all with the God of the Jews and their boastful claim that they were his Chosen People. There is a remarkable difference between what he read about the historical Moses and what he wanted Moses to be.

The Book of Exodus describes Moses as the son of a daughter of Levi. At the request of Pharaoh's daughter, who found him by the river, his natural mother became his nurse for his first years. When he grew up he was given to the princess and "became her son," an adopted Egyptian. Moses did not forget who his people were: "When Moses had grown up, he went out to his people and looked on their burdens" (Exodus 2:11). Angered by an Egyptian's abuse of the Hebrew people, he killed the man, was exiled, and fled to the land of Midian, where he settled and married. He was tending the flock of his father-in-law near Horeb, the mountain of God, when the Lord called him one day with strong words, which only a Jewish man could recognize: "I am the God of your father, the God of Abraham, the God of Isaac, and the God of Jacob. . . . Come, I will send you to Pharaoh that you may bring forth my people, the sons of Israel, out of Egypt" (Exodus 3:8, 10). When Moses asked how he could exert any authority over his fellow Jews, God spoke forcefully: "Say this to the people of Israel, 'The Lord, the God of your fathers, the God of Abraham, the God of Isaac, and the God of Jacob, has sent me to you': this is my name forever, and thus I am to be remembered throughout all generations" (Exodus 3:15).

Freud, however, did not want to remember this God of Moses and the Hebrew lineage of the man the Lord had called to his service. He was intent on transforming the Book of Exodus into "a historical novel." He had no other primary source to guide him: Exodus is the only extant text about Moses. Freud drew from the writings of contemporary Egyptian scholars,[15] some of whom later renounced their original work, but without persuading Freud to change his new version of Exodus.

He summed up his ideas in a letter to Andreas-Salomé on June 6, 1935, describing the view that "holds such a great fascination for me" (1966 [1972], p. 205):

> It started out with the question as to what has really created the particular character of the Jew, and came to the conclusion that the Jew is the creation of the man Moses. Who was this Moses and what did he bring about? The answer to this question was given in a kind of historical novel. Moses was not a Jew, but a well-born Egyptian, a high official, a priest, perhaps a prince of royal dynasty, and a zealous supporter of the monotheistic faith, which the Pharaoh Amenhotep IV had made the dominant religion round about 1350 B.C. With the collapse of the new religion and the extinction of the 18th dynasty after the Pharaoh's death this ambitious and aspiring man had lost all his hopes and had decided to leave his fatherland and create a new nation which he proposed to bring up in the imposing religion of his master. He resorted to the Semitic tribe which had been dwelling in the land since the Hyksos period, placed himself at their head, led them out of bondage into freedom, gave them the spiritualized religion of Aten and as an expression of consecration as

15. Freud made frequent allusions to the works of J. H. Breasted (*History of Egypt* [1906] and *The Dawn of Consciousness* [1934]); A. Weigall ("The Life and Times of Akhnaton" [1922]); and A. Erman ("Die Agyptische Religion" [1905]). He also read E. Sellin, "Mose un seine Bedeutung für die israelitische-judische Religionsgeschichte" (1922). It was Sellin who suggested that Moses was murdered. Freud built his theory on Sellin's ideas, which were not supported by later scholarship. I believe that Sellin in the end repudiated his theory. As he did with other Egyptologists, Freud made far-fetched inferences from their discoveries.

well as a means of setting them apart introduced circumcision, which was a native custom among the Egyptians and only among them. What the Jews later boasted of their God Jahve, that he had made them his chosen people and delivered them from Egypt, was literally true—of Moses. By this act of choice and the gift of a new religion he created the Jew. . . . Moses was probably killed a few decades later in a popular uprising. . . . Jahve became the national God of the Jewish people. . . . In the course of six to eight centuries Jahve had been changed into the likeness of the god of Moses. This process is typical. . . . Religions owe their compulsive power to the *return of the repressed*; they are reawakened memories of very ancient, forgotten, highly emotional episodes of human history. I have already said this in *Totem and Taboo.* (1966 [1972], pp. 204–5, my italics)

Freud's new version abounds in reversals of the biblical text. In particular, he shifts the text from the praise of God to the praise of a powerful man. Moses, not God, is the liberator of the Israelites. This Moses is not the son of a daughter of Levi but an Egyptian, who assigned himself the task of presenting a new and Egyptian god to the Israelites. Moses, then, created the Jewish God. Furthermore, he did not present a living God who spoke to him and to the Israelites through him but a new *idea* of God. God, the caller of Moses, is out; Moses the idea-giver is in. From the perspective of Freud's own theories about God as a father substitute the conclusion is obvious: Jakob Freud–God is out, Sigmund Freud–Moses is in.

Freud was unequivocal about the presence of the father in any god, specifically in the God of Moses. In individual development, the father "in the flesh" makes a significant contribution to the child's idea of God together with the inherited memory traces of the murdered father of the primal horde. It was the emotional recognition of that primal and repressed father that provided the Israelites with the "need" to believe Moses' idea of God: "The first effect of meeting the being who had so long been missed and longed for was overwhelming. . . . Admiration, awe, thankfulness for having found grace in his eyes—the religion of Moses knew none but these positive feelings towards the father-god. The conviction of his irresistibility, the submission to his will, could not have been more unquestioning in the helpless and intimidated son of the father of the horde.[16] . . . A rapture of devotion to God was thus the first reaction to the return of the grand father" (1939, pp. 133–34).

There are many contradictions in these accounts. To mention only two: first, Moses supposedly presented the *idea* of God. The Jews, however, then responded to the idea as though it was the return of the repressed image of the father. Secondly, Moses himself decided to create a people, after the death of his master and adoptive grandfather, the Egyptian Pharaoh. Freud says not a word about why enslaved people of another race would follow an Egyptian prince, the representative of the oppressor. There is no need for these theories to make sense; it is better to read them as a "historical novel," to try to understand what Freud tried to understand first in Michelangelo's *Moses* and then in the biblical Moses.

What impelled Freud to create this Moses and not another? What could he have been trying to do with the tormenting ghost?[17] The compulsion and the torments of "the unlaid

16. One may wonder what could intimidate the sons if the father had been murdered. Perhaps here, too, was the "unlaid ghost" of the father returned to them.

17. Others (Grubrich-Simitis, 1991; Krüll, 1986; Rice, 1990; Yerushalmi, 1991) have attempted to understand Freud's motive for writing *Moses and Monotheism*. I address here only his transformation of the story of Moses and the significance that it may have had for him.

ghost" made Freud a very poor reader of the Book of Exodus. He knew the bible well enough to quote it seventy-six times in *Moses and Monotheism.* In his lay readings, Freud was precise, observant, careful to notice nuances. These qualities vanished in the face of his need to disprove what the Book of Moses said about Jews' establishing their "sacred frenzies."

Why did Freud's Moses have to be an Egyptian? Freud had a strong Egyptian bias. According to him, the Egyptians invented monotheism and were highly cultured and creative, unlike their neighbor Palestine. In the only childhood dream he remembered, his mother was carried by Egyptian figures. Where could it have come from, this very early passion to substitute for what is Jewish the more highly valued Egyptian equivalent? Leaving aside the psychodynamic considerations for the moment, another question arises: what source provided the young dreamer and the adult man with the knowledge and the images he could use for his exaltation of the Egyptians, at the cost of the Jews? Such a source, of course, is the Philippson Bible, with its commentaries and illustrations. The vivid illustrations of Egypt and the Egyptians in the Bible must have impressed him, as his collection of antiquities demonstrates so eloquently.

The story of Moses, however, must have touched him personally, even as a child. Freud was born a Jew, as Moses was. Moses had two mothers, two cultures, two languages, and they served two different functions. One mother was Jewish, the other an Egyptian princess. Freud also had two mothers, Amalie and the ill-fated nurse. They had two languages, two cultures, and served different functions. One was Jewish, the other Czech. Moses went to Pharaoh's court with his adoptive mother; Freud went to impressive priestly services in the local church with his nurse. Moses, according to the biblical text and Freud's "novel," discovered his mission after the death of his adoptive master, Pharaoh. Freud, like the biblical Moses, had two sharply differentiated periods in his life, before and after "the catastrophe." Both Freud's Moses and Freud himself responded to the overwhelming collapse in identical manner. Freud's novel says that Moses "lost all his hope" after Pharaoh's death and, "ambitious" and "aspiring" as he was, decided to create a new nation with the god of his master. Freud debunked the source of mankind's pride and offered to lead a new group of men. Their god—Logos—would allow them to be honest with themselves and give them the courage to stand alone, without the infantile consolation of the Jewish, or any other, father-God.

Freud's Moses appears as Freud's family romance in displacement: Although he was a prince, the son of royalty, Moses was a self-made man; all he achieved he owed to himself. He had no debts to other human or divine beings. Disillusioned and betrayed by his people, he controlled his rage and channeled it into the service of his creation, the Jewish nation. Freud, too, contained his rage at the failures and betrayals of his people. He kept his promise to himself to become the leader of a more enlightened group of human beings.

Reading *Moses and Monotheism* in this manner leads inevitably to the conclusion that it is, in displacement, the closest thing we have to a psychological autobiography of Freud,[18] a man near death who feels the need for closure, the need to tell himself and others about his personal journey. Freud, with his love of secrecy (Barron el al., 1991) and his deep disdain for biographers, could never write so directly about himself. With the suffering of oncoming personal death and the overt persecution of the Jews that finally forced him out of his native land, the "unlaid ghost" of Moses returned, with both its rage and its self-containment. Freud's identification with the great Jewish

18. Grubrich-Simitis (1991) suggests that the book is an autobiographical essay.

leader was deep and lasting.[19] Keeping Moses as he is presented in the biblical narrative—a leader whose father-God made him what he was—was more than Freud could tolerate in a figure of identification. What was most difficult to bear was the notion that Moses had received his mission from God. Freud had to say to himself and to the world, in the confusing words of his "novel," that he had been a man alone all his life. There was neither God nor father "in the flesh" to help him. He and he alone had created the new human. Those who trusted in a fatherly God seemed infantile to him. Their religion was for him a "closed book." He could not experience the "despondency" that called for the "regressive revival" of the small child's father in the shape of a God. He experienced instead the rage of his loneliness and, with sober and heroic power, transformed it creatively into his great discoveries.

Where is the mother in Freud's theory of religion? Where was his real mother? Why did he not find help and protection in her? I shall attend to these questions in the next chapter.

19. Shengold (1972) describes how "Freud's family complexes were expressed and lived out in metaphors derived from the Bible and from Egypt" (p. 156).

chapter ten
Amalie Nathansohn Freud

Freud, the man who destroyed his personal papers so as to foil the efforts of his future biographers, succeeded in obscuring behind the words proud and beautiful a more complex portrayal of his mother. He never wrote about her or his feelings about her in the explicit and uncompromisingly self-revelatory way that he did about his father. We know virtually nothing from him about his mother, except that he was her favorite child. To throw some light on the matter, it is helpful to explore, first, what other relatives said about Amalie Nathansohn Freud and second, proceed to examine in detail most of the references Freud made to his mother and his few remarks about his nanny.

Freud's son Martin, his niece Judith Bernays Heller, daughter of his oldest sister, Anna, and his own daughter Anna had much to say about Amalie. What they perceived, from their own individual angles of vision, was a multifaceted woman. Martin Freud (1957) gives us precious information about his grandmother. Martin was born on December 7, 1889, when his grandmother was aged fifty-four, and was in his early forties when she died in 1930. Thus he had the opportunity to know her well in the context of the closely knit family encircling her as a matriarch.

It is clear that Martin did not like his grandmother, and he made no effort to hide his feelings:

I saw my Grandmother Amalia[1] often. Although she was an old woman when, as a small boy, I became conscious of her, I was already a middle-aged man when she died. She had had great beauty, but all traces of this had gone when I remember her first. It looked for some time as if she would live forever, and my father was terrified[2] by the thought that she might survive him and, in consequence, have to be told of his death.

Grandmother came from East Galicia, then still part of the Austrian Empire. She came of Jewish stock; and it might not be known by many people that Galician Jews were a peculiar race, not only different from any other races inhabiting Europe, but absolutely different from Jews who had lived in the West for some generations. They, these Galician Jews, had little grace and no manners; and their women were certainly not what we shall call "ladies." They were highly emotional and easily carried away by their feelings. But, although in many respects they would seem to be untamed barbarians to more civilized people, they, alone of all minorities, stood up against the Nazis. It was men of Amalia's race who fought the German army on the ruins of Warsaw; and it might, indeed, be true to say that whenever you hear of Jews showing violence or belligerence, instead of that meekness[3] and what seems poor-spirited acceptance of a hard fate sometimes associated with Jewish people, you may safely suspect the presence of men and women of Amalia's race.

These people are not easy to live with, and grandmother,

1. Martin Freud spells the name with a final *a*. In all other references, the accepted spelling is Amalie.

2. Martin's report makes it clear that Freud's "terror" was not only a subjectively experienced fear but that it was well-known by the family.

3. This picture contrasts the "belligerent" disposition of Amalie Freud with her husband's "meekness" when affronted on the street by a Christian.

a true representative of her race, was no exception. She had great vitality and much impatience; she had a hunger for life and an indomitable spirit. Nobody envied Aunt Dolfi, whose destiny it was to dedicate her life to the care of an old mother who was a tornado. Aunt Dolfi once took Amalia to buy a new hat—and she was not perhaps wise to recommend what seemed to her "something suitable." Studying carefully her image crowned by the hat she had agreed to try on, Amalia, who was on the wrong side of ninety, finally shouted, "I won't take this one; it makes me look old."

Memorable occasions were the family gatherings in Amalia's flat. These were on Christmas Day and New Year's Eve, for Amalia ignored Jewish feasts.[4] . . . As the evening went on, an atmosphere of growing crisis was felt by all as Amalia became unsettled and anxious. There are people who, when they are unsettled and disturbed, will hide these feelings because they do not want to disturb the peace of those around them; but Amalia was not one of these.[5] My father always came to these gatherings—I know of no occasion when he disappointed her—but his working day was a long one and he always came much later than any one else. Amalia knew this, or perhaps it was a reality she could never accept. Soon she would be seen running anxiously to the door and out to the landing to stare down the staircase. Was he coming? Where was he? Was it not getting very late? This running in and out might go on for an hour, but it was known that any attempt to stop her would produce an out-

4. The neglect of Jewish feasts must have come after Jakob's death in 1896; as we have seen, his granddaughter remembered that he recited the Jewish celebration by heart during Passover. Earlier, during his adolescence, Freud mentioned to Silberstein the family's celebration of Passover.

5. In contrast with her son Sigmund, Amalie did not restrain her feelings or show mastery over them.

burst of anger which it was better to avoid by taking as little notice as possible. And my father always came at very much his usual time, but never at a moment when Amalia was waiting for him on the landing. (M. Freud, 1957, pp. 10–12)

Amalie, according to Martin's description, must have been difficult to live with. He presents a belligerent woman—anxious, inconsiderate, easily angered, and vain, a woman fixated on her son and craving his presence. We have seen that Amalie stopped her daughters' piano lessons because Sigmund, trying to study, had threatened to walk out if they continued, and "she did not wish him to leave the house altogether" (Bernays, 1973, p. 142). She apparently needed Sigmund close to her and suffered when they were apart. Perhaps this throws some light on his fear of dying, for this would cause her terrible pain.

The letter Freud wrote to Silberstein on December 31, 1871, at age fifteen, documents the imperative nature of Amalie's wishes: "Mother was very cross when she heard that you did not want to come over. She had already told your mother that you would be with us on New Year's Eve. We expect you without fail. Remember how glorious it is to bring oneself to do something for others" (1871–81 [1990], p. 3). The closing ironic comment leaves no doubt that Amalie's demand for Silberstein's presence had to be obeyed.

Judith Bernays Heller (1973) introduced her observations of her grandmother by saying: "My life from the age of six on has swung back and forth between the Old World and the New" (p. 334). Judith was born on February 19, 1885, when Amalie was fifty. When her parents emigrated to the United States, Judith was left behind for a year in the care of her maternal grandparents. She recalls that physically Amalie cut an impressive figure: "She was still handsome and upstanding then, with a fine head of gray hair that was combed *à la Pompadour* every morning by a hairdresser" (p. 337).

Judith also discloses her feelings about her grandmother: "I really feared her, though I admired her stateliness and the nice clothes she wore when she went out with her friends" (p. 335). There seemed to have been good reasons for the fear:

> My grandmother . . . had a volatile temperament, would scold the maid as well as her daughters, and rush about the house. . . . I greatly envied my sister, who had been left in the Sigmund Freud household, where there were three boys and a girl to play with. . . . I hated to go back to my grand-parents', where there were only grown-ups, among them my somewhat shrill and domineering grandmother. . . .
>
> I cannot remember any special incident that might account for the prejudice that I had and continued to have against my grandmother. . . . Was it . . . that she preferred the male members of her brood to the female ones? . . . My grandmother did not like us to go off by ourselves; at the time I thought she was a most selfish old lady and altogether disapproved of her. And she no less of me. (pp. 336–37)

The disappointed granddaughter relates the predicament of her Aunt Dolfi, the sister selected by the family to care for Amalie:

> She [Amalie] had many friends and acquaintances and spent the afternoons playing cards with them. . . . My aunt, who did not play cards, would be forced[6] to go with her, whether she liked it or not. . . . Whenever Dolfi went out my grand-

6. Amalie's psychological power appears in this word *forced*. That a daughter in her sixties could not disobey such a simple order clearly indicates that those who dealt with Amalie dare not to oppose her wishes or commands. At the time of her last vacation, as we shall see, Amalie made everybody submit to her, and at a great expense.

mother would stand at the window watching for her return, and not be content or easy until she saw her there. . . . When grandmother at last died this poor aunt of mine, then not far from seventy herself, was completely broken[7] and left without any real purpose in life. (pp. 337–38)

Aunt Dolfi's predicament was the worst, but others were not free of trouble with Amalie: "She was charming and smiling when strangers were about, but I, at least, always felt that with familiars she was a tyrant, and a selfish one. Quite definitely, she had a strong personality and knew what she wanted" (p. 338).

On the occasion of Freud's seventieth birthday, for example, Amalie "insisted that she be bought a new dress and had to go to *Jause* [a coffee party] at his house," even though Freud was ill and did not want her to come. "She had to be carried down stairs from her own house and up the stairs to the Freuds', but she did not mind that so long as she could be present to be honored and feted as the mother[8] of her 'golden son'" (p. 338).

Another instance occurred shortly before her death, at ninety-five. Although she was very frail, "She had continued to make her will felt and had insisted that, instead of spending the summer in Vienna, she be taken to her beloved Ischl in the mountains as before. Everybody was against it: her sons, the doctor, her daughters. But she had her way. She had to be carried to the train on a stretcher, looked after in her sleeping car by her doctor, and taken to her country apartment in an ambulance. . . . Two weeks after she returned to Vienna she fell into a coma and died peacefully" (p. 340).

7. To submit to Amalie meant to be "completely broken." Unlike Dolfi, Sigmund seemed to have found in his secret and restrained defiance a way of handling his "clinging" and domineering mother.
8. This description echoes Amalie's reported dream about her Sigmund's death and funeral being attended by the European heads of state.

These descriptions clearly reveal that Amalie Freud knew what she wanted and demanded to have it, regardless of the personal or economic cost to others. She was a true matriarch. Judith Bernays Heller concludes her essay with a fitting line to mark the end of a matriarchy: "With her going, the strong and vivid bond that held the family together was broken" (p. 340). It seems that the fear of arousing Amalie's volatility and bad temper had kept her children—and her doctor, too—obeying her imperious demands in their seventies and sixties.

Bernays Heller highlights another facet of Amalie's character: her peculiar (and cruel) ways of avoiding suffering and death:

> She so successfully used her increasing deafness in order to avoid hearing what she did not want to hear—principally the report of any event that might require her to bestow an extra amount of sympathy or consolation[9] upon some members of the family. Thus, when a young granddaughter died tragically at the age of twenty-three,[10] and [Amalie] heard grief-stricken whispers all around her, she manifested no desire to learn their cause, nor was she expressly told of it. When the bereaved mother [Amalie's sixty-two-year-old daughter, Rosa Freud Graf] came to see her, she never asked about the girl, nor did she inquire afterwards about her, though this granddaughter had visited her frequently in the past. Ten years later, however, she began to talk again about "poor Cecily," revealing that she had been fully aware all along of what had happened. (p. 339)

9. *Consolation* is a critical word. This is what Freud believes people want from religion: protection and consolation.

10. Cecily Graf was Sigmund's "best niece." Unmarried and pregnant, she committed suicide on August 16, 1922, by taking an overdose of veronal (Gay, 1988, p. 418).

Freud told Ferenczi that he was "deeply shaken" by the event (letter of August 24, 1922, in Gay, 1988, p. 418), and his distress must have been apparent. That his mother remained oblivious to the death suggests that she did not ask him about it or that if she did, he lied to her about it. In the same letter, Freud described his bereaved sister Rosa, who had lost her only child, as "a virtuoso of despair." The phrase suggests that he may have identified with his mother's avoidant attitude in relation to consoling people in great pain.

In addition to her shortcomings, Amalie had some commendable traits. Judith concedes that Amalie was

> efficient and capable in the household, lively and sociable, much visited by friends, and loved and honored by her children. . . . She had a sense of humor, being able to laugh at and at times ridicule herself. . . . She was not a complainer.[11] Even when she broke her arm at eighty-five and had to give up her beloved crocheting and knitting, she did not waste time pitying herself, but praised the doctor, her children who had nursed her so patiently, and the friends who had come to help her pass the time. (pp. 336–38)

Amalie could be gracious, grateful, and brave, with a sense of distance about her own suffering. This contrasts sharply with her unresponsiveness to terrible grief and her urgent need that certain things be done exactly as she wanted them without regard for others.

Amalie organized her social life around her need to have the family with her. Judith Bernays Heller adds to Martin's description of holiday celebrations an account of a typical Sunday at Amalie's: "My grandmother's sitting room on Sunday morn-

11. Her son Sigmund seems to have identified with her. Schur (1972) documents Freud's extreme tolerance of pain and his disinclination to complain about physical distress.

ings was the weekly meeting place for her busy sons, her daughters and daughters-in-law, her grandchildren and their children. Even when convalescing from operations and illness, Professor Freud would always find time of a Sunday morning to pay his mother a visit and give her the pleasure of petting and making a fuss over him." The description presents Freud as the receiver of her affection. It says nothing about his showing affection for her. Other sources add further details about her influence on her famous son.

Ernest Jones, Freud's biographer, confirms the grandchildren's descriptions. For instance, he reports that Amalie complained six weeks before her death that her photograph in the paper was "a bad reproduction; it makes me look a hundred" (1953, p. 3). Amalie seems to have shared dreams of grandeur with her husband; when they translated the dates of their birth from the Jewish to the Gregorian calendar they made them coincide with the birthdays of two great men: Jakob with Bismarck's, Amalie with Emperor Franz Josef's (p. 192).

Sigmund was always "her" son. Jones notes: "It was strange to a young visitor to hear her refer to the great Master as "mein goldener Sigi" (1953, p. 3) and to insist on her right to see him because she was "the mother." As Freud's friend and official biographer, Jones of course met Amalie Freud and must have formed his own impressions about her. It is therefore curious that someone as attentive to detail as he was has supplied so little information about the formidable mother of the father of psychoanalysis. There must have been some censorship, a conspiracy of silence about her.

Paul Roazen, who interviewed several members of the Freud family, describes how Anna Freud would "bristle at the suggestion that in obscure ways unknown to himself, Freud might have been dependent on his mother." Anna wrote, describing her grandmother: "She was . . . rather infantile, if not childish, excessively devoted and proud of her sons, as Jewish mothers are, and unintellectual to a degree that even the word does not fit.[12] She probably had a good stock of common sense of a very primitive kind, but she was neither dictatorial nor self-sufficient and until her very old age, rather charmingly vain of her appearance. My father suffered her as a good Jewish son, but 'dependent on her??'" (letter to Kurt Eissler, December 7, 1969, quoted in Roazen, 1993, p. 191). This letter, written by Freud's daughter when she herself was seventy-four years old, supplies three new pieces of information: Amalie was "rather infantile,"[13] she was not self-sufficient, and Freud "suffered" his mother. Anna must have meant that Amalie was not emotionally self-sufficient. She could not tolerate even brief separations from those she felt she needed, such as her daughter Dolfi or her son Sigmund on Sunday mornings.

What have we learned about Amalie Freud from these scanty reports? The emerging picture shows a woman with marked narcissistic traits, whose wishes no one dared to oppose. She must have inspired true terror, even in her psychoanalyst son. The family's submission to her desires and their worry over her reactions if she were contradicted indicate the fear inspired by her capacity for narcissistic rage. The Freud household and the extended family included many strong characters. None of them, however, dared to confront Amalie, regarding either her control over Dolfi or her demands. Perhaps they also sensed some fragility in her, believing that she could not tolerate contradiction. Freud described her in a letter to Martha Bernays as "a fragile woman both physically and spiritually" (July 23, 1884, in E. Freud et al., 1985, p. 99). This is the only published

12. Anna Freud's comment supports Sigmund's complaint to Silberstein, at the age of seventeen, that his mother cared only physically for him.
13. The word *infantile*, from the pen of a prominent child analyst, must not be taken lightly. Anna Freud is known for her precision with words.

statement in which Freud describes his mother in human terms, without idealization.

This thin but consistent portrayal of Amalie Nathansohn Freud raises the question: what were the consequences of her personality for the son who was her favorite?

One of Freud's most incontrovertible discoveries is the ambivalence of feelings in human relations: "Psycho-analysis shows that almost every intimate emotional relation between two people which lasts for some time—marriage, friendship, the relations between parents and children—contains a sediment of the feelings of aversion and hostility, which only escapes perception as a result of repression." He added in a footnote, "perhaps with the solitary exception of the relation of a mother to her son, which is based on narcissism, is not disturbed by subsequent rivalry, and is reinforced by a rudimentary attempt at sexual object-choice" (1921, p. 101).

In the *New Introductory Lectures* (1933), without referring directly to himself, Freud affirms emphatically: "A mother is only brought unlimited satisfaction by her relation to a son; this is altogether the most perfect, the most free from ambivalence of all human relationships. A mother can transfer to her son the ambition which she has been obliged to suppress in herself, and she can expect from him the satisfaction of all that has been left over in her of her masculinity complex" (p. 133). These striking words contradict clinical experience about the complexities of mother-son relations.

As for the ambivalence of the son, Freud knew it well from his analytic practice. From his analysis of the "Rat Man," for example, he had omitted several notes on his patient's mother from the published case report. One such note mentions a transferential dream of the Rat Man in which Freud's mother was dead. Freud interpreted: "Hasn't it ever occurred to you that if your mother died you would be freed from all conflicts, since you would be able to marry?" (1909, p. 283). Freud felt this freedom when his mother died twenty-one years later. In his notes on a later session, Freud wrote about the Rat Man's conflict regarding "his mother's old scheme for him to marry one of R's daughters": "He had no notion that it was in order to evade this conflict that he took flight into illness" (p. 292). On the next page Freud noted: "In recent days, he has stood up *manfully* against his mother's lamentation over his having spent 30 florins of pocket-money during the last month instead of 16" (p. 293, my italics).

How could Freud talk so idyllically about the relationship between a mother and her son when the Rat Man, according to Freud, had to escape into illness to avoid overt conflict with his mother? Was the limited manliness the Rat Man could show her nothing more than holding his ground over his spending allowance? Perhaps what Freud should have noted was the tremendous power mothers have over their sons and the fear sons have of defying and disappointing their mothers. This illustration is but one of many that highlight the discrepancy between Freud's clinical findings and his idealization of maternal love. The repression he postulated for "feelings of aversion and hostility" between children and parents must have been at work between his mother and himself. How can we imagine Freud's not feeling hostility toward a mother who demanded that the entire family suppress their sorrow at the death of a child? Could it really be said, as Freud did, that a mother's love for her son "is altogether the most perfect, the most free from ambivalence of all human relationships"?

It appears that Amalie Freud was a highly narcissistic and socially ambitious person who placed all her hopes on her firstborn son. She selected Sigmund at birth to be a great man so as to satisfy, as he said, "the ambition which she has been obliged to suppress in herself." She reveled in his glory and expressed her sense of ownership over him privately and publicly, even when he was an elderly man.

His mother's favor was based on narcissism. Her character structure tolerated no opposition, no resistance. She refused to accept the absence of a desired companion and communicated anxiety in crescendo to the family when Sigmund was late or Dolfi went out on an errand. She did not, however, let her son see that anxiety; she just "fussed" over him when he finally arrived. She was not inclined to attend to the feelings of others, particularly those who required comfort and consolation. Amalie did not want to deal with death. The family understood this and acquiesced. No one dared to confront her, not even her daughter Rosa when she lost her only child to suicide. Freud, however, had a need to idealize his mother. The letter to Martha describing Amalie's physical and spiritual fragility introduces at once his remorse for the comment: "I offer her the most sincere apologies in case I have not done justice to her. I do not know one action of hers in which she has followed her own moods or interests against the interests or happiness of one of her children" (quoted in E. Freud et al., 1985, p. 99). Nowhere is it more obvious than in this letter that Freud had internalized his mother's demand that she not be criticized even for a moment.

A most intriguing sentence in the Freud-Fliess correspondence may throw some light on Freud's difficulty in confronting his mother, even in his imagination. The cryptic remark refers to what happens when mothers "become shaky." In this awkward communication, dated July 7, 1899, Freud changes the subject abruptly after the opening sentence. After a remark about mothers in general he speaks about the recovery from illness of Fliess's pregnant wife and his mother-in-law. I cite the letter in German first because the translations differ and are highly problematic: "Unheimlich, wenn die Mütter wackeln, die einzigen, die noch zwischen uns und der Ablösung stehen. Indes schreibst Du, es geht besser, beiden Müttern also" (1985, p. 392). Masson, the most recent translator of the letters, renders it: "It is frightening when mothers become shaky; they stand between us and demise. But then you write things are better for both mothers" (1887–1904, p. 358). An earlier translation by Mosbacher and Strachey, edited by Marie Bonaparte, Anna Freud, and Ernst Kris, omits these sentences altogether (1954, p. 284).

Schur (1972) renders the first sentence: "[How] uncanny, when the mothers are shaky, the only ones who still stand between us and redemption" (p. 353). The Schur translation does justice to the way Freud used the word heimlich—uncanny—in the essay he wrote on the subject in 1919. It is true that the word can be rendered as "it is frightening." The meaning, however, is best clarified by Freud's own explanation. In his essay he defines heimlich in several ways. The last (ninth) definition is as follows: "The notion of something hidden and dangerous. . . . Thus: 'At times I feel like a man who walks in the night and believes in ghosts; every corner is heimlich and full of terrors for him'" (Klinger, 1877, 298). Thus the meaning of heimlich develops in the direction of ambivalence, until it finally coincides with its opposite, unheimlich (Freud, 1919, p. 226). Several pages later Freud connects unheimlich to death: "Many people experience the feeling in the highest degree in relation to death and the dead bodies, to return of the dead, and to spirits and ghosts" (p. 241).

There is a great distance between Masson's "demise" and Schur's "redemption." The term Ablösung is used to mean redemption only for legal or commercial matters. The more common usage refers to removal and replacement, whether of a sentry on duty by another soldier or of a government official by a successor (Langenscheidt, 1974, p. 21). This clarification makes the sentence read like this: "How uncanny, when mothers are shaky; they stand between us and [our] replacement."

By linking this version of such a cryptic remark, stimulated by the illnesses of two mothers, with Freud's lifelong convoluted relations with his mother, with death, and with God (who decreed that we should become dust again), it is possible to conclude that Freud must have been afraid, at a primary, infantile, unconscious level, of the deadly power in his mother's hands, filled, as he saw it, with the dust of death. In "The Uncanny" (1919) he links death to the religious wish for survival (p. 242) and attributes the origin of these feelings to the "omnipotence of thoughts" and the "old animistic conception of the universe" (p. 240). The very young Freud must have unconsciously linked mother, death, and God—hence his great astonishment at this mother's demonstration of the earth in her hands.

The beliefs linked to this incident were never analyzed and remained with him in many manifestations. This psychic link brings to focus Freud's difficulties in exploring his relationship with his mother during his self-analysis. Many authors have remarked that Freud was not able to analyze his pregenital issues, including his relationship with his mother. Anzieu (1986), in his exhaustive study of Freud's self-analysis, documents the point in detail.

The sentence referring to the illnesses of Fliess's mother and wife must have reflected unconscious feelings in Freud about Amalie's frequent illnesses during his childhood and youth. Freud's sister Anna, as mentioned earlier, said that Amalie became ill every Easter and would go to Roznau for three months, taking one child and leaving the others behind. Freud himself has documented in letters to Silberstein, Martha, and Fliess several occasions on which his mother suffered from a lung condition.

Freud's dream about his mother's death after the death of her father may have organized his complex feelings about her illnesses, their separations when she went to Roznau without him, and what happens to sons when mothers are "shaky." This is the other side of the liberation he experienced with her death—the fear of his own demise. Freud never wrote about this childhood fear.

His ambivalence toward his mother also appears in his own character. In spite of the fact that his mother obviously favored him and regardless of his assertion that favored sons are optimists, Freud was prone to pessimism. I have been unable to find any text in which Freud said he loved his mother or that she loved him—only that she favored him. The word love in connection with his mother appears only twice in his writings. The first time is in a letter to Silberstein in which he says that they should not love their mothers any less if they acknowledge their shortcomings in comparison with Frau Fluss. And Freud uses the word beloved when describing, as an adult, his anxiety dream about his mother's death.

Perhaps Anna Freud was right when she said that he suffered his mother and was not dependent on her. Amalie was not emotionally self-sufficient and depended on him for narcissistic supplies. The fact that she enjoyed "petting and making a fuss over him" did not make him less "terrified" of this overbearing, emotionally exhausting, willful mother, a mother who could see herself in her children but could not see them in their own right. She was especially incapable of attending to their emotional pain. She offered no consolation or protection. Instead, she demanded to be protected from any knowledge that would cause her pain or remove her from center stage. This

Amalie is a very different person from the "beloved" mother of the anxiety dream and drifts very close to the dangerous Fates. It is even possible to wonder whether the dream about his mother's death was, as Freud claimed about dreams in general, a wish-fulfillment, expressing the desire for the freedom he obtained only at the age of seventy-five when she actually died. After all, the dream itself was triggered by the death of his mother's father.

Anna Freud must also have been right when she called her grandmother "infantile." Amalie was efficient, clear in her wishes, socially integrated, and mundane in her involvements with people. She had a sense of humor and was not a complainer. But she was infantile in an emotional sense, in that her love objects became narcissistic objects, not full objects for mutuality of thoughts and feelings. This slant on her personality makes it possible to understand the great mystery of her marriage to a man forty years her senior. As mentioned earlier, Jakob Freud had an endless sense of fun and a capacity to enjoy the fantastic. Their mutual attraction must have been based on Amalie's enormous zest for life and his fantastic realities. She was the dominant member of the couple, the one who, like many Jewish women of the period, carried the weight of the household. The arrangement seems to have worked for them.

Sigmund, however, found himself, with his brilliant mind and his passionate disposition, at the center of his parents' great ambitions.[14] Much as they must have loved him in their own way, he felt, as he said to Martha in a rare moment of self-reve-

14. Freud wondered in The Interpretation of Dreams "Could this have been the source of my thirst for grandeur?" He was referring to two predictions about his life. The first was a peasant woman's prophecy to his mother that she had brought a great child into the world. In the second, an itinerant poet predicted to both of his parents that he would grow up to be a cabinet minister (1900, pp. 192–93).

lation, that he had never been a child. Jones noted that he did not like to talk to his children about his youth and early years.

His silence about his early years, his dislike of music, his inexperience with "oceanic feelings," his lack of a sense of orientation (Jones, 1955, p. 393), all point in the direction of unresolved pregenital issues that interfered with regression to primary states of closeness to the mother. More conflictual attitudes about loving women appear in the "extraordinary precautions he took to conceal a most innocent and momentary emotion of love in his adolescence," as well as in his secrecy about such private events as wedding anniversaries (p. 409).

Further evidence for the avoidance of the early mother is provided by Freud's response to Amalie's death. He did not undertake self-analysis as he did when his father died. Instead, he wrote a paper on "Female Sexuality" in February 1931, five months after her death. Discussing the girl's sexual development, he asks. "How does she find her way to the father? How, when, and why does she detach herself from her mother?" (1931, p. 225). He reflected: "Everything in the sphere of this first attachment to the mother seemed so difficult to grasp in analysis—so grey with age and shadowy and almost impossible to revivify—that it is as if it had succumbed to an especially inexorable repression" (p. 226). Freud reflected about the especially intimate relation between a girl's attachment to the mother and hysteria, suggesting that "In this dependence on the mother we have the germ of later paranoia in women. For this germ appears to be the surprising, yet regular, fear of being killed (? devoured) by the mother" (p. 227).

Finally, Freud was able to speak about the terrors of childhood by displacing them onto little girls, attributing the cause of such fears to the girl's hostility to the mother for the frustrations she imposes, though these are identical for children of both sexes: "It is plausible to assume that this fear corresponds to a hostility which develops in the child towards the mother in consequence of the manifold restrictions imposed by the latter in the course of training and bodily care and that the mechanism of projection is favoured by the early age of the child's psychical organization" (p. 227).

The source of the fear lies mostly in the child. Freud acknowledges, however, that there is another probable source: "It is impossible to say how often this fear of the mother is supported by an unconscious hostility on the mother's part which is sensed by the little girl" (p. 237). Thus, mothers can harbor hostility toward their girl children, while mothers of sons "have the most free from ambivalence of all human relationships."

Men, Freud said in a parenthesis, do fear being devoured by the father. He suspected that this was "the product of transformation of oral aggressivity directed to the mother" (p. 237). The only being exempted from the mother's hostility is the little boy. The conclusion seems to follow that Freud was compelled to create, while mourning his own mother, a theory that supported his denial of the possibility that his mother could hold hostile feelings toward him, much less kill or devour him. "That happens only to girls! Boys are not at risk of being devoured by their mothers," his defenses said to him. His infantile fear, the terrors of childhood, still whispered: "Mother made Julius disappear, maybe she killed him. Mother is dangerous."

Freud's written references to his mother are few, in remarkable disproportion to his references to his father (Mahl, 1985). However, he frequently wrote about mothers in general and about the mothers of those whom he admired. In his paper on Leonardo da Vinci (1910) he speaks explicitly about mothers and the origin of religion: "We recognize the roots of *the need for religion* in the parental complex; the almighty and just God, and

kindly Nature,[1] appear to us as grand sublimations of father and mother, or rather as revivals and restorations of the young child's ideas of them" (p. 123, my italics).

In this chapter I shall explore Freud's relations with his mother and with nature. In addition I shall examine his understanding of himself as a "natural scientist," a "godless medical man," and "a godless Jew," a man who did not need the "grand sublimations" of "God and kindly Nature."

Freud admired Leonardo's bold research, his modes of thought, and his rejection of authority. Leonardo, in Freud's opinion, "became the first modern natural scientist, . . . the first man since the Greeks to probe the secrets of nature[2] while re-

1. "Kindly Nature" has other characteristics, such as "terrifying" powers and an inclination to keep secrets.
2. Freud uses the word *nature* in both lower and uppercase. When he uses lowercase he seems to refer to natural phenomena. When he uses uppercase

lying solely on observation and his own judgment." Freud believed that Leonardo's rejection of authority stemmed from the lack of a father; thus he "escaped being intimidated by his father during his earliest childhood," and "nature once more becomes the *tender and kindly mother* who had nourished him" (pp. 122, 123, my italics). Freud doubted that one who was free of paternal authority could have remained religious, although he had to acknowledge that Leonardo "expresses his admiration for the Creator, the ultimate cause of all these noble secrets [of Nature]." Freud concluded: "But there is nothing which indicates that he wished to maintain any personal relation with this divine power" or expected any "*alleviation* from the goodness or grace of God" (pp. 124–25, my italics). The "alleviation" Leonardo did not expect, according to Freud, was relief from subjection to Ananke, "the laws of nature." He described Leonardo as an old man resigned to the human condition of being subjected to nature. I believe that here Freud was talking about himself.

Like Leonardo, Freud became a natural scientist deeply committed to uncovering the secrets of nature. In his autobiography (1925a) he described his decision "to become a medical student" at the age of seventeen, after attending the reading of an essay "On Nature" erroneously attributed to Goethe.[3] In *The Interpretation of Dreams* (1900), Freud refers to "Goethe's short but exquisitely written essay," confirming its impact on him (p. 411). The essay presents nature as enigmatic, alluring, unassailable, and reluctant to surrender her secrets:

he seems to refer to Nature as the governing principle of existing things. The spelling in the quotations follows in each case Freud's capitalization.

3. James Strachey comments (Freud 1925a, footnote 4, p. 8): "According to Pestalozzi (1956) the real author of the essay (written in 1780) was G. C. Tobbler, a Swiss writer. Goethe came across it half a century later, and, by a paramnesia, included it among his own works."

Nature! We are surrounded and embraced by her: powerless to separate ourselves from her and powerless to penetrate beyond her. Without asking or warning, she snatches us up into her circling dance, and whirls us on until we are tired[4] and drop from her arm. . . .

She is ever shaping new forms; what is, has never yet been; what has been, comes not again. Everything is new, and yet nought but the old. . . .

We live in her midst, and know her not. She is incessantly speaking to us, but betrays not her secret. We constantly act upon her, and yet have no power over her. . . . She is always building up and destroying; but her workshop is inaccessible.

Her life is in her children; but where is the mother? She is the only artist . . . always veiled under a certain softness. . . .

She loves herself, and her innumerable eyes and affections are fixed upon herself. . . .

She rejoices in illusion.[5] Whoso destroys it in himself and others, him she punishes with the sternest tyranny. Whoso follows her in faith, him she takes as a child to her bosom. . . .

To none is she altogether miserly; but she has her favourites, on whom she squanders much, and for whom she makes great sacrifices. Over greatness she spreads her shield. . . .

She is vanity of vanities; but not to us, to whom she has made herself of the greatest importance. . . .

We obey her laws even when we rebel against them; we

4. This is certainly no kindly nature!
5. Freud became insistent that human beings are not to rejoice in the greatest illusion of all, religion. The essay "On Nature" affirms, however, that nature rejoices in illusion.

work with her even when we desire to work against her. . . .
She is cunning, but for good ends; and it is best not to notice her tricks. (Goethe, 1869)

On May 1, 1873, shortly after the reading, Freud wrote to
Emil Fluss in Freiberg: "Today it is as certain and as fixed as any
human plan can be (any being can turn into a tower of Babel). . . . I have decided to be a Natural Scientist and herewith
release you from the promise to let me conduct all your law-
suits. It is no longer needed. I shall gain insight into the age-
old dossiers of Nature, perhaps even *eavesdrop* on her eternal
process, and share my findings with anyone who wants to
learn" (1969, p. 424). Freud's three references to the essay—
in the 1873 letter to Fluss, the Goethe dream at age forty-two,
and his biography (1925a, p. 8), written when he was sixty-
nine—confirm its profound significance for him.

The psychoanalytic reader can recognize in the description
of nature many aspects of Freud's relationship to his mother
and of Amalie Freud's character traits: we are "powerless to separate ourselves from her," "she snatches us up into her circling
dance," "she is ever shaping new forms [babies]," "she loves
herself, and her innumerable eyes and affections are fixed upon
herself," "over greatness she spreads her shield," "she is vanity
of vanities; but not to us, to whom she has made herself of the
greatest importance," "we obey her laws even when we rebel
against them; we work with her even when we desire to work
against her. . . . She is cunning, but for good ends; and it is best
not to notice her tricks." Freud must have recognized, if only
preconsciously, his predicament with his mother. The sudden
and deep commitment he developed after hearing the essay on
nature points to his readiness to find in the task of "eavesdropping on nature" a preexisting desire that he had not consciously
recognized. The desire must have been a wish to figure out the

riddle of his mother's behavior and his relationship with her. In the end, he failed. After astonishing discoveries about the human mind and the unconscious, the now elderly Freud posed to Marie Bonaparte "the great question that has never been answered and which I have not yet been able to answer, despite my thirty years of research into the feminine soul: . . . 'What do women want?'" (Jones, 1955, p. 421).

In Freud's mind, nature as a subject of scientific research was opposed to "kindly Nature," the "great sublimation" at "the roots of the need for religion." He concluded his essay on Leonardo with: "The protection against neurotic illness, which religion vouchsafes to those that believe in it, is easily explained: it [religious belief] removes their parental complex, on which the sense of guilt in individuals as well as in the whole human race depends, and disposes of it, while the unbeliever has to grapple with the problem on his own" (p. 123).[6]

What kind of unbeliever was Freud, and how did he deal with his "parental complex" when he renounced "God and kindly Nature" to devote his life to "eavesdropping" on nature? Freud's path led him away from the benefits religion offered to others: no parental couple would take care of him. Instead, it was he who aimed to penetrate and thus gain mastery over Mother-Nature and her secrets. He wished to be in charge, have control, and trust only his own judgment. He did not depend on help from nature. He saw himself as an active agent to whom even nature would yield. He would be the parent to himself. He would also defy what she delighted in: illusion. His life commitment was to live without illusions, particularly the religious illusion of "God and kindly Nature." Thus, he affirmed with defiant pride in *The Future of an Illusion*: "No, our science is no illusion" (1927, p. 56).

6. Strachey notes that the last sentence was added in 1919.

Nature, however, is far from kindly. Freud asserted that civilization provides a service to mankind by protecting it from the "superior powers of nature" (1927, p. 16). The functions of the gods include the power to "exorcise the terrors of nature" and to "reconcile men to the cruelty of Fate, particularly as it is shown in death" (p. 18). Children are especially vulnerable to fate: "The derivation of religious needs from the infant's helplessness and the longing for the father aroused by it seems to me incontrovertible, especially since the feeling is not simply prolonged from childhood days but is permanently sustained by fear of the superior power of Fate. I cannot think of any need in childhood as strong as the need for a father's protection" (1930a, p. 72). It is significant that the mother does not function as protector of the helpless infant and child against the terrors of nature, death in particular.

The analytic observer will note the correspondence between Freud's elaborations about nature and his relation to his mother. In exploring what is known about that relationship, I shall let Freud speak for himself. The quotations that follow are from different periods of his writings; they are presented chronologically, not in the order of their original appearance, but in reference to Freud's developmental life.

The first reference is to Freud at one year old. It appears in *The Interpretation of Dreams* in relation to the "Dishonesty Dream," which Freud had in May 1898. He barely analyzes this dream, which contains many allusions to early childhood events:

> The place was a mixture of a private sanatorium and several other institutions. A man servant appeared to summon me to an examination. I knew in the dream that something had been missed and that the examination was due to a suspicion that I had appropriated the missing article. Conscious of my innocence and of the fact that I held the position of a consultant in the establishment, I accompanied the servant

quietly. At the door we were met by another servant, who said, pointing to me: "Why have you brought him? He is a respectable person." I then went, unattended, into a large hall, with machines standing in it, which reminded me of an Inferno with its hellish instruments of punishment. Stretched out on one apparatus I saw one of my colleagues, who had every reason to take some notice of me; but he paid no attention. I was told I could go. But I could not find my hat and could not go after all. (1900, p. 336)

Freud believed that the dream thoughts contained a contradiction indicating that, after all, he was not an honest man (p. 337). A footnote links the dream directly to his early childhood:

In the complete analysis <of the dream> there was a reference to an event in my childhood, reached by the following chain of association. "Der Mohr hat seine Schuldigkeit getan, der Mohr *kann gehen*" ["The Moor has done his duty, the Moor *can go*." ‹a misquotation from Schiller's play *Fiesco*. . .][7] Then came a facetious conundrum: "How old was the Moor when he had done his duty?"—"One year old, because then he could go ['*gehen*'—both 'to go' and 'to walk']." (It appears that I came into this world with such a tangle of black hair that my young mother declared I was a little Moor.)[8] . . . The end of this dream also concealed a rejection of some melancholy thoughts about death: "I am far from having done my duty, so I must not go yet."—Birth and death were dealt with in it (1900, p. 337; square brackets Freud's, angled brackets mine).

7. The Moor in the play will do anything for money. In act 3, scene 4, the Moor, after doing what was requested of him, says: "Der Mohr hat seine Arbeit getan, der Mohr kann gehen." Freud unconsciously substituted "Schuldigkeit" (duty) for "Arbeit" (work) (Grinstein, 1980, p. 272).
8. Jones reports that to be born with a caul was "an event which was believed to ensure him future happiness and fame" (1953, p. 4).

The following events may be related to the dream: The names of Amalie Freud, her maid, and her child, Sigmund, were entered in the Register of Spa Visitors to Roznau on June 5, 1857 (Krüll, 1986, table 13). Freud was exactly thirteen months old and his mother was in the fifth month of her pregnancy with Julius. There were two servants in the dream, just as there were two women with him in the spa, one of them a "servant" whose respectability is affirmed while Freud's honesty is in question. One servant is dismissed, and Freud continues "unattended."

This may be a displacement of the question he was to wrestle with in October of the year of the dream. Who did in fact steal the zehners, the crime for which his nurse was dismissed, she or he? The dream reenacts her dismissal. The scene Freud saw in the hall reminded him of "an Inferno," a realm to which his nurse had introduced him. In the dream he does not obtain the attention he wants and is then dismissed. The fact that Amalie was at the time visibly pregnant and that she took the maid with her suggests that she must have delegated at least some of her son's care to the maid. He was told to go but he could not. In Schiller's play, when the Moor actually goes, he is embarking on the road to his death. This may relate to a condensation and telescoping of Julius's death and the other deaths in the family at the time, thus connecting birth and death, mother and nurse, and the "melancholic thoughts about death." In short, Freud's first written mention of his mother ends with his reflections about death.

His mother told an anecdote that Freud "had often heard repeated in my childhood": "At the time of my birth an old peasant-woman had prophesied to my proud mother that with her first-born child she had brought a great man into the world. . . . Could this have been the source of my thirst for grandeur?" (1900, p. 192). In a footnote to *The Interpretation of Dreams* added in 1911, Freud said: "I have found that people who know that they are preferred or favored by their mother give evidence in their lives of a peculiar self-reliance and unshakable optimism which often seem like heroic attributes and bring actual success to their possessors" (1900, p. 398).

In his essay on Goethe, Freud (1917) repeated the same idea, referring to the poet: "If a man has been his mother's undisputed darling he retains throughout life the triumphant feeling, the confidence in success, which not seldom brings actual success along with it. And Goethe might well have given some such heading to his autobiography as: 'My strength has its roots in my relationship to my mother'" (p. 156).

Freud's mother never deviated from her glorious vision of her firstborn. As an old woman close to death, Amalie Freud had a dream about Sigmund's death: "In her dream she was at Sigmund's funeral, and around his casket were arrayed the heads of state of the major European countries" (Roazen, 1975, p. 41). Roazen suggests that Amalie's reporting a dream of such a catastrophe reveals "her own yearnings which had been satisfied through her son's career" (p. 42). To this one could add Freud's own question: were his proud mother's reports "the source of my thirst for grandeur"? This becomes particularly poignant because Freud was terrified of dying before his mother. Jones reports that in May 1918, a few years before Amalie's dream, Freud wrote: "My Mother will be eighty-three this year and is no longer very strong. I sometimes think I shall feel a little freer when she dies, for the idea that she might have to be told that I have died is a terrifying thought" (1955, p. 196).

The next reference to his mother and to his nurse appears in the letter to Wilhelm Fliess of October 3, 1897, in which he reports on the awakening of his "libido toward matrem . . . on the occasion of a journey [by train] with her from Leipzig to Vienna, during which . . . there must have been an opportunity of seeing her *nudam*"[9] (1887–1904, p. 268). Freud's use of Latin to describe his naked mother to Fliess suggests the need to find affective distance from the discovery of his childhood libidinal attachment to her (Amati-Mehler et al., 1993).

On October 15, 1897, Freud reported to Fliess that his mother, in response to his questions about the nurse, had told him that at the time of his sister Anna's birth (December 31, 1858) the nurse was discovered to be "a thief, and all the shiny new kreutzers and zehners and all the toys that had been given to you were found in her possession. Your brother Philipp himself fetched the policemen; she then was given ten months in prison" (1887–1904, p. 271). Freud reported to Fliess having had a dream about "my taking money from the mother of a doctor." Using the information provided by his mother he concluded that "the correct interpretation is: I = she [the nurse], and the mother of the doctor equals my mother." Freud reflected that his misinterpretation of the dream indicated how far he was "from knowing she was a thief."

That a woman is sent to jail for stealing coins from a boy is plausible. It has, however, the features of a story made up to "help" Freud understand that she had wronged him. In *The Psychopathology of Everyday Life*, written four years after his letter to Fliess describing his mother's report of the incident, Freud said that the nurse had "carried out considerable thefts" (1901, p. 51). The letter continues with an insight into a previously unexplained recurrent memory from childhood: young Sigmund's desolation at the occasional and temporary disappearance of his mother: "I must have heard that the old woman had been locked up and therefore must have believed that my mother had been locked up too" (1887–1904, p. 272).

9. This trip took place in the winter of 1859. His sister Rosa was born on 21 March 1860. It is obvious that the naked mother was pregnant at the time.

A few lines later Freud recognized the universality of the childhood predicament he had just discovered in himself: "I have found, in my own case too, [the phenomenon of] being in love with my mother and jealous of my father. The switch from missing the nurse to being in love with the mother suggests the need to cover up the sad feelings of separation from the nurse with new feelings for the mother."

Freud found a rival for his mother's attention in his own half-brother Philipp, the man who had the power to make the nurse disappear. In a footnote added to *The Psychopathology of Everyday Life* in 1924, Freud described his childhood suspicions about Philipp's relationship with Amalie, who was only a few months older than he:

> The child of not yet three had understood that the little sister who had recently arrived [Anna] had grown inside his mother. He was very far from approving of this addition to the family, and was full of mistrust and anxiety that his mother's inside might conceal still more children. . . . [He] turned to his big brother, who (as is clear from other material) had taken his father's place as the child's rival. Beside the well-founded suspicion that his brother had had the lost nurse "boxed up," there was a further suspicion against him—namely that he had in some way introduced the recently born baby into his mother's inside. . . . His great satisfaction over his mother's slimness on her return can only be fully understood in the light of this deeper layer. (pp. 51–52)

These childhood miseries contrast with his report of his idyllic early childhood in the previously cited letter to the mayor of Příbor-Freiberg. No father is mentioned, neither Philipp nor Jakob. Mother and child are recalled as happy together in the retrospective idealization of the past.

The next explicit reference to his mother is the "very vivid" anxiety dream that Freud claims he had in his seventh or eighth year. In fact, we know that he was at least nine and a half because the dream was a response to the death of his maternal grandfather, on 3 October 1865. In the dream, Freud said: "I saw my beloved mother, with a peculiarly peaceful, sleeping expression on her features, being carried into the room by two (or three) people with birds' beaks and laid upon her bed" (1900, p. 583). His associations to this dream, as we have seen, evoked the falcons' heads illustration in the Philippson Bible, as well as the memory of a certain Philipp from whom Freud learned the vulgar term for copulation, vögeln. His associations reveal that: "the expression on my mother's features in the dream was copied from the view I had had of my grandfather[10] a few days before his death as he lay snoring in a coma. The interpretation . . . must therefore have been that my mother was dying. . . . I awoke in anxiety. . . . I remember that I suddenly grew calm when I saw my mother's face, as though I needed to be reassured that she was not dead" (1900, pp. 583–84).

A few lines later Freud denies that the anxiety had to do with his mother's dying. It was, he says, displaced from "sexual cravings." The associations, surprisingly, make no mention of his half-brother Philipp, who supposedly put babies into his mother's womb, certainly an act of "vögeln."

The next documents related to his mother appear in Freud's adolescent correspondence with Eduard Silberstein. The letter of September 4, 1872, contains the most explicit comments Freud ever made about his mother. He had been visiting Freiberg, his native town, as a guest of the Fluss family. His hostess made a tremendous impression on young Sigmund, and her

10. This is the only reference in Freud's writings to his maternal grandfather or to any member of his mother's immediate family.

daughter, Gisela, appealed to his heart. "My life in a large family circle . . . has sharpened my eye," he informed Silberstein. He described Frau Fluss:

> I am full of admiration for this woman whom none of her children can fully match.[11] . . .
>
> Would you believe that this woman from a middle class background, who once lived in fairly straitened circumstances, has acquired an education? . . . She has read a great deal, including the classics, and what she has not read she is conversant with. . . . She is even knowledgeable about politics. . . . She plays as large a part in running the business as Herr Fluss . . . and . . . all the factory workers obey her. . . . And you should see how she has brought up and continues to bring up her seven children. . . . I have never seen such superiority before. Other mothers—and why disguise the fact that our own are among them? We shan't love them the less for it—care only for the physical well-being of their sons; when it comes to their intellectual development the control is out of their hands. Frau Fluss knows no sphere that is beyond her influence. And you should see the love of the children for their parents.[12] . . . She punishes her children with looks and by withholding little favors, working on their sense of honor and not on their behinds. . . . A few days ago I had a terrible attack of toothache. . . . She cared for me as for her own child. . . . She fully appreciates that I need encouragement before I speak or bestir myself, and she never fails to give it. That is how her superiority shows itself: as she directs so I speak and come out of my shell. . . .
>
> She can never have been beautiful, but a witty, jaunty

11. It seems clear that in Freud's mind Eleanor Fluss was superior to Gisela.
12. The admiration seems to extend to Herr Fluss, who, unlike Jakob Freud, succeeded in his Freiberg business.

fire must always have sparkled in her eyes, as it does now. (pp. 17–18)

This description makes several comparative points with "other mothers," including Freud's own. Although Frau Fluss is not beautiful, her eyes sparkle; she is educated; she is involved with the family business and the world; she controls her children with her eyes without spanking them; she is caring, considerate, and knows how to draw people out. The extreme admiration the young Freud felt seems to have originated in his surprise that a woman so similar in background to Amalie and yet so different from his mother could exist and, of all places, in Freiberg. Amalie Freud spoke Galician Yiddish (T. Reik in Freeman, 1971, p. 80) and, as mentioned earlier, was preoccupied with her own beauty.

In 1873, Freud was planning to visit his half-brothers in England. Silberstein knew about the plan, but Freud admonished him to "tell no one about it. My mother would be the last person I would want to know until it is definitely settled" (p. 21). This may well reflect an adolescent's need to separate from his mother, but it certainly contrasts with Freud's pleasure in his interaction with Frau Fluss: "as she directs so I speak and come out of my shell."

The letter to Silberstein of February 27, 1875, refers to Amalie Freud's lung ailment, mentioned in two previous letters: "My mother is suffering from a protracted illness admitting of no quick improvement: infiltration of the lungs; she is bedridden and weak, and will be going to Roznau at the beginning of May. You will make her happy if you added some news of your mother."

Several years went by before Freud made another known reference to his mother. In September–October 1898 Freud had the dream of "The Three Fates," in which he found himself back in Vienna, returning without his wife after a holiday with her in Bosnia-Herzegovina (Anzieu, 1986, p. 362). The dream relates directly to his mother in his specific association to an event when he was six years old. Several authors have reinterpreted this dream. Here I attend exclusively to what pertains to Freud's mother, in the first part of the dream. Freud introduces the dream:

> Tired and hungry after a journey, I went to bed, and the major vital needs began to announce their presence in my sleep; I dreamt as follows: I went into a kitchen in search of some pudding. Three women were standing in it; one of them was a hostess of the inn and was twisting something about in her hand, as though she was making Knödel [dumplings]. She answered that I must wait till she was ready. (These were not definite spoken words.) I felt impatient and went off with a sense of injury. (1900, p. 204)

Freud's first association was to a novel he read at age thirteen. In it "the hero went mad and kept calling out the names of three women who had brought out the greatest happiness and sorrow into his life."[13]

The next association deserves careful scrutiny:

> In connection with the three women I thought of the three Fates who spin the destiny of man, and knew that one of the three women—the inn-hostess in the dream—was the mother who gives life, and furthermore (as in my own case)

13. Grinstein (1980) suggests that the novel is *Hypatia*, "by the Reverend Charles Kingsley, published in 1853," a book that "enjoyed tremendous popularity" in many languages (p. 179). It is a historically based romance taking place in fifth century Alexandria. The core of the story is about people's struggles and personal and ideological commitments to their conflicting religions: Christianity, Judaism, and paganism. There are several connections between women and religion.

gives the living creature its first nourishment. Love and hunger, I reflected, meet at a woman's breast.[14] . . . One of the Fates, then, was rubbing the palms of her hands together as though she was making dumplings: a queer occupation for a Fate, and one that cried out for an explanation. This was provided by another and earlier memory of my childhood. When I was six years old and was given my first lessons by my mother[15] I was expected to believe that we were all made of earth and must therefore return to earth. This did not suit me and I expressed doubts of the doctrine. My mother thereupon rubbed the palms of her hands together—just as she did in making dumplings, except that there was no dough between them—and showed me the brackish scales of *epidermis* produced by the friction as a proof that we were made of earth. My astonishment at this ocular demonstration knew no bounds and I acquiesced in the belief which I was later to hear expressed in the words: "Du bist der Natur einen Tod schuldig."[16] So they really were Fates that I found in the kitchen when I went into it—as I had so often done in my childhood when I was hungry, while my mother, standing by the fire, had admonished me that I must wait till dinner was ready. (1900, pp. 204–5)

Freud did not report the full analysis of this aspect of the dream "because the personal sacrifice demanded would be too great" (p. 206).

He continued with other associations and returned to the subject of death: "For one of the thoughts which my hunger introduced into the dream was this: `One should never neglect

14. This is Freud's only allusion to his knowledge that he was breast-fed.
15. It must have been the biblical lesson about the punishment of Adam and Eve after their sin.
16. As discussed in Chapter 6, Freud exchanged Nature for God in the quotation of 1 *Henry IV.*

an opportunity, but always take what one can even when it involves doing a small wrong. One should never neglect an opportunity, since life is short and death inevitable'" (p. 207).

Freud reported this dream to illustrate the emergence of infantile material. The dream has great significance for understanding his relationship with his mother. First, it is the only adult dream in which he reports an explicit association to his mother. Second, it is the only place in his entire body of writings in which he describes an actual interaction with his mother. Third, the dream locates his mother as the deliverer and teacher of God's terrible punishment: "You shall eat bread till you return to the ground, for out of it you were taken; you are dust, and to dust you shall return" (Genesis 3:19). Fourth, it connects God to feeding as Genesis does ("you shall eat bread"), to death, and to a Fate-mother-feeder who is a messenger of death.

In 1913, Freud established the connection between the Three Fates, death, and mother in his essay "The Theme of the Three Caskets"(1913a):

> What is represented here are the three inevitable relations a man has with a woman—the woman that bears him, the woman who is his mate and the woman that destroys him; or that they are *the three forms taken by the figure of the mother* in the course of a man's life—the mother herself, the beloved one who is chosen after her pattern, and lastly the Mother Earth who receives him once more. But it is in vain that an old man yearns for the love of woman as he had it first from his mother; the third of the Fates alone, the silent Goddess of Death, will take him into her arms. (p. 301, my italics)

Freud had referred to "wicked Fate" as early as 1873, in a letter to Emil Fluss on June 16: "That I sometimes have good and sometimes bad luck goes without saying: on such important occasions kind Providence and wicked Fate are invariably involved" (1960, p. 3). The words anticipated his writings about the illusory wish for a kind Providence and the "wickedness" of Fate. Together, they sound like the much later parental figures transformed in his theoretical writings into God and nature.

The dream of the Three Fates deals with other issues as well, but here I am focusing selectively on the significance of Freud's connection of death, God, and mother in his explicit associations to the dream. Reflecting on the same matter, Erikson concludes: "The associating dreamer thus puts nature, that is, a maternal figure, in the place of God, implying that a pact with a maternal woman is a pact—with death" (1964, p. 182). Anzieu (1968) writes that "Freud's replacement of God by Nature is indicative not so much of atheism as of a disturbing mother figure" (p. 365). Freud's own childhood memory and "astonishment" combined with the feeling of "owing" death to Nature rather than God suggests that at the age of six he was already struggling with the issue of death in connection with his mother and refusing to believe the decree of God and mother that he must return to dust. Furthermore, the memory is unmistakable evidence that, in his six-year-old mind, God, death, and mother gathered together in a single unity of intention: Mother Earth gladly waits to give us her deathly embrace. How else could he have interpreted his mother's instantaneous demonstration of God's will when she carried the dust of death in the same hands that fed the hungry Sigmund?

Many years later, on August 21, 1925, at the age of sixty-nine, Freud wrote to his nephew Samuel Freud in Manchester. Amalie, he said, had admitted at her birthday party on August 18 to being ninety years old. He also revealed the significant accommodations all the family members made to shield Amalie from news of death: "We made a secret of all the losses in the family . . . my daughter Sophie [died in 1920], her second son Heinerle [died in 1923], Teddy [the son of Freud's sister Mitzi] in Berlin [date of death unknown], Eli Bernays [died in 1923] and your parents [Emmanuel and Marie Freud]. . . . We had to use many precautions not to be discovered" (Clark, 1980, p. 481).

Once more, Freud links Amalie with death and the deceased. This time she requires a conspiracy of silence, literally an international family plot to keep her from knowing the obvious. What was the message she delivered about death that prompted the father of psychoanalysis—the unveiler of all secrets, the eavesdropper on Nature, the destroyer of illusions—to require that the family deny the death of members and pretend that they were still alive? The only person who could have assessed the answer to this question, Freud himself, opted to acquiesce rather than confront his mother.

Freud's last reference to his mother has to do with her own death. Gay (1988) cites a condolence letter Freud wrote to Max Eitingon when Eitingon's mother died that shows the weight Freud accorded to such an event: "The loss of a mother must be something quite remarkable, not to be compared with anything else, and awaken excitations that are hard to grasp" (p. 573). In August 1930 Freud visited his vacationing mother to congratulate her on her ninety-fifth birthday. He wrote to Samuel: "She is very weak, at times apathetic, but not out of her senses. She recognizes people and is accessible to all kinds of emotions." Amalie Freud returned to Vienna, where she died on September 12, 1930. Freud informed Samuel: "Mother died peacefully this morning in her bedroom in Vienna. The funeral may be on Saturday. At 95 she well deserved to be relieved" (Clark, 1980, p. 482).

Four days later he disclosed his feelings about her death in his response to Ferenczi's "beautiful words" of condolence: "It has affected me in a peculiar way, this great event. No pain, no grief, which probably can be explained by the special circumstances—her great age, my pity for her helplessness toward the end; at the same time a feeling of liberation, of release, which I think I also understand. I was not free to die as long as she was alive, and now I am. The values of life will somehow have changed noticeably in the deeper layers. I did not go to the funeral; Anna represented me there, too" (1960, p. 400).

It is striking to see that his mother's death gives Freud permission to die—the more so if one recalls that Amalie dreamt with pleasure about Sigmund's death and her joining with heads of state to mourn her famous son. Freud wrote to Jones on September 15, "It was always an abhorrent thought that she would learn of my death" (Gay, 1988, p. 573). Why was Freud so determined not to die before her? We know that Amalie refused to acknowledge the death of others as close to her as her granddaughter and great-grandson. Perhaps Freud feared his mother's rage if he died first. Perhaps he feared the ultimate oblivion of a death unmourned. Did Amalie forget Julius, her second-born son, as Sigmund never could? These thoughts must remain speculations. However, one well-documented fact remains: Freud brooded over his inevitable death and even predicted that he would suffer an early death. In his June 9, 1901, letter to Fliess, Freud comments about his past fears:

You have reminded me of that beautiful and difficult time [April 1894?] when I had reason to believe that I was close to the end of my life, and it was your confidence that kept me going.[17] . . . I have always lacked your optimism. It is certainly foolish to want to vanquish suffering and dying

17. Fliess fulfilled a function for Freud in his adult life similar to that which his nurse fulfilled for him in his early childhood. They both helped him to keep going.

from this world, as we do in our New Year's wishes; it was not for this that we did away with our dear Lord God only to lift them both from us and from our dear ones and dump them on strangers. (1887–1904, p. 443)

The connection between the fear of dying, inevitable death, and "our dear Lord God" is very clear. Freud implies that doing away with God will convince people that they are mortal. This is an amazing reversal of the biblical and graphic kitchen lesson with which his mother astonished him. The reasoning, once more, connects death, God, and mother.

The death of Freud's daughter Sophie, on January 25, 1920, opened again the issue of death and God. On February 4, 1920, Freud confided to Ferenczi: "For years I was prepared for the loss of my sons; now comes that of my daughter. Since I am the deepest of unbelievers, I have no one to accuse and know that there is no place where one can lodge an accusation" (Gay, 1988, p. 393). The world *accusation* has weight: it implies that Freud had the wish to accuse somebody of Sophie's death. His unbelief denies him a target for his anger.

When his grandson Heinerle died of miliary tuberculosis at the age of four and a half, Freud confided to Jones that this death "had killed something within him for good." It was the only time, Robert Hollitscher told Jones, "when Freud was known to shed tears." Freud later told Marie Bonaparte that "he had never been able to get fond of anyone since that misfortune" (Jones, 1957, p. 92).

Freud's need to avoid the pain of loss is documented in a much later episode described by his son Martin Freud (1957). When Martin's son was behaving foolishly, "Father said in effect that there was not the slightest sense in becoming attached to a boy who must sooner or later kill himself in dangerous escapades" (p. 193).

Freud was a healthy man who did not have any serious illness until his advanced sixties. He was, however, preoccupied with his health and his anticipation of death and was ever attentive to such physical symptoms as heart disrhythmias, intestinal disorders, constipation, and a Sunday morning indigestion that he attributed to a heavy dinner on Saturday. The condition "became a family joke" (Jones, 1955, p. 391). The analytic observer must question the connection between the visit to his mother and a digestive condition. "Throughout his life," Jones writes, "Freud was much preoccupied with thoughts about death. There were reflections of it and later on the wish for it. He often spoke and wrote about it to us, the burden of his remarks always being that he was growing old and had not long to live" (p. 392).

In 1929 Freud became Max Schur's patient. At their first meeting, Freud requested the truth and then said: "Promise me one more thing: that when the time comes you won't let me suffer unnecessarily." They shook hands on the promise (Schur, 1972, p. 408). When his actual death came near, on September 21, 1939, Freud took Schur's hand and said: "My dear Schur, you certainly remember our first talk. You promised me then not to forsake[18] me [mich nicht im Stiche zu lassen; the word can also be rendered as *abandon*] when my time comes. Now it is nothing but torture and makes no sense anymore" (Schur, 1972, p. 529). Schur gave him two heavy doses of morphine twelve hours apart. Freud died on September 23, 1939, at three in the morning.

In summary, Freud wrote very little about his mother. Most of what he wrote linked her to death and to God. There are still-unpublished letters to Martha Bernays that might add another dimension to this persistent link. It is possible that the same ter-

18. Promise and forsake are words found in the Psalms, frequently used in Hebrew Liturgy: "Do not forsake us Lord."

ror of dying before her or remembrance of her reactions to the death of others contributed to Freud's habitual internal censorship of thoughts and feelings about his mother. His public description portrayed Amalie as the proud, youthful mother of a "happy child," and he asserted that mothers' favorite sons are optimistic; yet he, the "goldener Sigi," was not an optimist. His first reported dream was an anxiety dream about his mother's death. He had a persistent fear of dying and found the idea of dying before his mother "terrifying." His mother's death, when he himself was elderly, gave him "a feeling of liberation, of release." In view of all these facts, it must be asked: What was the nature of his attachment to his mother? What gave him such a preoccupation with death? In what way did his mother imprison him? What was the nature of his liberation? Was his private experience of his mother comparable with his experience of nature, which, "without asking or warning, . . . snatches us up into her circling dance, and whirls us on until we are tired and drop from her arms"?

Freud's writings about his nurse, like those about his mother, are sparse but revealing. Some repetition of material already mentioned is unavoidable in order to demonstrate the nurse's significance in Freud's psychic life. The facts known so far are that she was with him until the birth of his sister Anna, when he lost her abruptly. She was accused of stealing money from Sigmund and sent to prison after Philipp reported her to the police. Sigmund never saw her again or talked about her until the time of his self-analysis following another major loss, the death of his father.

During the self-analysis Freud reported to Fliess in three letters his discoveries about the nurse. The letter of October 3, 1897, refers to Freud's exploration of his awakening sexuality. He must have written it after he spoke with his mother about the nurse because he used her words in describing the nurse as "an ugly, elderly, but clever woman" (p. 268). His description of her as "the prime originator" reveals that Sigmund's first conscious oedipal attachment was to his nurse, and only later did he form such an attachment to his mother. The language referring to the nurse is colloquial and direct, suggesting the reawakening of ego-syntonic emotions; the language referring to the mother is filtered through adult Latin expressions. Freud could not say "naked mother." A censor interposes the adult scientist between Sigmund the child and his memory of his childhood mother.

The description also reveals that the nurse offered him narcissistic enhancement and a connection to the invisible realms of heaven, hell, and God. Later in the same letter, Freud wrote again about the nurse. The words are moving and yet vague, suggesting cryptic meanings: "I have not yet grasped anything at all of the scenes themselves which lie at the bottom of the story. If they come [to light] and I succeed in solving my own hysteria, then I shall be grateful to the memory of the old woman who provided me at such an early age with the means for living and going on living. As you see, the old liking is breaking through again [die alte neigung schlagt heute wieder durch]" (p. 269).

Freud's "hysteria" and the "bottom" of his "story" relate directly to his nurse rather than to his mother. He says his early living depended on the "means" the nurse provided. What were those means, and why did she provide them when his own mother, father, and extended family were close by? The phrasing "the old liking" suggests in the original German (alte Neigung) affection for and attachment to the nurse. It alludes to a close involvement between nurse and child that alleviated Freud's childhood depression. They also indicate the sad fact that his conflicts with living and dying started in his toddler years. Yet while he associates his mother with death, he unconsciously links "living" and "going on living" with his nurse. Could it be that the nurse offered him an antidote to what he sensed and feared in his mother? There is no final answer to the question, but the evidence is there.

The next-day letter to Fliess, dated October 4, 1897, confirms that the nurse "was my teacher in sexual matters" and adds that she "complained because I was clumsy and unable to do anything" (p. 269). "A genuine ancient discovery" appeared in Freud's self-analysis: "she washed me in reddish water in which she had previously washed herself." Freud then described his stealing the zehners for her as compensation for bad treatment she had received: "Just as the old woman got money from me for her bad treatment, so today I get money for the bad treatment of my patients" (p. 269). Freud identifies directly with the nurse: they both treat their charges badly and get paid for it. In the next letter, dated October 15, 1897, Freud reports "a memory of my taking money from the mother of a doctor—that is, wrongfully. The correct interpretation is: I = she, and the mother of the doctor equals my mother" (p. 271).

Once more the manifest dream content interposes Freud the adult doctor between his mother and himself as a child. On the other hand, he remains close to his nurse in the memory of how he stole to help her. Freud seems to need the protection of his adult self in relation to his mother. In these memories, he cannot safely experience himself as a child with her. It is as though in his self-analysis Freud the adult shifts back and forth between allowing himself to experience his affection and his deep identification with his departed nurse and a strategy of distancing from his feelings toward his present-day mother. The next paragraph in the same section refers specifically to that point.

Early in this letter Freud talked about three days when he felt "tied up inside" and "really desolate." He asked his mother directly about the nurse to find "a few real points of reference." When Amalie commented on the nurse as old and clever, on her son's preaching God upon his return from the Catholic church, and on the nurse's conviction for stealing at the time when Anna was born, she made no reference to the relationship between Sigmund and the nurse. Freud, however, reflected: "I said to myself that if the old woman disappeared from my life so suddenly, it must be possible to demonstrate the impression this made on me" (p. 271). He found the answer in a scene which "in the course of twenty-five years has occasionally emerged in my conscious memory without my understanding it." "It" was the already mentioned scene of Freud "crying in despair" because he feared that his mother had also been sent to jail.

What this memory revealed only indirectly is how deeply he missed his nurse. Searching for his mother may have been his indirect way of continuing to search for the vanished nurse. According to Hardin (1985, 1987, 1988a, 1988b), who has studied the effect on attachment to the mother when a toddler loses a primary substitute caretaker, the loss is always traumatic. Hardin's main points are that (1) there is "estrangement from biological mothers and intolerance of intimate relationships in patients with an early history of surrogate mothering," and (2) in psychic experience "the image of the surrogate is screened by that of the mother"; the "biological mother play[s] a significant role in perpetuating the concealment of the surrogate" (1985, p. 628). Hardin suggests that Freud, like many of his patients in this situation, lost much of his "ability to adapt to his mother, to cue with her, because his involvement with the nurse maid resulted in some separation from his mother" (1987, p. 641). These observations help to explain Freud's difficulties in talking and writing about his mother and correlate with Anna Freud's assertion that Freud "suffered" his mother. Schur (1972) concurred indirectly with Anna's description: "Whatever Freud's early relationship to his mother had been, during her last years it was, at least outwardly, one of filial duty" (p. 423).

Freud does not seem to have attached emotionally to his mother in the way small children do. He tolerated her fussing over him but could not respond to it. Even his discovery of oedipal love is reported to Fliess in the October 15 letter in an indirect manner: "I have found in my own case, too, [the phenomenon of] being in love with my mother and jealous of my father" (p. 272).

Freud was a dutiful son. He was respectful toward his mother and obeyed her persistent demands for his presence, but it was at a price. As mentioned earlier, he came away from the Sunday visits with digestive upsets. The family joke about it noted the connection as well as the fact that it was not heavy meals that cause him dyspepsia.

To fully understand Freud's emotional distance from his mother, it is important to keep the whole picture in mind. It is true that Amalie was self-centered, difficult to live with and relate to. It is also a fact that during Sigmund's early years his mother was confronted with overwhelming changes and losses: she lost her immediate family in Vienna by moving to Freiberg and acquired a new and very complex family—two stepsons and a daughter-in-law of her own age, and a year-old step-grandson—before she had become a mother herself. The family lived very close to each other, and Amalie, at the age of twenty, must have had to learn to deal with an entire group whose interactions preceded her appearance. She became pregnant with Sigmund immediately after her marriage, and in the seventh month of her pregnancy her father-in-law died. Freud was born in early May 1856. Amalie became pregnant again in January 1857, when Sigmund was eight months old. Her favorite brother, Julius, died in March 1858, five months after the birth of the baby named after him; baby Julius died of an acute intestinal infection exactly a month later, when Amalie was in the first month of her pregnancy with Anna. It was during this terrible period, filled with birth and death, that Sigmund was being cared for by his nurse. Soon after Anna was born, on the last day of December 1858, the nurse was dismissed, never to be seen again. Amalie could not have been fully available to her spirited first-born, caught, as she was, in major life changes, pregnancies, and the consecutive loss of three major family figures. Freud's maternal attachment must have been restricted by her emotional and physical condition. The summary gives a context to Freud's assertion that he had never been a child and that the nurse provided him with the means to go on living. It also highlights the depth of his loss after her departure.

Seventy-three years later, when his mother died, Freud was the only member of the immediate family who did not attend her funeral. He sent his favorite daughter, Anna, to represent him. Hardin (1988a) considers Freud's behavior a parapraxis, offering his mother a surrogate mourner who "could grieve without the constraints her father experienced because of his lifelong alienation from her grandmother" (p. 85).

In the final chapter I shall discuss the ways that Freud's relationships with his mother, his nurse, and his father affected his lack of belief in God and "kind Providence."

chapter twelve
Why Did Freud Reject God?
a psychodynamic interpretation

The terrifying impression of helplessness in childhood aroused the need for protection—for protection through love—which was provided by the father. Freud, 1927, p. 30

A personal God is, psychologically, nothing other than an exalted father. . . . The almighty and just God, and kindly Na-

ture, appear to us as grand sublimations of father and mother, or rather as revivals and restorations of the young child's ideas of them. Freud, 1910, p. 123, my emphasis

Freud's groundbreaking and strikingly original analysis of the psychodynamics of religious beliefs and emotions is a lasting contribution to the study of religion. By linking the representations of God to the paternal figure and connecting religious feelings to experiences and attachment to the father, Freud affirmed that the developmental process conditions religious belief. In this chapter I shall apply Freud's insights to his own unbelief, for the psychic rules that facilitate belief must also condition unbelief (Rizzuto, 1979, pp. 201–3).

Freud encountered God when he was a small child, scarcely able to understand the meaning of the word. He responded to the encounter with childish and enthusiastic imitation of the preaching he had heard in church. The early excitement of telling "all about the Almighty" (1887–1904, p. 271) finds its counterpoint in the injunction of the mature Freud urging human beings to give up their childish clinging to God. How did Sigmund, the toddler preacher, become Freud, the man for whom religious experience was a "closed book"?

Freud theorizes that the child forms the representation of God early in life by "exalting" the earliest caretakers, most specifically the father, to the rank of God. Sigmund's visits to the Catholic church with his nurse afforded him multiple encounters with an invisible God, explicitly mentioned in the preaching and ceremonies. His playful imitation of the priest suggests how impressed he was with what he saw and heard. Small as he was, Sigmund must have listened very attentively and must have found the preaching worth repeating. He identified with the preacher and with those attending the service.

The experience must have left its psychic mark. The analyst must infer that two-year-old Sigmund formed a very early representation of the invisible God by linking the word *God* to the representation of visible and experiential objects. Thus "God" acquired its first meaning for his infantile discourse and emotional investment. The adult Freud affirmed that the father is always the early object to become "exalted" and "sublimated" into a divine being. Was this the case with him? The attempt to answer this question poses great difficulties in view of the scanty biographical data. The researcher, however, may extrapolate from existing psychoanalytic knowledge and from Freud's own statements.

Freud postulated that the child's helplessness and the adult's acknowledgment of his own helplessness prompt a defensive reaction, a search for protection, that leads to "the formation of religion." He claimed that "in this function [of protection] the mother is soon replaced by the father" (1927, p. 24). The choice of the mother as protector indicates an "anaclitic object choice," which prefers "objects which ensure the satisfaction of . . . [narcissistic] needs" (pp. 23–24). Research on the formation of the God representation demonstrates the great significance of the maternal object for the small child's conception of God. Positive attachment resulting from adequate maternal satisfaction of the small child's narcissistic and relational needs facilitates the later formation of an ego-syntonic God representation based on the emotional characteristics of the mother-child affective exchanges (Rizzuto, 1979, pp. 177–211). This early attachment, if positive, creates the psychic conditions of trust that later facilitate religious belief in God. Conversely, profound disturbances in emotional attachment between mother and child interfere with the capacity to entrust oneself to others and the later formation of an ego-syntonic God representation deserving belief. The research demonstrated that the maternal figure provides the emotional and representational psychic conditions and material for the formation of the first representation of God.

In his theories, Freud soon discarded the maternal component in connection with the need for religion and God: "the mother is soon replaced by the stronger father" (p. 24). The father became for Freud the only significant source to form the God representation. The word *replace* does not do justice to Freud's own theories about unconscious processes. Object representations and the affective responses of object relations cannot be "replaced." Once a representation has been formed, it continues to influence the psychic life of the individual and his relationships with people, unconsciously and consciously. An object representation can be transformed only as a process of reorganization of memory (1887–1904, p. 207). Freud acknowledged the lasting power of the object representations originating in the relationship with the first objects: "All of his [the child's] later choices of friendships and love follow upon

the basis of the memory-traces left behind by these first pro-
totypes . . . the imagos—no longer remembered" (1914b,
p. 243).

The libidinal attachment to objects may shift, but the earlier
memories of the objects never disappear from the psychic field.
They remain ever-present as preconscious or unconscious representational memories exercising a silent or overt influence in
unconscious and conscious processes. The God representation
"created" by the child to flesh out the invisible God presented
by adults is shaped by the same psychic laws that regulate the
representational transformation of the primary objects. Two-
year-old Sigmund must have found in the early representation
of—in his case—maternal objects the bases for trust or mistrust
that were to color his early formation and later transformation
of his God representation.

What primary object did young Sigmund link to his playful, preachable God? There is no direct answer to this question.
The theoretical response is complex because Freud had two
mother figures, a father, and two half-brothers who were his
mother's contemporaries. The two mothers were in charge of
the bodily ministrations that Freud saw as the foundation for
anaclitic attachment. The interactions involved in the physical
care of the infant and toddler create the essential conditions for
the formation of the child's sense of self and of the first object
representations.

Freud's own writings document that he perceived his nurse
and not his mother as the caretaker. Although Sigmund was his
mother's firstborn, he was her central focus for only eight
months, at which point she became pregnant with Julius.
Freud's writings never mention any physical connection between himself and his mother except a passing and impersonal
sentence about his having been breast-fed. The two adjectives
he used to describe her, "young" and "beautiful," do not refer

to any concrete physical attribute that suggest their bodily contact. He left no personal depiction of his mother as he did with his father. When he recognized his childhood sexual excitement about her he had to resort to Latin—a dead academic and adult language, which he first heard in church with his nurse— to describe her. All these facts suggest Freud's emotional distance from his mother even as a small child.

The situation with the nurse was very different. She was the "primary originator" who initiated him in "sexual matters," washed him "in reddish water in which she had previously washed herself," complained about his being "clumsy and unable to do anything," reprimanded him if he "failed to reach the required standards of cleanliness," and instilled in him "a high opinion" of his capacities. She also told him about God, heaven, and hell. Freud's descriptions of her speak of bathing, toilet ministrations, shared tasks, and conversational involvement. Freud described the consequences of such intimate contact: "A child's intercourse with anyone responsible for his care affords him an unending source of sexual excitation and satisfaction from his erotogenic zones. This is especially so since the person in charge of him, who, after all, is as a rule his mother, [1] herself regards him with feelings that are derived from her own sexual life: she strokes him, kisses him, rocks him and quite clearly treats him as a substitute for a complete sexual object" (1905b, p. 223). In Freud's case, as he recognized in his self-analysis, the nurse became his primary sexual object. His mother came to his oedipal awareness later, after the nurse's disappearance. Freud uses colloquial and direct language in talking to Fliess about his nurse, suggesting ego-syntonic affects. He himself drew an inference in his self-analysis: "It is reason-

1. The expression "as a rule" implies exceptions. Perhaps Freud was alluding to himself.

able to suppose that the child loved the old woman" (1900, p. 248). He never said he loved his mother.

Freud's early psychic living depended on the "means" the nurse provided. The words speak of childhood depression and reveal that Freud's problems with living and dying started in his toddler years. He unconsciously connected "living" and "going on living" with his nurse, while he linked his mother to death. Did he feel that the nurse offered him the counterpart of a death he sensed and feared in his mother? There is no final answer to the question, but the fact remains that when he challenged the biblical story about turning to dust, his mother showed him that she had the dust of death in her hands. Freud's misquotation of the 1 *Henry IV* line when he was an adult strongly suggests the unconscious representational admixing in his mind of mother, nature, and God. They must also be linked to his earliest representations of God: the life-giving and preachable representation of God was connected to the nurse; an owed death connected another representation of God to his mother.

Freud's overt identification with his nurse and distancing from his mother are confirmed by his dream about getting money "for the bad treatment of my patients" (1887–1904, p. 269). The identification with the nurse is direct: they both treat their charges badly and get paid for it. In his letter to Fliess on October 15, 1897, Freud made the equation "I = she [the nurse], and the mother of the doctor equals my mother" (p. 271). It is as though in his self-analysis, Freud the adult was rediscovering his affection for the nurse and his identification with her, and on the other hand, the need to keep his mother distant. This suggests a fear of regressing to childhood experiences with the mother.

Freud recalled his early childhood experience of loss and separation, which had left him vulnerable to similar experiences later. Two instances illustrate this point. The first involved his falling in love with Gisela during his first visit to Freiberg at age seventeen: "It was my first calf-love and sufficiently intense, but I kept it completely secret. After a few days the girl went off to her school . . . and it was this separation after such a short acquaintance that brought my longings to a really high pitch. I passed many hours in solitary walks through the lovely woods" (1899, p. 313).

The second instance was his acute and bewildered reaction to the feared loss of his fiancée Martha to her friend Fritz Wahle, whom Freud viewed as a potential rival. He tormented her with his doubts about her love and his fear that he could not retain her affection. Freud believed that Wahle told her to give him up. "This aroused an appalling dread. Then, her letter assuring Fritz that their friendship was quite unchanged drove him into a frantic state in which he wandered through the streets for hours in the night" (Jones, 1953, p. 113). Freud's desperate nocturnal wanderings echo the "despair" in his earlier search for his mother after the nurse's disappearance. The intensity of his childhood despair, and its repetition in facing the impending loss of another beloved woman suggest that the nurse's disappearance represents for him "the terrifying impression of helplessness in childhood" that calls for the protection of the father.

Freud's relationship with his mother suffered no final disruption, even though she left him many times for a period of weeks to go to Roznau. There is no indication that Freud was affected by these separations. Amalie, on the other hand, needed Sigmund to stay close when she wanted him. From the beginning he was her favorite. She exalted him from the moment of his birth to the condition of a golden child. Such preference had its risks, as demonstrated by Dolfi's wasted life spent in caring for her mother. Unlike Dolfi, Sigmund found in his secret and restrained defiance a way of handling his "clinging" and domineering mother. He remained a responsible son who kept his emotional distance while performing his "filial duty" (Schur, 1972, p. 423).

The examination of Freud's relationships with his mother and his nurse indicates that Freud's primary attachment was to his nurse. He apparently did not form an emotional attachment to a mother who, at least in his unconscious perception, demanded death. This conclusion coincides with Hardin's finding of "estrangement from biological mothers and intolerance of intimate relationships in patients with an early history of surrogate mothering" (1985, p. 628).

What contribution did mother and nurse make to Freud's first inchoate conception of God? A meaningful response may be found in Freud's own writings. Amalie Freud had an intensely traumatic life during Freud's first three years and must have been unable to be fully attentive to his emotional needs. Chapters 10 and 11 suggest that her attachment to him was of a narcissistic nature. These experiences may have contributed to an aspect of the God representation that prompted Freud to wish to be liberated from a possessive, demanding, and emotionally unavailable mother-God. Freud must have felt the burden of being the special child for his mother. He said, after all, that he had "never been a child." Freud's childhood situation gives psychodynamic meaning to his feelings of "liberation, of release" and the absence of "pain" and "grief" upon her death. It also gives meaning to Freud's absence from her funeral—it was the first time he could afford not to be there when she wanted him to.

Freud's attachment to the nurse, by contrast, was deep and lasting. It contributed to his sense of grandeur, stimulated his sexuality, contributed to his sense of self, and brought him to the realm of the divine. The attachment persisted as an "old liking" when he was in his forties.

We can thus formulate a hypothesis about the formation of Freud's earliest God representation. In the same way that he had two very different mothers, he seems to have formed a composite representation of mother-God. One, originating in his relationship with his mother, was a God linked to death: it was colored by the early deaths in the family and was consolidated during his latency by the graphic demonstration of deadly dust in her hands. Such God representation must have already inspired in Freud the disbelief that prompted him to question his mother about God's imposed death. His mother's intense need for him may have contributed to his wish to liberate himself from a possessive, demanding, and emotionally unavailable God-mother representation.

The God of imitational excited preaching found its affective source in the bodily ministrations of the nurse, their spirited relationship, their conversations about religion, and their joint visits to the church. That childish but emotionally exciting God won Sigmund's approval. The nurse's abrupt and shameful departure brought him to the brink of despair. He was now left alone with his mother, who was nursing newborn Anna. Sigmund's "means for living and going on living" had disappeared. The phrasing indicates how lost he felt without his nurse's nurturance. He might also have feared death from his mother, who, after all, had not provided Julius with the "means for living and going on living." It was at that point of his brief and already painful life of loss and separation that he experienced the "terrifying helplessness of childhood." He had now a great need for a protector. Sigmund did not know how to defend "against the superior powers of Nature" (Nature-mother) in facing a life that must have been "hard to bear." He must have felt that his pain came from the desertion of his nurse and the God linked to her: "We naturally feel hurt that a just God and a kindly providence do not protect us better from such influences

[fate] during the most defenseless period of our lives" (1910, pp. 136–37).

Furthermore, the loss of the nurse must have been complicated by the concurrent loss of the Czech language they shared in life and in church. Amati-Mehler, Argentieri, and Canestri (1993) have demonstrated that language encodes human relations and their affects. When the language is lost, the memories and emotions it encoded may become segregated from conscious access and not be available for psychic integration. Indeed, the nurse disappeared from Freud's conscious recollection until the time of his self-analysis. The exciting component of his God representation must have suffered a deep blow with her disappearance. Sigmund was left bereft of supports— nurse, church, and God—feeling "hurt" and vulnerable in the hands of his mother and those aspects of the God representation linked to her and to death. His mother's preference for him could not assuage the terrors of his childhood situation.

It is fair to assume that, mourning and desolate, Sigmund turned to his lighthearted father for protection and help. The attachment became deep and lasting, coloring every aspect of Freud's life to the last moment (Schur, 1972). The autobiographical account of "Screen Memories" presents Freud's first reported memory of his relationship with his father: "I believe now that I was never free from a longing for the beautiful woods near our home, in which (as one of my memories tells me) I used to run off from my father, almost before I had learnt to walk" (1899, pp. 312–13). The memory discloses affectionate intimacy and playfulness between father and small child, but also a wish for distance and separation. Jakob, with his imposing physical figure, his jocular disposition, and his expressed love for Sigmund, could offer the boy a feeling of security. He needed that feeling because, in his bereavement, he was searching for someone to provide him with the means "to go on living." He also needed to find some new shape for a "God" that had let him down so cruelly. He could have said about himself, at that point in his life, what he said in 1927 about all human beings: "As we already know, the terrifying impression of helplessness in childhood aroused the need for protection—for protection through love—which was provided by the father; and the recognition that this helplessness lasts throughout life made it necessary to cling to the existence of the father, but this time a more powerful one. Thus the benevolent rule of a divine Providence allays our fear of the dangers of life" (1927, p. 30).

Freud suggests that the helpless child connects the father with the gods who are supposed to "exorcise the terrors of nature" (p. 18). When the protection through love could not come from his nurse or his mother, Freud, in his desperate search for a protector, must have found in Jakob a keeper who was already there. At this moment of Sigmund's development Jakob became an optimal object to modify and update his preexisting God representation into a great and powerful father-God.

Soon, Jakob's reassuring presence and the joyful and carefree sharing between the small child and the impressive father changed for the worse. The "catastrophe" showed Sigmund's father losing "all his means," unable to support the family, and forcing them to "move to a large town" where they lived in poverty (1899, p. 312). Meanwhile, Jakob and his wife continued bringing new babies into the family. Sigmund could no longer blame Philipp for placing babies in his mother's womb; he now knew that his father was responsible for siring the new infants of whom Sigmund disapproved, as he described so graphically when his sister Anna was born.

Freud did not lose his father in the way he had lost the nurse. He did, however, lose the admired man who could be "exalted" into God himself. The Jakob of Vienna could not sustain the status of the respected merchant of Freiberg. Sigmund, who was now entering latency, had to drastically reassess his beloved father. Freud, as mentioned earlier, described that moment of childhood transformation for all boys, but he seems to be describing himself when he says that the child "cannot fail now to make discoveries which undermine his original opinion of his father and which expedite his detachment from his first ideal. He finds that his father is no longer the mightiest, wisest and richest of beings; he grows dissatisfied with him, he learns to criticize him and to estimate his place in society; and then, as a rule, *he makes him pay heavily for the disappointment* that has been caused by him" (1914b, p. 244, my italics). Freud's suffering and the disruption of his admiration for his father during the "long and difficult years" that followed the "catastrophe" were intense. He explicitly said that there was nothing in those years "worth remembering."

When Sigmund was in latency, his father started teaching him to read and write and introduced him to the God of Israel as presented in the Philippson Bible. Sigmund became deeply involved in the "biblical story," which left a lasting impression on him. Father and child must have discovered together the excitement of contemplating the lives and the lands of the exotic biblical characters. They no doubt experienced a deep pleasure in their shared study. Sigmund must have found admirable, perhaps awesome, his father's profound knowledge of the book and his "deep wisdom" in this area. Jakob, the respectable and impressive man of the Bible, was teaching him about the great God of Israel. It was Sigmund's second opportunity to learn about the Almighty.

During their common study Sigmund may have experienced the same rush of emotion that the adult Freud believed the Israelites, as remote descendants of the early horde, experienced in facing the return of a "single god" who had all power:

> The first effect of meeting the being who had so long been missed and longed for was overwhelming and was like the traditional description of the law-giving from Mount Sinai. Admiration, awe and thankfulness for having found grace in his eyes—the religion of Moses knew none but these positive feelings towards the father-god. The conviction of his irresistibility, the submission to his will, could not have been more unquestioning in the helpless and intimidated son of the father of the horde—indeed those feelings only become fully intelligible when they are transported into the primitive and infantile setting. A child's emotional impulses are intensely and inexhaustibly deep to a degree quite other than those of the adult; only religious ecstasy can bring them back. A rapture of devotion to God was thus the first reaction to the return of the great father. (1939, pp. 133–34)

Did Sigmund experience "a rapture of devotion" when presented with the God of Israel? Did he consciously link this impressive God to the "God Almighty" of his nurse? There is no answer. Freud left no documentation of his reaction to the biblical teachings. But Freud's theories of religious development indicate that at the time of the resolution of the Oedipus complex the child renounces libidinal attachment to the parents and identifies with the parent of the same sex. The child then finds, by sublimating the paternal representation into a God, the possibility of loving the father in displacement through religious fervor (1918, pp. 114–15). In Freud's case evidence exists that he identified with many significant aspects of his father's personality. Like Jakob, Sigmund was very kind and playful with children, illustrated his theories with stories, loved jokes, and could be, at times, quite lighthearted in his ironic remarks. Moreover, he acquired the "vice" of smoking from his father. In short, he identified with those aspects of his father that he continued to love and admire to the end of his father's life.

Freud described his disappointment in his father only through the disclosure of his deep ambivalence about him. His complaints about his father's failure were disguised in his cryptobiography "Screen Memories" (1899) as the comments of a patient. He had good reason to be restrained because his father's order not to criticize him had been explicit and without appeal. This prohibition did not diminish Freud's special role in the family. His mother and father delegated to him the supervision of his sisters' readings and gave him an authoritative voice in the "family council." Furthermore, he was entrusted at the age of ten with finding a name for his father's new son. Sigmund selected the name of Alexander in the conscious hope of giving his brother a model of courage, to induce him not to be like their father.

As we have seen, two months before the birth of Alexander, in April 1866, the *Neue Freie Presse* had reported the trial and conviction of Joseph Freud, Sigmund's favorite uncle, for dealing in counterfeit rubles. The shame felt by the family must have been deep and difficult to bear. For Sigmund, being disappointed by another paternal model must have caused a new and deeper injury. The men in the family could offer neither protection nor integrity.

Finally, it was around this time that Jakob described to Freud his submissive response to the Christian who knocked off his cap in the street. Sigmund's violent internal reaction to this deflated picture of his father immediately brought identification with Hannibal, whose father, Hamilcar Barca, made his son swear revenge on the offending Romans. Sigmund wanted a different father, one who could protect him and make him proud to be his son. There was no reason for pride in Jakob at this period in Freud's development, nothing the father could do to restore his early image. Once more, now at the end of his latency years, Sigmund was without protection or consolation, emotionally alone, in charge of himself. He had no father to idealize or "exalt" into a God. No other male was available to him for pride or identification. He was alone in the world while he was himself idealized by his parents. He had already begun to replace his father as the person in charge of the family. Later, from his late twenties to the marriage of his sisters and the death of his parents, he would be the main provider for the whole family. Like the biblical Joseph, Freud fed his "starving" siblings.

Freud's aloneness was paradoxical. His mother had a profound need for his presence, his success, his being there for her. His father, in his more subdued manner, also favored him and unabashedly expressed his deep love for him. Sigmund was therefore surrounded by their great affection and attachment to him, yet he felt perpetually constrained to be a caretaker, thus forgoing the freedom of childhood. A reversal of idealizations occurred in which the father progressively idealized the son and delegated the paternal duties to him. This description leads to the conclusion that Freud was what is now called a parentified child. To an ordinary observer, Freud must have appeared to be well cared for by his parents. At the psychic level, however, Freud could not count on them but had to be there to respond to their need for him.

In the end, he did become the father—and even mother—of the whole family. There was no one who could offer him consolation. Two episodes from different periods of his life throw some light on this point. The first reveals how early in life Freud experienced the reversal of roles: "It appears that when I was two years old I still occasionally *wetted the bed*, and when I was reproached for this I *consoled* my father by promising to buy him a nice *new red* bed in N., the nearest town of any size" (1900, p. 216). This story happened in the days when Sigmund thought that Jakob was a great man; yet, he still felt the need to console and compensate his father with an action that only an adult can carry out. The second circumstance that highlights Freud's unmet needs is his amazement during adolescence at the personal interest of Frau Fluss in getting him to express his ideas, to come out of his "shell." The experience led him to complain to Silberstein about "our mothers" because they did not offer the same support.

Adolescent Transformation of the God Representation

Blos (1979) describes the developmental task of adolescence as "the disengagement of libidinal and aggressive cathexes from the internalized infantile love and hate objects" (p. 179). At the end of adolescence, the transformations brought about by separation from the internal objects permit the establishment of more integrated self and object representations as the foundation of character structure. The adolescent Freud documented aspects of this transformational process in his correspondence with Eduard Silberstein. The two friends elected to impersonate the two dogs in Cervantes's story that narrated the betrayal of parents and owners. As typical adolescents, Freud and Silberstein must have found in the dogs' complaints an acceptable displacement of their own barely expressed grief about their parents. In the late part of adolescence, Freud seemed to be at sea about career opportunities until he heard the lecture "On Nature." The intensity of his reaction, the "recognition" of what he wanted to do, and his lasting commitment suggest that the description of nature became an organizing metaphor for unconscious feelings and sustaining adolescent ego ideals. The early unconscious connection mother-nature was there waiting for this recognition.

What happened during adolescence to Freud's earlier internal representation of his parents and of God in its multilayered structure of mother-nature-God-nurse-father? Little is known about his relationship with his parents during this period. There is no indication of overt adolescent rebelliousness, with the exception of his complaints about the meals on religious holidays and mothers who attend only to their children's physical needs. In this, as in many other realms of his self-disclosure, he fulfilled his wish to keep his biographers wondering. His wrestling with God, however, is well documented in the letters to Silberstein and Fluss. As we have seen, Freud was studying the Old Testament at the Gymnasium and learning the Jewish traditions and prayers. He identified with Job in describing his powerlessness to make light and with God by giving himself the life-giving and life-taking position of God in relation to the defunct school newspaper—a Jew knew there was no greater blasphemy than this. The new and great reversal of roles, full of playful irreverence, suggests displacement, reaction formation, and sublimation in the process of transforming parental, self, object, and God representations. It signals what Freud had said earlier to Silberstein: that he had lost his childhood fear of the gods and of their "envy." This transformation requires a reevaluation of parents and recognition of their limited power over destiny. It also presupposes a shift in the God representation from a fear-inspiring God to one that cannot harm.

God had lost his power for Freud. The reversal of roles with his actual parents appeared now in the reversal of roles with God. God is irrelevant, Sigmund is in charge. The adolescent Freud says nothing about his father's incompetence and failure. The forbidden criticism of the father remains ego-syntonic.

The "exalted" father-God receives an emotionally tamed but firm and lasting demotion. God is ineffective and has to accept overt lighthearted blasphemy. Freud suggests God's ineffectiveness in his ironic suggestion to his friends Fluss and Silberstein that they pray just in case something should happen. Freud was teasing them and God. At first he was mocking and taunting God, but finally he declared God a "nothing," a being that does not deserve his attention. Seven weeks before blessing himself, in the January 8, 1874, letter, Freud had called himself for the first time "the godless medical man and empiricist" (p. 70). Finally, the father who could not accept the child's criticism was made "to pay heavily" for all the miseries he had inflicted on his child in the form of a demoted father-God. The "exalted" father paid in adolescence for the suffering inflicted by the real father. As Freud had predicted, his own view of God evolved alongside his relationship with his father: the demoted father called forth a demoted God.

These conclusions address the paternal component of the adolescent Freud's God representation. What became of the earlier components of that representation, linked to his nurse, his mother, and his preoedipal father? Blos (1979) describes adolescence as involving a necessary regression to early objects: "The process of disengagement from infantile objects, so essential for progressive development, renews the ego's contact with infantile drive and infantile ego positions. . . . Adolescence can be contemplated as offering a second chance for coming to terms with overwhelming danger situations (in relation to id, superego, and reality) that have survived the periods of infancy and childhood" (pp. 150, 155).

These situations are precisely those Freud invoked as being the source of the need for religion: the helplessness and terrors of childhood and the need for consolation. Freud himself had seen the source of religion in the regressive move to earlier developmental moments. In Freud's case the revival of the "young child's ideas" of father and mother could only bring pain, suffering, and the revival of the "terrors" of childhood: death, loss, despair, desolation, and later "catastrophe." In the same way that there was nothing worth remembering about the catastrophic years, there was nothing worth reviving about his early objects that could be transformed into a God representation that could offer consolation and protection. Freud's only psychic choice was the one he made: he became "godless."

The early pain of loss, terror, and desolation reappeared in his bewildered reaction to the fear of losing a woman again, as illustrated in his adolescent wandering through the woods after separating from Gisela. Ten years later, the regressive pull that found no sublimation of maternal objects in religion expressed itself in absolute demands for Martha's love. On one occasion, when he believed his fiancée had thought first of her mother rather than of him, he described himself as "uprooted"[2] and wrote to her: "If that is so, you are my enemy. . . . You have only an Either-Or. If you can't be fond enough of me to renounce for my sake your family, then you must lose me, wreck my life, and not get much yourself out of your family" (Jones, 1953, p. 130).

The demand for absolute devotion suggests the depth of his vulnerability to the loss of the attention and love of the woman he had selected as his spouse. The "revival" of the childhood objects appeared in all instances as fear of loss. The revival of maternal objects could not help transform their early abandoning representations into the ego-syntonic God representation of his infantile preaching. Again, Godlessness was the adolescent Freud's only choice.

Infantile longings, however, do not disappear. Sigmund's

2. Freud used the same word sixteen years later when his father died.

rush of emotion following the lecture On Nature and his instantaneous decision to devote his life to the study of nature
demonstrate his capacity to integrate in sublimated form the
discomfort of his infantile longings for a maternal object. The
sublimation, once more, is a reversal of roles. Freud styled himself as the grand revealer of nature's secrets. He would not be
her plaything. He was determined to master her ways.

Nor did Sigmund's godlessness erase those components of
the God representation that had a certain positive appeal. Traces
can be found in the adolescent and adult letters where Freud
uses expressions such as "the dear Lord," a common German
expression. They remained marginal references to emotional
sources that could not be allowed entrance into his conscious
awareness without causing a storm. The storm came when the
adolescent Freud found Franz Brentano, the philosophy professor who was committed to proving the existence of God.
Freud's admiration for Brentano's brilliance, integrity, kindness, and the clarity of his argument brought him to a religious
crisis. He confessed to Silberstein that Brentano's unimpeach-
able reasoning had made him a "theist by necessity," although
he had "no intention of surrendering so quickly or completely"
to his teacher's arguments (1871–81, p. 104). Freud was following the path he was to describe in his mature years: a father
substitute may force the young person to revise his stance in relation to God. Freud could not refute Brentano's arguments, but
on the basis of his emotional developmental history he could
not believe, either. The issue found no closure in his correspondence. The rest of his life would be a constant confirmation that, in spite of his compelling need to reject religion, he
could not stop thinking about it. That was his manner of
wrestling with the psychic pain inflicted on him by his early
objects: he could not revive them, transform them into an emo-

tionally tolerable God, or reject them so completely that he could stop thinking about God and religion.

Freud's description of his adolescent grief about the loss of his mysterious biblical study suggests the depth of his involvement in searching for meaning in scriptural sources. It also points to the other aspect of his attachment to Jakob, which found no sublimation in religion: the intense involvement in biblical learning.

By the end of adolescence, Freud had become a confirmed atheist, "a godless Jew." His adolescent ego ideal became absolute self-sufficiency and stoical acceptance of reality and fate. The other side of his ego ideal, the roots of which were already present in childhood, was the identification with great leaders of humankind and the determination to liberate humankind from the powers of nature. The translation of his unconscious motivations could be phrased thus: I don't need the protection of a father; I'll tame Mother Nature myself.

This conclusion seems to be supported by one of Freud's well-known character traits, "his great dislike of helplessness and his love of independence" (Jones, 1953, p. 129). Echoes of the same trait appear in Freud's *Autobiographical Study* (1925a), where he commented: "There was something positively seductive in working with hypnotism. For the first time there was a sense of having overcome one's helplessness" (p. 17).

Adulthood

Freud maintained his atheistic stance until death. His mature years confirmed and consolidated the ego ideal that he formed at the end of adolescence. He accepted no other guide to an understanding of life's mysteries but the "soft voice" of his self-sufficient intellect. He accepted with stoical integrity his share of human suffering. He kept his ego-ideal mission to the end: his task was to free human beings from their self-deceptions, their high opinions of themselves, and their enslavement to religious illusions. This ego ideal sustained him and his atheistic views to the last moment of his life.

There is little evidence that Freud paid much attention to the religious issues of his adolescent crisis until his father's death. The case histories in *Studies on Hysteria* (1893–95) make no mention of the patient's religious concerns. But Josef Breuer, his coauthor, refers to "the torments of religious doubts" as an aspect of the conflict between "irreconcilable ideas" in hysteric patients (p. 210).

Freud described the death of his father as "the most important event, the most poignant loss, of a man's life" (1900, xxvi), one that left him with "a quite uprooted feeling." Gay (1988) observes, "This was hardly a characteristic response for a middle-age son contemplating the end of an aged father who had 'long outlived himself.' Freud's mourning was exceptional in its intensity" (p. 88). Freud attributed his reaction to survivor guilt, deep ambivalence, and his having surpassed his father, but these components of Freud's experience do not suffice to explain the powerful effects of his father's death. Freud's immediate response to Jakob's death showed a revival of religious thinking modulated by negation, displacement, and sublimation. Freud denied pondering where his father had gone: "[I] am not in the least interested in life after death." But he could not stop the return to consciousness of derivatives of unconscious God representations. His preoccupation with God and the underworld appeared in displaced and sublimated form in the four mottoes for future works mentioned in Chapter 1, referring to gods, accountability to God, doomsday, and infernal regions.

Freud's active response to the loss of his father included major physical and psychic shifts. He moved to a new office in less than three weeks and "adorned" it with "plaster casts of Florentine statues" that proved "extraordinarily invigorating" for him. Six months later, Freud thanked Fliess for being "a kindly disposed audience," explaining that "without such an audience I cannot function" (1887–1904, p. 243). He also felt "impelled to start working on the dream [book]" and to explore his inner world. This he did, by creating self-analysis. Before the anniversary of Jakob's death he was already immersed in the exploration of his childhood period in Freiberg. On October 3, 1897, he recalled the existence of his nurse for the first time. After continued self-analysis he discovered how much she had meant to him. All these moves, external and internal, point to a driven effort to reorganize his inner world after his father's disappearance.

The day after his father's funeral,[3] Freud had the dream with the sign requesting "to close the eyes." He already knew that dreams were wish fulfillments. He analyzed the dream only as the "self-reproach that regularly sets in among the survivors." But this interpretation does not suffice to explain the dream or his driven inner search. A more fitting explanation may be that Freud had to close his own eyes to certain things but that he also had a regressive wish—normal in a state of deep mourning— to return, to see again those aspects of his father that he needed for survival, in order to "go on living." The move to the new room may have included aspects of reenactment and reversal of the fateful move that brought about the irreversible "catastrophe"; the Florentine casts may have evoked the studying of the Philippson Bible shared with his father. It also brought into his study in a symbolic form a semblance of the presence of his

3. In Chapter 6 of *The Interpretation of Dreams* Freud changes the date: "During the night *before* my father's funeral."

father. It must have been, together with his self-analysis and the dream book, a way of keeping his father psychically alive and physically present.

All these considerations point to the same conclusion: Freud needed his father's presence. Jakob's physical disappearance brought about, once more, Freud's frantic reaction to the loss of a loved object. Why did he need his father? Why did he revive in suppressed but undisguised form the imagery of gods, God, and the underworld? Why did he have to say in his urgent search, "Flectere si nequeo superos, Acheronta movebo," indicating his determination to search heaven and hell for what he needed?

The most cogent answer is that the death of his father revived the feelings of terror and helplessness that Freud experienced after the most traumatic event of his early childhood, the loss of his life-giving nurse. If my hypothesis is correct that Freud turned to his father when he lost his nurse, it follows that the loss of the father rekindled a state of despair. Freud, at age forty, was once more alone with his mother, still fearfully associated with death and danger, but without Jakob's deep affection, his playfulness, and his lightheartedness, helping Sigmund to "go on living." With his father gone, Freud, under the sway of unconsciously revived infantile needs and terrors, urgently needed to find a new way to restore his father's presence. Most people, in circumstances of acute object loss, renewed their devotion to God, the exalted father. Freud's available God representations could not be called to psychic duty to sustain him. His earliest infantile and exhilarating God representation could not be revived to help him. First, it was not linked to the father; second, having been codified mostly in Czech, a language Freud had lost, it was not accessible for consolation or preconscious transformation; third, the earlier God was also linked to the deadly maternal God representation and the loss of the nurse; and fourth, no God representation could be consciously acceptable to Freud after the formation of his ego ideal with its fierce rejection of dependence and need for consolation. Finally, the "exalted" God-father representation of the latency child and biblical student had lost its appeal in early adolescence and was finally rejected in late adolescence.

In short, the renewed preconscious presence of God representations in Freud's mind after the death of his father could not offer him any psychic services. They returned in disguised form in his associations, bringing with them even the early hell and the ponderings of an afterlife. They reappeared as part of the necessary psychic revival of early objects in the regression of mourning. They had to be repressed once more. Freud, however, needed a presence to help him "go on living" and escape the unconscious infantile terror of God-Nature-mother-death.

The previously described dream of the Three Fates, which Freud had in the summer of 1898, less than two years after his father's death, strongly supports this interpretation. In its manifest content and associations, the dream seemed to have organized Freud's primary connection between his mother and death. Freud's associations led him to the first novel he read (see Chapter 11, note 13), which ends with the hero "calling out the names of the three women who had brought the greatest happiness and sorrow into his life." It was at that point that Freud recalled the childhood memory of his mother showing him the dust of death in her hands, to his boundless astonishment. He concluded: "So they really were Fates that I found in my kitchen." Freud's associations led him to his famous misquotation of Shakespeare: "Du bist der Natur [Gott] einen Tod schuldig" (Thou owest nature [God] a death). In this dream, Amalie-Fate-Nature-God demonstrated her power to give life and to take it away.

Other associations led Freud to think of plagiarizing and stealing: "I was treated as though I were the thief who had for some time carried on his business of stealing overcoats in lecture rooms" (p. 205). Surprisingly, Freud did not connect this association to his infantile stealing for his nurse. Her presence, however, can be sensed in Freud's identification with her as a thief. The dream unmistakably presents Freud's mother as one of the Fates, who had in their hands the entire life of each human being: "*Clotho* who spins the thread of life, *Lachesis* who determines its length, and *Athropos*, the inexorable, who cuts it off" (Grinstein, 1980, p. 162). It seems obvious that eight months after having recovered the memories of his early childhood, his nurse, her painful loss, and his early mother, Freud was processing feelings connecting his mother to death and to God.

Freud's inner experience demanded a protector who could ward off the dangers of the Fates. The need was now most urgent because for the first time in his life he was alone with the Fate-mother. In this state, he unconsciously called Jakob back by reproducing in his collection the illustrations they had looked at together in the Philippson Bible. From now on, the illustrated pages of the bible became the three-dimensional figures of the collection. Freud's need for his father's presence found satisfaction in the collecting of antiquities. Schur (1972) has documented with the precision of a clinician how Jakob was a constant presence in Freud's living and dying: "His reference to his father's manner of meeting death and the memory of his father's shrinking steadily into pneumonia and that fateful date [of Jakob's death] were to be of great significance in Freud's own last years" (p. 193). The antiquities, however, brought him unmatchable joy, as his friends knew so well. They acted as an antidepressant, as he said to Fliess in August 1899, speaking about Egyptian antiquities: "These things put me in a good mood and speak of distant times and countries." Egypt was accessible to Freud, but he did not even think of visiting it. Thus "distant times and countries" must have referred to the distant times and lands of his latency, when he and his father visited the dreamlike lands portrayed in the Philippson Bible.

Freud the scientist, who demanded of men that they grow up and face the world alone, without the infantile crutch of an exalted father-God, could not himself do without the presence of his father. It must be granted that he sublimated his father's presence into an age-appropriate collection of transitional objects in the shape of antiquities. They offered him what God offers to believers: the assurance of a constant presence and the joy of sublimated emotional contact with the enticing father. The way Freud "played" with his collection as an audience, his affection for the "grabby gods," his smiling back at one statuette and "sacrificing" another, and his grateful acceptance of Athena's protection at age eighty-two—these give witness to the double function of the antiquities: they were always there as a needed presence serving the same function that God's presence has for the believer. They permitted Freud to retrieve the playfulness he shared with his father and provided a necessary complement to the debunking of God in life. He had denounced the failure of a father-God but kept a more ego-syntonic sublimation of his father's protective presence in the form of the collection. The only protection that presence could offer was what most believers find so appealing about God: the simple fact that he is there (Rizzuto, 1979). Jakob's tender dedication remained alive in the objects: "Your father who loves you with *eternal* love." It can be said that Freud was never alone as long as he was with his gods and his antique objects. Jakob remained with him in this sublimated form until his son joined him in death.

The death of his mother only "liberated" him. Soon, however, he started to read about Moses in preparation for writing

Moses and Monotheism. The book was to prove once more that a man, Moses, had invented God, and that God—this time perhaps God-mother-Fate-death—did not exist. This last effort to dismiss God was perhaps necessary to undo the deadly power held by that unconscious representation of God-nature-mother-death.

But Freud may not have been able to fully settle the question about God's existence. As has been noted, Freud responded to Jones's (1957) suggestion that his inclination to accept occult beliefs could lead him to believe in angels with the jocular remark: "Quite so, even *der liebe Gott*" (p. 381).

Freud's collecting of antiquities was a compulsory activity motivated by irresistible and unrecognized deep emotions, emotions that were assuaged only by the presence of the objects and their reassuring psychic meaning. They held psychic meaning for Freud because they conjured up the psychic protection of the father. This psychic presence became Freud's substitute for the protection afforded by religion.

Further confirmation of this point may be seen in Freud's unconscious use of biblical quotations. The chronological study of all Freud's writings, from correspondence to published works, reveals that biblical citations occur in most of them and that Freud cites the Bible more frequently than any other source, including Shakespeare (Pfrimmer, 1982). Pfrimmer reports that Freud quoted from twenty-one of the thirty-nine books of the Hebrew Bible. His conclusion supports the interpretation of the transitional function of the collection: "Their frequency is greater during the moments of crisis in Freud's life: during his systematic self-analysis [death of father] as witnessed by the letters to Fliess and *The Interpretation of Dreams,* during the great 1911–1914 crisis of the analytic movement, and, again, just after the war when Freud suffered the cruel losses of Anton von Freund, then, his daughter Sophie, his Sunday child. . . . His book *Moses and Monotheism* (1939) contains 76 quotations from the Old Testament" (p. 283).

Pfrimmer makes an important contribution by suggesting that Freud unconsciously returned to biblical sources at moments of psychic distress. We can now read in a different light Freud's 1935 statement, "My deep engrossment in the Bible story (almost as soon as I had learnt the art of reading) had, as I recognized much later, an enduring effect upon the direction of my interest." Engrossment in the Bible not only focused Freud's intellect, it also supported him emotionally. Similarly, the antiquities helped Freud to tolerate the pain of loss and offered him some solace in times of crisis.

Freud never acknowledged the emotional significance of his reading the Philippson Bible with his father or of receiving it as a special gift from him. I have attempted to show that the deep emotional bond between the early father and the loved traits of the later father, linked to the Philippson Bible and the "exalted" father-God representation, persisted as a sublimated and sustaining presence in Freud's remembrance of the biblical texts. In vain Freud rejected religion and God to free himself from "clinging" to the father he had so sharply criticized. In his own creative, stoical, and sublimated way, he, too, held fast to his father's presence.

Freud's adolescent ego ideal interfered with his recognition of the need for his father's presence. He defined himself as different from common men and as the new Moses, who was to lead a new type of human being to be free of infantile longings and moral feebleness. He said with firm conviction to his imaginary interlocutor in a debate on religion: "Observe the difference between your attitude to illusions [religious] and mine [scientific]. You have to defend the religious illusion with all your might. If it becomes discredited . . . then your world collapses. . . . From that bondage [religion] I am, we [psychoanalysts?] are free. Since we are prepared to renounce a good part of our infantile wishes, we can bear it if a few of our expectations turn out to be illusions" (1927, p. 54).

Freud (1925b) demonstrated that he could "bear" the hardships of his position in his paper "The Resistances to Psycho-Analysis": "Nor is it perhaps entirely a matter of chance that the first advocate of psychoanalysis was a Jew. To profess *belief* in this new theory called for a certain degree of readiness to accept a situation of *solitary opposition*—a situation with which no one is more familiar than a Jew" (p. 222, my italics). Freud's "belief" and his reliance on the "soft voice" of the intellect had, surprisingly, "the same aims as those whose realization you expect from God . . . namely the love of man and the decrease of suffering" (1927, p. 53).

Freud was aware of doing it alone, of being the exception among his contemporaries. His singular status among men held true also for his moral commitments. We have mentioned his painfully strong words to Pfister describing most human beings as "trash" while claiming that he himself subscribed to "a high ideal" that placed him in opposition to those others whom he cannot respect. Freud seems to suggest that this is not inherited morality but his own creation. He liberated himself from the oppression of religion. He and he alone had created the new human. Freud's contempt for the feeble morality of human beings sounds like a muffled complaint about his family. Like others who have no one to appeal to, he found his consolation in himself and his creations.

Freud's ego ideal sustained him and gave him remarkable intellectual and moral courage to the last moment of his life. The analyst who hears Freud's self-descriptions cannot ignore the rejection of parental guidance and the ties it represents. He never complained overtly about his parents, but the forcefulness of his sentences hints at suppressed suffering and rage displaced onto God and the absence of protection. But his "wrath," he said to Lou Andreas-Salomé, "was not so much directed against him [the Almighty] as against the gracious Providence and moral world-order for which he is, to be sure, responsible" (December 11, 1927, p. 172).

Speaking theoretically, he declared:

Superstition derives from suppressed, hostile and cruel impulses. Superstition is in large part the expectation of trouble; and the person who has harbored frequent evil wishes against others, but has been brought up to be good and therefore repressed such wishes into the unconscious, will be especially ready to expect punishment for his unconscious wickedness in the form of trouble threatening him from without. (1901, p. 260)

When the concept applied to him he did not attribute the source of his superstition "to frequent evil wishes against others": "My own superstition has its roots in suppressed ambition (immortality) and in my case takes the place of that anxiety about death which springs from the normal uncertainty of life" (p. 260, note 2). Freud had a certain right to deny that his superstitions were linked to "evil wishes," for, like Michelangelo's Moses, he had effectively restrained his rage at having been let down by his family. Freud used the psychic and moral vigor of such self-restraint to create a new realm of knowledge and to sustain himself in his lonely career. His suppressed rage, now in a sublimated form, remained in the service of sustaining his ego ideal.

Freud's superstitions also functioned to dispose of his own fear of death and of the early representation mother-Nature-God-Fates. For this too, he created his own belief "in the supremacy of the ego, of the intellect, of *Logos*, the only force with which he could face *Ananke*" (Schur, 1972, p. 332).

Meissner (1984) reached the conclusion that Freud's stance on religion reflected his personal situation: "There can be little doubt that Freud's religious views, which maintained an admirable consistency from his earliest writings on the subject through the final pages of *Moses and Monotheism*, reflected at every step deep psychological forces and unresolved conflicts within his psychic economy" (1984, p. 55). In my book *The Birth of the Living God: A Psychoanalytic Study* (1979) I described the developmental conditions necessary for belief or unbelief in the divinity. When the concepts expounded there are applied to Freud, it becomes obvious that Freud could not believe. The conditions for belief in God were not present in him. In that book I described four categories of people in their relation to belief in God. Freud belongs in the category of those who cannot believe and who look with surprise or curiosity at others who do. Freud told Romain Rolland: "To me mysticism is just as closed a book as music" (1960, p. 389).

Each individual belief or disbelief in an existing God is based on complex developmental and dynamic processes. Psychically, most children in the Western world form God representations in their interactions with primary objects. The psychic formation of God representations does not by itself elicit belief. Belief and unbelief are always the result of dynamic processes in which the sense of self and the prevailing God representation are linked in a dialectic of compatibility or incompatibility in the satisfaction of relational needs. Belief "is not a matter of maturity. Some people cannot believe because they are terrified of their God. Some do not dare to believe because they are afraid of their own regressive wishes. Others do not need to believe because they have created other types of gods that sustain them equally well. Maturity and belief are not related issues. Only detailed study of each individual can reveal the reason for that person's belief in his God" or unbelief (Rizzuto, 1979, p. 47).

The research results presented in *The Birth of the Living God* (Rizzuto, 1979) describe the conditions for belief and unbelief at each stage of development (pp. 206–7). During the oral stage and early infancy the subjective experience that later allows for belief is expressed as: "I am held, fed, nurtured. . . . I see me on your face (you make me in your image)." These conditions were satisfied in Freud through the mediation of his nurse and his mother. There is not yet a God representation during this period, but there are basic emotions of trust and relatedness that later will color the emerging God representation. During the anal stage the condition for belief is conveyed by the feeling "I feel you are with me." Unbelief, on the contrary, is based in the opposite experience: "I cannot feel you are there for me. I despair." Freud and his nurse attended religious services together and were physically involved with each other during her ministrations to him. As a result, the young churchgoer could "believe" enthusiastically, if childishly, in "God Almighty," however he conceived of it. Toddler Freud, when he lost his nurse, must have experienced the contrary feeling: "I cannot feel you are with me. I despair." Sigmund's God representation related to his nurse, and his own self-representation of an abandoned child must have absorbed the repercussions of the loss, leading to his first steps toward later unbelief.

The phallic stage brings great emotional excitement. The sense of self of that moment is conveyed in the sentences "I am wonderful. I can do great things." Complementing it, there is in the child's mind an idealized, great, powerful primary object, frequently the father. The representation of that object, in conjunction with other earlier object representations, is susceptible to transformation into a God representation. When the affects are positive they lead to a feeling about God that says "You are wonderful, the Almighty." The object's failure to sustain the child's admiration prompts a reaction that may extend to God in the form of doubt or unbelief: "I thought you were omnipotent. You failed." Freud's prototypical description of God as an exalted father must refer to his own experience during the period when he believed Jakob to be the greatest of men and his own wise and kind protector.

During the oedipal stage the aggrandized opposite-sex parental imago, experienced as "You are lovable and exciting," and the complementary sense of self, "I am attractive. You should love me first," when properly sustained, facilitate the child's belief in his updated God representation. The oedipal situation places the child in direct conflict with the parent of the same sex. During this period of development the child's God representation, linked to both parents, changes with the modality of resolution of the oedipal conflict. In the end, as Freud suggested, the necessary sublimations and transformations of attachment to the parents and object love for them have a direct impact in the child's now more organized representation of God.

The resolution of the oedipal crisis leaves an indelible mark in the way God is conceived. Freud's oedipal strivings toward his mother became manifest in their train trip, where he believed he saw her naked. Even at that early moment, Freud's narrative of the trip places side by side his excitement about his mother with "souls burning in Hell." The experience left him with a lasting anxiety about traveling that may be related to his unconscious fear of the maternal oedipal object.

During the oedipal and latency periods the parent of the opposite sex must support the child's sense that he is a deserving love object. Failure to confirm the child's value may cause a deep narcissistic hurt. The opposite-sex parent has to be renounced as a libidinal object while the parent of the same sex becomes an object for identification. Problems in identifying

with that parent may bring about complex difficulties and narcissistic injury. Freud experienced that injury when his father
said he would come to "nothing." His father had in fact come
to nothing in the young Freud's eyes. Jakob's devaluation of Sigmund became an intolerable and lasting narcissistic injury. Both
factors, the narcissistic humiliation of the son by the father and
the son's recognition of his father's improvidence, must have
interfered with Freud's capacity to "exalt" the representation of
the father to an oedipal emotionally believable God representation.

During latency the prevailing sense of self affirms: "I am a
child. I will grow up and be and do like you." The experience
of the child says: "You are my parent. You are big and powerful. You protect me." When these conditions are fulfilled the
child is inclined to believe in a God who is a protector. When
the conditions are not fulfilled or worse, when great disappointment comes from a previously much admired parent, unbelief in God may be the only available alternative to handle the
despair internally, while remaining obedient and noncritical of
the needed parent. In this case, the child may say to God unconsciously or consciously what he cannot say to the parent: "I
don't need you. You don't help me." The child may add: "I take
care of myself."

Finally, in adolescence, the deep and prolonged process of
separating from the internal object leads to multiple searches
that eventuate in the formation of a more complex and multilayered God representation. The early adolescent says to the
parental objects: "You are limited. You have faults. Let me be."
In late adolescence the ambivalent wish to learn from the parent of the same sex emerges with the request: "Teach me to be
a man, a woman." When the experience of adolescence keeps
the parental imagos as acceptable, if flawed, the conditions for

belief in God are present, even when in actual behavior the young person may or may not believe. When the adults have failed the adolescent in a deep and essential manner, unbelief in God is frequently an explicit reaction. The adolescent says to God: "I don't need you. I have myself." Then, all the hopes are placed in the possibility of finding a partner to love and to be loved by.

In Freud's case, the entire psychic stage was set for unbelief. His father could not teach him to be a man. The memories of the nurse were not affectively available until his self-analysis. Her disappearance had left him with an indelible unconscious fear of loss. His maternal representation linked fear of death to God. During latency he had already become a functional adult within the family, on his way to being the provider of the family for decades.

Freud was adamant about not being like his father and complained that his mother attended only to his physical needs. There was nobody else to father or mother him. He had only one choice: to accept that he was alone, unprotected, without models, and that the obvious affection of his parents could not help him. Freud's final stance was one of deep disillusion. The only consolation available to him and to mankind was to be stoically self-reliant. There is no God, no benevolent Providence. The pain of the small child led to the vehement insistence that we all must give up a Father-God, incapable of delivering any protection or consolation. Freud's personal suffering had become articulated in his theory about religion for all humankind. Like Michelangelo's Moses, he could only suppress the rage at his predicament. He could substitute his own determination to have no God for the representation of a feared, abandoning and improvident God. In his case, he was right: there was no God to console or protect him. His defiant unbelief was the measure of his psychic integrity. It was also the measure of his courage and his capacity for sublimation: to transform the deep suffering of the child and adolescent into a new science that opened the unexplored horizons of the human mind. God had been replaced by Freud's reason. The unprotected man had created his own self-protection. Later in life he could say with conviction about his great sublimation: "No, our science is no illusion. But an illusion would be to suppose that what science cannot give us we can get elsewhere" (1927, p. 56).

Freud generalized into universal principles his personal religious evolution. He firmly believed that his personal stance must be normative. By losing perspective about his own personal suffering, he became blind to the "variety of religious experiences" that William James, his contemporary, described so well. Freud claimed that human beings must be stoical, renouncing their wishes for protection and consolation. They must stop clinging to their father and to God, his substitute. The best they can and must do is to face their fate and believe in science. That would make them true adults, committed, as Freud was, to a stark and stoical realism, in which no consolation is expected other than pride in being able to accept suffering and terror.

Freud did not make his father "pay heavily" for the brutal disillusion of his latency and later life. God was made to pay in displacement for the failure of all his primary objects: his mother, his nurse, and his father. Instead of keeping the "exalted" representation of the primary objects and of the father in the shape of God, Freud insisted that God is only an illusion. His personal God had no reliability. It did not deserve belief. Strong unbelief was the only protection against the intense pain of unsatisfied infantile, adolescent, and adult longings. Freud's life experiences did not provide him with the psychic conditions for belief in God. Thus Freud, the great trailblazer and leader, contained his suffering and rage and transformed them into masterpieces. He could not, however, avoid revealing, in disguised and sublimated ways, his own urgent need for unmet protection.

epilogue

In this book I have traced the private pathways of Freud's unbelief. I have followed him closely as a child, an adolescent, and an adult, "eavesdropping," as he taught me to do, listening to the cries and whispers of his struggle with his private God and God himself. I have come to the end of my journey, a journey made difficult because I could not talk to Freud directly but had to content myself with the crumbs of self-revelation he left for his biographers. I have gathered the muffled hints and crumbs and placed them together as a narrative of his internal transformations toward his final stance of unbelief. He guided my search with his own theories about the formation and transformation of God representations and the powerful emotions linked to them. I hope to have demonstrated, using Freud as a concrete example, that psychodynamic understanding of religious development offers a powerful tool to understand belief and unbelief.

What Freud did not reveal to his biographers in personal detail about his religious evolution appeared in his theoretical conceptions of the formation and transformation of religious belief. Freud's religious theories can be read as an unintended psychobiography of his private and unwitting transformation into a "godless Jew."

Amati-Mehler, J., Argentieri, S., and Canestri, J. (1993). *The Babel of the unconscious: Mother tongue and foreign languages in the psychoanalytic dimension.* Madison, Conn.: International Universities Press.

Anzieu, D. (1986). *Freud's self-analysis.* Madison, Conn.: International Universities Press.

Astropoulos, S. (1989). Psyche in ruins: Sigmund Freud and the impact of archaeology on psychoanalysis. *Journal of Art* 2, 26–27.

Aurbach, J. (1858). *Kleine Schul- und Haus-Bibel.* Leipzig: Brockhaus.

Barron, J. W., Beaumont, R., Goldsmith, G., Good, M., Pyles, R. L., Rizzuto, A-M., and Smith, H. F. (1991). Sigmund Freud: The secrets of nature and the nature of secrets. *International Review of Psychoanalysis* 18, 143–63.

Bernays, A. F. (ca. 1930). *Erlebtes.* Vienna: Kommissionnsverlag der Buchhandlung Heller.

———. (1973) [1940]. My brother, Sigmund. In H. M. Ruitenbeek, ed., *Freud as we knew him.* Detroit: Wayne State University Press.

Bernays Heller, J. (1973) [1956]. Freud's mother and father. In H. M. Ruitenbeek, ed., *Freud as we knew him.* Detroit: Wayne State University Press.

Berthelsen, D. M. (1986). J'étais la bonne de docteur Freud. *Figaro-Magazine,* March 1.

Blond, S. (1974). *Tysmenieca: A memorial book.* Tel Aviv (in Hebrew and Yiddish).

Blos, P. (1979). *The adolescent passage: Developmental issues.* New York: International Universities Press.

Cassirer Bernfeld, S. (1951). Freud and archeology. *American Imago* 8(2), 127.

Cervantes Saavedra, M. de. (1967). *Coloquio que pasó entre "Cipión" y "Berganza": Obras Completas.* Madrid: Aguilar.

Clark, R. W. (1980). *Freud the man and the cause: A biography.* New York: Random House.

Corcoran, L. H. (1991). Exploring the archeological metaphor: The Egypt of Freud's imagination. *Annual of Psychoanalysis* 19, 19–32.

de Mijolla, A. (1981). *Les visiteurs du moi: Fantasmes d'identification.* Paris: Société d'edition "Les Belles Lettres."

Doolittle, H. (1956). *Tribute to Freud*. Boston: David R. Godine.

Erikson, E. H. (1964). *Insight and responsibility: Lectures on the ethical implications of psychoanalytic insight*. New York: W. W. Norton.

Freeman, E. (1971). *Insights: Conversations with Theodor Reik*. Englewood Cliffs, N.J.: Prentice Hall.

Freud, E. L. (1956). Sigmund's Freud's family bible. *National Jewish Monthly*, May.

Freud, E., Freud, L., and Grubrich-Simitis, I. (1985). *Sigmund Freud: his life in picture and words*. New York: W. W. Norton.

Freud, M. (1957). *Glory reflected: Sigmund Freud, man and father*. London: Angus and Robertson.

Freud, S. (1871–81) [1990]. *The letters of Sigmund Freud to Eduard Silberstein, 1871–1881*. W. Boehlich, ed., A. J. Pomerans, trans. Cambridge: Belknap Press of Harvard University Press.

———. (1887–1904) [1985]. *The complete letters of Sigmund Freud to Wilhelm Fliess, 1887–1904*. Jeffrey Moussaieff Masson, ed. and trans. Cambridge: Belknap Press of Harvard University Press.

———. (1899). Screen memories. Standard Edition, vol. 3. London: Hogarth Press.

———. (1900). *The interpretation of dreams*. Standard Edition, vols. 4 and 5. London: Hogarth Press.

———. (1901). *The psychopathology of everyday life*. Standard Edition, vol. 6. London: Hogarth Press.

———. (1903–4). Contributions to the Neue Freie Presse. Standard Edition, vol. 9. London: Hogarth Press.

———. (1905a). *Jokes and their relation to the unconscious*. Standard Edition, vol. 8. London: Hogarth Press.

———. (1905b). *Three essays on the theory of sexuality*. Standard Edition, vol. 7. London: Hogarth Press.

———. (1907). Obsessive actions and religious practice. Standard Edition, vol. 9. London: Hogarth Press.

———. (1909). Notes upon a case of obsessional neurosis. Standard Edition, vol. 10. London: Hogarth Press.

———. (1910). Leonardo da Vinci and a memory of his childhood. Standard Edition, vol. 11. London: Hogarth Press.

————. (1911). Psycho-analytic notes on an autobiographical account of a case of paranoia. Standard Edition, vol. 12. London: Hogarth Press.

————. (1912). Remembering, repeating, and working-through. Standard Edition, vol. 12. London: Hogarth Press.

————. (1913a). The theme of the three caskets. Standard Edition, vol. 12. London: Hogarth Press.

————. (1913b). *Totem and taboo.* Standard Edition, vol. 13. London: Hogarth Press.

————. (1914a). The Moses of Michelangelo. Standard Edition, vol. 13. London: Hogarth Press.

————. (1914b). Some reflections on schoolboy psychology. Standard Edition, vol. 13. London: Hogarth Press.

————. (1914c). On narcissism. Standard Edition, vol. 14. London: Hogarth Press.

————. (1917). A childhood recollection from Dichtung und Wahrheit. Standard Edition, vol. 17. London: Hogarth Press.

————. (1918). From the history of an infantile neurosis. Standard Edition, vol. 17. London: Hogarth Press.

————. (1919). The "uncanny." Standard Edition, vol. 17. London: Hogarth Press.

————. (1920). Beyond the pleasure principle. Standard Edition, vol. 18. London: Hogarth Press.

————. (1921). *Group psychology and the analysis of the ego.* Standard Edition, vol. 18. London: Hogarth Press.

————. (1922). Medusa's head. Standard Edition, vol. 18. London: Hogarth Press.

————. (1923). A seventeenth-century demonological neurosis. Standard Edition, vol. 19. London: Hogarth Press.

————. (1925a). *An autobiographical study.* Standard Edition, vol. 20. London: Hogarth Press.

————. (1925b). The resistances to psycho-analysis. Standard Edition, vol. 19. London: Hogarth Press.

————. (1927). *The future of an illusion.* Standard Edition, vol 21. London: Hogarth Press.

———. (1930a). *Civilization and its discontents.* Standard Edition, vol. 21. London: Hogarth Press.

———. (1930b). The Goethe prize. Standard Edition, vol. 21. London: Hogarth Press.

———. (1931). Female sexuality. Standard Edition, vol. 21. London: Hogarth Press.

———. (1933). *New introductory lectures on psycho-analysis.* Standard Edition, vol. 22. London: Hogarth Press.

———. (1939). *Moses and monotheism: Three Essays.* Standard Edition, vol. 23. London: Hogarth Press.

———. (1940 [1938]). An outline of psycho-analysis. Standard Edition, vol. 23. London: Hogarth Press.

———. (1941 [1938]). Findings, ideas, problems. Standard Edition, vol. 23. London: Hogarth Press.

———. (1954). *The origins of psychoanalysis: Letters to Wilhelm Fliess.* E. Mosbacher and J. Strachey, trans. New York: Basic.

———. (1960). *Letters of Sigmund Freud.* E. Freud, ed., T. Stern and J. Stern, trans. New York: Basic.

———. (1966 [1972]). *Sigmund Freud and Lou Andreas-Salomé letters.* Ernest Pfeiffer, ed., W. Robson-Scott and E. Robson-Scott, trans. New York: Harcourt Brace Jovanovich.

———. (1969). Some early unpublished letters of Freud. *International Journal of Psycho-Analysis* 50, 419–27.

———. (1970). *The letters of Sigmund Freud and Arnold Zweig.* E. L. Freud, ed., E. Robson-Scott and W. Robson-Scott, trans. New York: Harvest.

———. (1985). *Sigmund Freud Briefe an Wilhelm Fliess, 1887–1904.* Frankfurt am Main: S. Fischer.

———. (1991). Le Testament de Freud: Presenté par Paul Roazen. *Revue Internationale d'histoire de la Psychoanalyse* 4, 635–41.

Freud, S., and Breuer, J. (1893–95). *Studies on hysteria.* Standard Edition, vol. 2. London: Hogarth Press.

Freud, S., and Jung, C. G. (1974). *The Freud/Jung letters: The correspondence between Sigmund Freud and C. G. Jung.* W. McGuire, ed., R. Manheim and R. F. C. Hull, trans. Bollingen Series, 94. Princeton: Princeton University Press.

Freud, S., and Pfister, O. (1963). *Psychoanalysis and faith: The letters of Sigmund Freud and Oskar Pfister.* H. Meng and E. L. Freud, eds., E. Mosbacher, trans. New York: Basic.

Friedmann, F. (1929). *Doe galizischen Juden im Kampfe um ihre Gleichberechtigung, 1848–1868.* Frankfurt.

Gamwell, L. (1989). The origins of Freud's antiquities collection. In L. Gamwell and R. Wells, eds., *Sigmund Freud and art: His personal collection of antiquities.* New York: State University of New York Press; London: Freud Museum.

Gardiner, M. (1971). *The wolf-man by the wolf-man.* New York: Basic.

Gay, P. (1987). *A godless Jew: Freud, atheism, and the making of psychoanalysis.* New Haven: Yale University Press; Cincinnati: Hebrew Union College Press.

———. (1988). *Freud: A life for our time.* New York: W. W. Norton.

———. (1989). Introduction. In L. Gamwell and R. Wells, eds., *Sigmund Freud and art: His personal collection of antiquities.* New York: State University of New York Press; London: Freud Museum.

Gicklhorn, R. (1965). Eine Episode aus Sigmund Freuds Mittelschulzeit. *Unsere Heimat* 36, 18–24.

———. (1976), *Sigmund Freud und der Onkeltraum: Dichtum und Wahrheit.* Vienna: Eigenverlag, Druck Berger.

Ginsburg, L. M., and Ginsburg, S. A. (1987). A menagerie of illustrations from Sigmund Freud's boyhood. *Psychoanalytic Study of the Child* 42, 469–86.

Goethe, J. W. (1869). Nature, aphorisms by Goethe. T. H. Huxley, discussant. *Nature,* November 4, pp. 9–11. [Incorrectly attributed to Goethe; actual author was G. C. Tobler (1780).]

Goldsmith, G. N. (1992). Freud's aesthetic response to Michelangelo's Moses. *Annual of Psychoanalysis* 20, 245–69.

Grinstein, A. (1980). *Sigmund Freud's dreams.* New York: International Universities Press.

Grubrich-Simitis, I. (1991). *Freud's Moses-Studie als Tagtraum: Ein biographischer Essay.* Weinheim: Verlag Internationale Psychoanalyse.

Halevi, M. (1958–59). Discussion regarding Sigmund Freud's ancestry. *YIVO, Annual of Jewish Social Sciences* 12, 297–300.

Hardin, H. T. (1985). On the vicissitudes of early primary surrogate mothering. *Journal of the American Psychoanalytic Association* 33, 609–29.

———. (1987). On the vicissitudes of Freud's early mothering. I: Early environment and loss. *Psychoanalytic Quarterly* 56, 628–44.

———. (1988a). On the vicissitudes of Freud's early mothering. II: Alienation from his biological mother. *Psychoanalytic Quarterly* 57, 72–86.

———. (1988b). On the vicissitudes of Freud's early mothering. III: Freiberg, screen memories, and loss. *Psychoanalytic Quarterly* 57, 209–23.

Heller, J. B. (1973) [1956]. Freud's mother and father. In H. M. Ruitenbeek, ed., *Freud as we knew him*. Detroit: Wayne State University Press.

Jones, E. (1953). *The life and work of Sigmund Freud*. Vol. 1. New York: Basic.

———. (1955). *The life and work of Sigmund Freud*. Vol. 2. New York: Basic.

———. (1957). *The life and work of Sigmund Freud*. Vol. 3. New York: Basic.

Kallen, H. M. (1990). The bearing of emancipation on Jewish survival. In D. D. Moore, ed., *East European Jews in two worlds*. Studies from the YIVO Annual. Evanston: Northwestern University Press.

Klinger. (1877). Illustration of *heimlich*. In J. A. W. Grimm, ed., *Deutsches Wörterbuch*, vol. 4, part 2., pp. 873 ff. Leipzig.

Kohut, H. (1978). Beyond the bounds of the basic rule. In P. H. Ornstein, ed., *The search for the self*, pp. 275–303. New York: International Universities Press.

Krüll, M. (1986). *Freud and his father*. New York: W. W. Norton.

Laible, E. (1993). "Through privation to knowledge": Unknown documents from Freud's university years. *International Journal of Psycho-Analysis* 74, 775–90.

Langenscheidt. (1974). *Encyclopedic Muret-Sanders German Dictionary*. O. Springer, ed. Berlin.

Lehmann, A. (since 1859). *Allgemeiner Wohnungs-Anzeiger nebst Gewerbe-*

Adressbuch der kk. Reichchaupt- und Rezidenzstadt Wien. Vienna. [Published since 1859, with a few exceptions.]

Liebert, R. S. (1983). *Michelangelo: A psychoanalytic study of his life and images.* New Haven: Yale University Press.

Mahl, G. F. (1985). Freud, Father, and Mother: Quantitative aspects. *Psychoanalytic Psychology* 2, 99–113.

Mahler, R. (1990). The economic background of Jewish emigration from Galicia to the United States. In D. D. Moore, ed., *East European Jews in two worlds.* Studies from the YIVO Annual. Evanston: Northwestern University Press.

Mahony, P. (1982). *Freud as a writer.* New York: International Universities Press; expanded ed. New Haven: Yale University Press, 1987.

Meissner, W. W. (1984). *Psychoanalysis and religious experience.* New Haven: Yale University Press.

Niederland, W. G. (1988). Die Philippsonsche Bible und Freuds Faszination Für die Archeologie. *Psyche* 42(6), 465–70.

Ostow, M. (1989). Sigmund and Jakob Freud and the Philippson Bible. *International Review of Psycho-Analysis* 16, 483–92.

Pestalozzi, R. (1956). Article in *Neue Zürcher Zeitung* 8 (July 1).

Pfrimmer, T. (1982). *Freud, lecteur de la Bible.* Paris: Presses Universitaires de France.

Philippson, J. (1962). The Philippsons, a German-Jewish family, 1775–1933. *ZATW* 16–17, 95–118.

Philippson, L. (1855). *The development of the religious idea in Judaism, Christianity, and Mahomedanism.* Anna Maria Goldsmith, trans. London: Longman, Brown, Green and Longmans.

Pinsent, J. (1969). *Greek mythology.* London: Paul Hamlyn.

Rainey, R. M. (1975). Freud as student of religion: Perspectives on the background and development of his thought. Dissertation series 7. Missoula, Mont.: American Academy of Religion and Scholars Press.

Rice, E. (1990). *Freud and Moses: The long journey home.* Albany: State University of New York Press.

Rizzuto, A-M. (1979). *The birth of the living God: A psychoanalytic study.* Chicago: University of Chicago Press.

Roazen, P. (1975). *Freud and his followers*. New York: Da Capo.

———. (1993). *Meeting Freud's family*. Amherst: University of Massachusetts Press.

Roback, A. A. (1957). *Freudiana*. Cambridge, Mass.: Sci-Art.

Rosenfeld, E. M. (1956). Dream and vision: Some remarks on Freud's Egyptian bird dream. *International Journal of Psycho-Analysis* 37, 97–107.

Sachs, H. (1944). *Freud: Master and friend*. Cambridge: Harvard University Press.

Sajner, J. (1968). Sigmund Freuds Beziehungen zu seinem Geburtsort Freiberg (Příbor) und zu [Mähren]. *Clio Medica* 3, 167–80.

———. (1981). Drei dokumentarische Beiträge zur Sigmund Freud-Biographik aus Böhmen und Mähren. *Jahrbuch der Psychoanalyse* 13, 143–52.

———. (1989). Die Beziehungen Sigmund Freuds und seiner Familie zu dem mährischen Kurort Roznau. *Jahrbuch der Psychoanalyse* 24, 73–96.

Salisbury, S. (1989). In Dr. Freud's collection, objects of desire. *New York Times*, September 3.

Schafer, R. (1970). The psychoanalytic vision of reality. *International Journal of Psycho-Analysis* 51, 279–97.

Schönau, W. (1968). *Sigmund Freuds Prosa: Literarische Elemente seines Stils*. Stuttgart: J. B. Metzlersche Verlagsbuchhandlung.

Schur, M. (1972). *Freud: Living and dying*. New York: International Universities Press.

Shengold, L. (1972). A parapraxes of Freud's in relation to Karl Abraham. *Imago* 29, 123–59.

Spector, J. J. (1975). Dr. Sigmund Freud, art collector. *ARTnews*, April.

Wells, R. (1989). Interview with Lynn Gamwell and Richard Wells, co-curators of the exhibition. Unpublished.

Wittels, F. (1924). *Sigmund Freud: His personality, his teaching, and his school*. T. Eden and C. Paul, trans. London: Allen and Unwin.

Yerushalmi, Y. H. (1991). *Freud's Moses: Judaism terminable and interminable*. New Haven: Yale University Press.

Zborowski, M., and Herzog, E. (1952). *Life is with people: The Jewish little town of Eastern Europe*. New York.

index

Bernays, Anna Freud (*continued*)
Vienna move, 89; and book
with colored plates, 90, 101;
and Silberstein, 147; and Julius
Freud's death, 232

Bernays, Eli, 223

Bernays, Minna, 21

"Beyond the Pleasure Principle"
(Freud), 117

Bible: Freud's early exposure to,
48, 67, 79, 113, 244–45; and
death, 93, 94; and Amalie
Freud, 93, 113; and Freud's
imagination, 112; and Gymnasium, 141; Freud's mentions
of, 145–52, 181, 183,
260–61; loss of biblical study,
145–46, 149, 253; and man's
dominion, 157. *See also* Hebrew
Bible; Philippson Bible

Bismarck, 42, 174, 194

Blos, P., 248, 250

Bonaparte, Marie, 14, 20, 199,
209, 225

Brehm, Alfred E., 100–101

Brentano, Franz, xxi, 147,
150–51, 153, 154, 168–69,
252

Breuer, Josef, 176, 254

Breuer, Leopold, 139–40

Busch, Wilhelm, 100

Canestri, J., 242

Catastrophe: and poverty, 44, 46,
52–53, 98n4, 243; and Vienna,
44–46; and Freud's oedipal development, 52, 102; and Jakob

Freud's paternal authority, 54;
effects of, 63, 92, 184, 255;
and loss, 243–44, 251

Cervantes, Miguel de, 100,
144–45, 248

Charcot, Jean Martin, 7, 89

Childhood: and father's protection, 85, 161–62, 168, 210;
helplessness in, 85, 167, 168,
210, 233, 234, 239, 243, 250;
and unconscious processes, 90,
117, 251; and lack of protection, 161, 162, 167, 168; terrors of, 210, 250–51

Childhood of Freud: and
Freiberg, 43–44, 89–90, 134,
215; and Freud's mother-son
relationship, 44, 204, 215,
238; and Bible stories, 48, 67,
79, 113, 244–45; and protection, 61, 67, 171, 247; reti-
cence about, 62–63, 89,
116–17, 203, 244; and Freud's
father-son relationship, 63, 87,
89, 91–92, 103, 215; and
helplessness, 64, 85, 241, 256;
male role models of, 64, 87;
terrors of, 64, 204, 242, 256,
257; and role reversal, 66,
202–3, 240, 247–48,
249–50; and death, 89,
228–29, 238; and separation,
89, 238; visual memories of,
89–90; and Philippson Bible
illustrations, 113–16; and
Philippson Bible, 119, 139; and
God representation, 136, 236,

Freud, Amalie Nathansohn
(continued)
222–23; and Vienna move, 89;
and "dust to dust" demonstration, 93, 113, 138, 200, 220,
220n15, 221, 222, 238, 241,
257; and nanny/nurse, 135,
214; and Anna Freud, 186,
194–95, 195n12, 202, 224,
232; Judith Bernays Heller on,
186, 189–94; Martin Freud
on, 186–89; disposition of,
187, 187n3, 189, 190–92; appearance of, 189–90, 218; narcissistic traits of, 195–98, 201,
202, 240; and nature, 208–9.
See also Mother-son relationship
of Freud

Freud, Anna: and antiquities collection, 22; and Philippson
Bible, 56–57n4; and Freud's
cancer, 171; and Amalie Freud,
186, 194–95, 195n12, 202,
224, 232; and Fliess correspondence, 199; on Freud's mother-
son relationship, 201, 230

Freud, Dolfi: birth of, 46; and
Freud as provider, 56, 61, 66;
in Vienna, 80; and Amalie
Freud, 188, 190–91, 190n6,
195, 239

Freud, Emmanuel: and Jakob
Freud, 23, 30, 45; in Freiberg,
34, 38; business of, 36; in Manchester, England, 38, 44, 45,
51, 89; and Joseph Freud,
49–50, 49n2, 51, 61; Freud's

visit to, 55, 66, 218; as male
role model, 64, 87; and Freud's
mentions of God, 138; Freud's
relationship with, 143; death
of, 223

Freud, Ephraim, 24, 29

Freud, Ernst, 24n1, 26, 77–78, 79

Freud, Fanny, 33, 35

Freud, Heinerle, 223, 225

Freud, Jakob: death of, 1–5, 9, 66,
80–83, 254–57; submissiveness to Christian, 10, 13, 51,
58, 64, 66, 187n3, 246; occupations of, 12, 31–36, 45–46,
61–62; children of, 23; father's
death, 24, 26–27, 65, 89; family background of, 29–36, 65;
in Freiberg, 31, 33, 34, 35, 38;
and Philippson Bible, 33–34,
42, 60, 70–78, 103, 113, 160,
174, 255; marriage of, 34, 36,
37–38, 65, 202; appearance of,
36, 59; and Haskala, 41–42,
63; and Bismarck, 42, 194; failure as provider, 46, 61, 62, 92,
103, 174, 243; and Joseph
Freud's arrest, 50–51; paternal
authority of, 53, 54, 62, 246,
249; childish nature of, 64–65,
102; and Philippson Bible illustrations, 101, 102–3; and complaints, 177n11. *See also* Catastrophe; Father-son
relationship of Freud

Freud, John, 36, 38, 43–44, 55,
86–87

Freud, Joseph: family background

Freud, Sigmund (continued)
of Freud; Nanny / nurse of
Freud; Self-analysis; and spe-
cific works
Freud, Sophie, 223, 225, 260
Freud, Teddy, 223
Freud, Walter, 87n1, 225
Freud Museum, 15, 22, 119
Freund, Anton von, 260
"From the History of an Infantile
Neurosis" (Freud), 162
Future of an Illusion, The (Freud), xix,
166, 170, 209

Gamwell, Lynn, 5, 8, 9, 19
Gay, P., 152, 223, 254
German language: and Jewish
public schools, 28–29; and
Jakob Freud, 30, 63; and
Philippson Bible, 33, 41, 107,
108; Ludwig Philippson, 106
Ginsburg, L. M., 100
Ginsburg, S. A., 100
God: Freud's conception of, xix,
78; Brentano's proof of existence of, xxi, 147, 150–51,
153, 154, 168–69; and infantile beliefs, xxi, 78, 174, 184,
185; accountability to, 2; and
Freud's mottoes, 3, 3n2, 4, 254;
and Freud's reaction to father's
death, 4, 85; Freud assuming
Godlike power, 12–13, 148,
149, 249; Job's impotence
compared to, 12; Philippson
on, 39–40; Freud's rejection
of, 67, 93, 103, 269–70, 271;

and Philippson Bible, 70–77,
93; and antiquities collection,
131; and nanny / nurse, 136,
137, 237; Freud's mentions of,
138, 142–44, 145–52, 252;
and religion, 139–40, 162,
253; and Moses, 140, 182,
185, 245, 260; and nature,
140, 209, 220n16, 222, 238,
257; jokes concerning,
156–57; as human invention,
157, 177; as father substitute,
160–63, 164, 170, 181–82,
233, 234, 245, 269; and protection, 168, 170, 263, 267,
268; and Jews as chosen people, 179; and Freud's "Three
Fates" dream, 222; and death,
225, 238, 241; Freud's mother-
son relationship linked with,
226; and Freud's preaching
experience, 233–34; developmental conditions for belief /
unbelief in, 264–67
God representation: and Freud's
childhood, 136, 236, 238,
240, 241; and nanny / nurse,
136, 228, 234, 238, 241, 242,
245, 250, 265; and Freud's
adolescence, 144–52,
248–53, 267–68; formation
of, 164, 264, 271; and mother,
164, 165, 235, 236, 241, 250,
256, 263; and father, 165–66,
174, 181, 233, 235, 243, 257,
261, 265–66, 267; and oedipal
development, 165–66, 245,

266; and unconscious pro-
cesses, 236, 255, 260, 267;
transformation of, 244,
248–53, 271; and consolation,
251; and Jakob Freud's death,
256; and belief, 265, 266
Gods: and Freud's mottoes, 2, 4,
254; and antiquities collection,
18, 236; and Philippson Bible
illustrations, 41; and father-son
relationship, 85; of Egypt, 131,
132, 174; Freud on, 148, 249;
and consolation, 166; and nature, 166–67, 210
Goethe, Johann Wolfgang von,
3–4, 63, 84, 166, 206–8, 213,
248
Goldsmith, Anna Maria, 39
Goldsmith, G. N., 136
Graf, Cecily, 192, 192n10
Graf, Rosa Freud: birth of, 46; and
Freud as provider, 56, 61; and
Silberstein, 147; and loss,
192–93, 198; mother pregnant
with, 214n9
Grinstein, A., 95, 136, 219n13
Guilt: and religion, 158–59,
161, 209; and oedipal period,
165
Gymnasium: religion classes in,
12, 113–14, 131, 138–39,
146, 148, 249; Freud in, 47,
52, 138, 142, 146, 148; and
Hebrew language, 140–41

Haizmann, Christoph, 8–9,
163–64

Halevi, Mayer, 41
Halpen, Abraham, 33
Hammerschlag, Samuel, 140,
141–42
Hannibal, 10, 52, 64, 136n4, 246
Hardin, H. T., 230, 232, 240
Harlow, Jules, 26
Hasidism, 30, 31, 41
Haskala, 41–42, 46, 63, 105
Hebrew Bible, 71n1, 139, 260. See
also Philippson Bible
Hebrew language: and Jakob
Freud, 24, 26, 30; and Philipp-
son Bible, 24, 26, 33, 41, 68,
107, 109, 111; and Jews, 28,
140; and Sigmund Freud, 30,
31, 67, 77, 113, 138, 140,
141, 142; and Moses Philipp-
son, 105; and Gymnasium,
140–41
Heine, Heinrich, 156–57
Heller, Judith Bernays, 30, 54, 59,
78, 186, 189–94
Herdan, M. N., 33
Hinterberger, Heinrich, 21n6
Hoffer, Otto, 3n2
Hofmann, Siskind, 29, 30, 31, 32,
35, 65
Hollitscher, Robert, 225
Homberg, Naphtali Herz, 28, 30
Hypnotism, 253

Illusion: and religion, 167, 168,
169, 171, 207n5, 254; and
science, 169, 209, 261–62,
269; and nature, 207, 207n5,
209

Freud's religious theory, 146,
172–85, 178n12, 182n17,
260–61, 264
"Moses an Egyptian?" (Freud),
178n12
"Moses Created the Jews"
(Freud), 178
"Moses of Michelangelo, The"
(Freud), 174–75
Mother: and religion, xxi, 84,
160, 164, 167n6, 185, 205;
and protection, 85, 167–68,
167n6, 234–35; and God representation, 164, 165, 235,
236, 241, 250, 256, 263; and
oedipal period, 165; and love,
167, 197, 204; fear of, 203–4;
and sexuality, 214, 237; and
fate, 221, 260; and belief, 235;
infantile longings for, 251–52
Mother-son relationship: and narcissism, 196; and maternal
love, 197, 204; of Leonardo da
Vinci, 205–6; and Goethe, 213
Mother-son relationship of Freud:
death linked with, xxi, 95, 138,
199–200, 212, 222–23, 226,
229, 238, 240, 241, 256,
257–58, 268; and mother's tuberculosis, 37; mother's favoritism, 38, 53, 189, 191,
194, 195n12, 196, 197–98,
201, 213, 239, 242, 247; and
Freud's childhood, 44, 204,
215, 238; and Freud's education, 47; Freud's financial support, 56, 61–62, 66; deaths

hidden from Amalie Freud, 62,
222–23; and mothering figures, 86–87, 183, 232, 236;
and Philipp Freud, 88; and
nanny/nurse, 88, 229, 232,
236; and mother's grief, 89;
and dreams, 94, 183, 212, 216,
218–22, 227; and Vienna train
trip, 136–38, 213–14, 266;
mother's blessings on Freud,
156; Freud's references to, 186,
205, 226, 227, 228, 237;
Freud's fear of his death preceding hers, 187, 189, 201,
213, 224, 227; and Freud's defiance, 191n7, 239–40; Anna
Freud on, 194–95; Freud's idealization of mother, 198; and
thirst for grandeur, 202n14,
212; and mother's death,
203–4, 216, 223–24, 227,
232, 240, 259; and nature,
208–9, 210–12, 227; and
mother's disappearance, 214,
230; and Freud's Manchester
visit, 218; God linked with,
226; and separation, 230, 239;
Freud's emotional distance
from, 231; and love, 238

Nanny/nurse of Freud: and
Freud's preaching episode, xxi,
135–36, 230, 233–34, 241;
and Mariae Geburt Church
visit, 43, 44, 134–35, 183,
230, 234; as mothering figure,
86, 183, 232, 236, 240; loss of,

87–88, 135, 136, 137–38,
215, 230, 232, 239, 241–42,
256–57, 265, 268; and stealing, 87, 212, 214, 227, 229,
230, 258; and self-analysis,
135, 227, 229, 237–38, 242,
255, 268; and Freud's God representation, 136, 228, 234,
238, 241, 242, 245, 250, 265;
and Freud's sexuality, 137–38,
227, 229, 237–38, 240; and
dreams, 212, 214, 238; and Vienna train trip, 213–14; Fliess
compared to, 224n17

Napoleon I, 4, 52

Nathansohn, Jacob: and Freud's
anxiety dream, 31, 96, 99, 216,
216n10; business of, 36; and
daughter's marriage, 37; in Vienna, 45; funeral of, 97–98;
and catastrophe, 98n4

Nathansohn, Julius, 36, 43, 89,
231

Nathansohn, Sara Wilenz, 36, 37,
45

Nature: and Job's impotence, 12;
and Freud's medical career, 84,
166, 206, 248, 252; and God,
140, 209, 220n16, 222, 238,
257; "kindly nature," 160,
160n2, 162, 166–67n5, 205,
205n1, 207n4, 209, 210, 233;
and civilization, 166; and gods,
166–67, 210; Goethe on, 166,
206–8, 206n3, 248; and Providence, 167; and science, 169,
205, 206, 208, 209; limitations

in, 170n8; Freud's conception
of, 205–10, 205–6n2, 253;
and illusion, 207, 207n5, 209;
and Freud's mother-son relationship, 208–9, 210–12,
227; and religion, 209; and
protection, 241; and unconscious processes, 248–49, 253

New Introductory Lectures (Freud),
196

"Notes upon a Case of Obsessional Neurosis" (Freud), 162

Object representations, 235–36,
248

"Obsessive Actions and Religious
Practices" (Freud), 158–59

Oedipal development: and Jakob
Freud's catastrophe, 52; and
Freud's anxiety dream, 95, 99,
102; and God representation,
165–66, 245, 266–67; and
nanny/nurse, 228; and love of
mother, 231, 237; and Vienna
train trip, 266

On Aphasia (Freud), 57–58

"On Narcissism" (Freud), 157

"On the History of the Psychoanalytic Movement" (Freud), 4

Orthodox Jews, 29, 38, 41, 63,
134, 136, 152

Ostow, M., 68, 70

"Outline of Psycho-Analysis"
(Freud), 172

Palestine, 173–74, 183

Paneth, Josef, 150, 152

Sachs, Hanns, 84

Sajner, J., 37

Satin, Allan D., 107n1

Schatzky, Jacob, 21n6

Schiller, Friedrich, 211, 212

Schliemann, Heinrich, 6, 7

Schönau, Walter, 3

Schreber, Daniel Paul, 162, 163

Schur, Max, 6, 21, 170, 193n11, 199, 226, 230–31, 258

Science: and Jews, 160; and religion, 168; and illusion, 169, 209, 261–62, 269; and nature, 169, 205, 206, 208, 209; and consolation, 170; belief in, 269

"Screen Memories" (Freud), 46, 55, 89, 242, 246

Self-analysis: and Jakob Freud's death, 2, 4–5, 84, 255, 256, 260; and archaeology, 7; and nanny/nurse, 135, 227, 229, 237–38, 242, 255, 268; and Freud's mother-son relationship, 200; and mother's death, 203–4

Separation: and Freud's childhood, 89, 238; and nanny/nurse, 136, 215; and Amalie Freud, 195; and Freud's mother-son relationship, 230, 239; and Freiberg visit, 239; and Freud's father-son relationship, 242

"Seventeenth-Century Demonological Neurosis" (Freud), 163

Sexuality: and antiquities collection, 17; female sexuality, 20,

203–4; and anxiety dream, 94, 95, 99, 216; and nanny/nurse, 137–38, 227, 229, 237–38, 240; and Vienna train trip, 137, 213–14; and religion, 158, 159; and mother, 214, 237

Shakespeare, William, 93, 173n10, 220n16, 238, 257, 260

Silberstein, Eduard: and Job, 12–13; and Amalie Freud, 37, 189, 195n12, 200, 216–18; and Fluss, 45; and Freud's family life, 53, 54–55; and Gymnasium, 142; and Freud's religious evolution, 144–52; and Freud's adolescent God representation, 248–50, 252

Solitary opposition, 169n7, 262

Spanish language, 31, 141, 144–45

Spector, J. J., 14, 15

Sphinx of Giza, 130n5, 180

Stoicism, 169–70, 253, 268, 269

Strachey, James, 172, 206n3

Studies on Hysteria (Freud), 139, 254

Superstition, 263

Swift, Jonathan, 99

Tenner, Nathan, 33

"Theme of the Three Caskets, The" (Freud), 221

Tobbler, G. C., 206n3

Torah, 27–28, 33, 42

Totem and Taboo (Freud), 159–60, 165, 181

Ulrich, Johann Jakob, 134
"Uncanny, The" (Freud), 200
Unconscious processes: and
    Freud's mottoes, 2–4; and
    childhood, 90, 117, 251; and
    Philippson Bible illustrations,
    100, 104, 117; and antiquities
    collection, 117–18, 131; and
    Freiberg, 136; and Freud's
    mother-son relationship, 200,
    266; and God representation,
    236, 255, 260, 267; and na-
    ture, 248–49, 253; and Jakob
    Freud's death, 256, 257; and
    Freud's biblical quotations,
    260–61

Vienna: and catastrophe, 44–46,
    89; Freud in, 79–80, 89; train
    trip to, 136–38, 213–14, 266
Virgil, 3

Wahle, Fritz, 239
Weich, Osias, 48
Wells, Richard, 17
Wittek, Resi, 37, 43, 86. *See also*
    Nanny/nurse of Freud
Wittels, F., 54
Women: female sexuality, 20,
    203–4; and Ludwig Philipp-
    son, 106; and God representa-
    tion, 164; and feminine soul,
    209; and religion, 219n13
Wurmser, Leon, 3n2

Zajic, J., 38
Zajic, Monika, 43, 86. *See also*
    Nanny/nurse of Freud
Zweig, Arnold, 158, 172, 173,
    177–78
Zweig, Stefan, 6